BET·ON·IT

THE ULTIMATE GUIDE TO
NEVADA

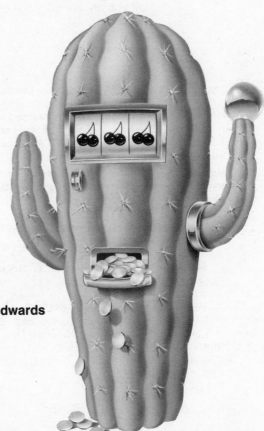

Mary Jane & Greg Edwards

Mustang Publishing Co.
Memphis, TN

For all our friends in aprons behind the tables.
May you always have first count.

All rights reserved, including the right of reproduction in whole or in part in any form. Published in the United States of America by Mustang Publishing Company, Inc., P.O. Box 3004, Memphis, TN 38173. Manufactured and printed in the U.S.A.

Distributed to U.S. bookstores by National Book Network, Lanham, Maryland. For information on distribution outside the U.S., contact the publisher.

Library of Congress Cataloging-in-Publication Data

Edwards, Mary Jane, 1938-
    Bet on it! : the ultimate guide to Nevada / Mary Jane and Greg Edwards.
    p. cm.
    ISBN 0-914457-44-6 (pbk.) : $10.95
    1. Gambling -- Nevada -- Guidebooks. 2. Games -- Nevada.
3. Card games -- Nevada. 4. Nevada -- Description and travel --
1981- -- Guidebooks. I. Edwards, Greg, 1940- . II. Title.
GV1301.E38 1992
795' . 109792 -- dc20   90-50863
                                                          CIP

Printed on acid-free paper.   ∞

10 9 8 7 6 5 4 3 2 1

Note: Maps are not drawn to scale.

Acknowledgments

Our gratitude and thanks to the gracious and helpful people at the Nevada State Gaming Control Board in Carson City, the Reno-Sparks Convention & Visitors Authority, the Henderson Chamber of Commerce, the Carson City Chamber of Commerce, the Las Vegas Tourist and Visitors Bureau, and the Laughlin Chamber of Commerce. Special appreciation to all the marketing and media relations people and all the hotel and casino employees whose help was invaluable.

Special thanks also to John and Evelyn Jackson who kept us apprised on Reno, Dale and Jennifer Edwards for their generosity and hospitality in Las Vegas, Lynn Smotherman for her research in the Reno-Sparks area, and our good friends Gregg Blando and Chris Steiglitz for all their help at Lake Tahoe.

Living and working in a place can take away the mystique and dull the magic. We thank Rollin Riggs, our publisher, for recognizing the beauty and fun of Nevada and helping us bring its magic to our readers.

Mary Jane & Greg Edwards

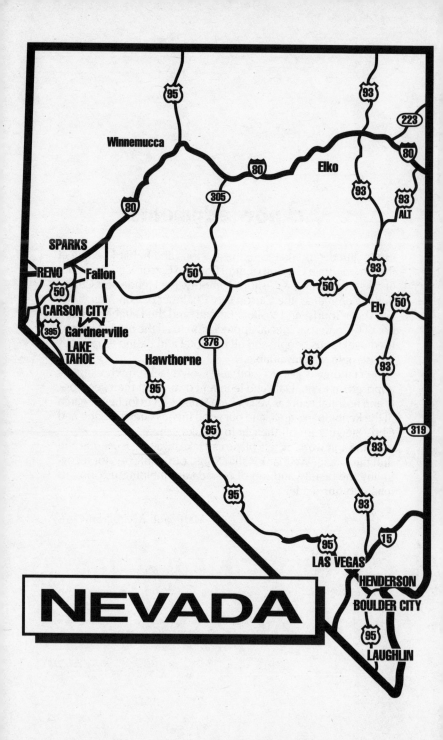

Contents

Introduction:
Nevada—For the Fun of It!

A casino is a magical place where there are no clocks and time matters least of all. Colored lights flash from every corner, an undercurrent of conversation hums, the stickman on the craps table shouts "Yo 'leven! Winner, winner, winner!", bells ring on hundreds of slot machines, a voice from the paging system calls out names, laughter and "All-l-l-l right!" come from a happy player somewhere in the distance, ice cubes tinkle in glasses at the bar, music plays—sometimes blaring, sometimes subdued, but always there. Pretty young dealers wear silk blouses, diamond jewelry, and expensive perfume that floats above the tables. The pit bosses are handsome in designer suits; the cocktail waitresses are leggy, full-figured, and friendly.

And there's something else: the sound of money. Sometimes it's a soft sound, like a whisper, when the dealer pulls a bill between two fingers before it disappears into the slot on the table. Sometimes it's a clattering, when quarters fall from a slot machine into the metal tray. The chips click as they're stacked on the layout, the little ball skips and snaps in the roulette wheel, and the keno machine whirs.

You might find the casino intimidating, and it's the fear of all the glitz that we hope to allay with this book. The beauty of the huge rooms is awesome, but the lavishness is part of the fun. The different themes are amazing. Caesars Palace is exactly as it sounds—a palace decorated for a Roman emperor. The Mirage offers white tigers and an erupting volcano. The Las Vegas Excalibur has jousting, court jesters, and knights in armor. Then there's Circus Circus, with trapeze acts flying over your head while you play and a mezzanine that lets you stand on eye-level with the acrobats—it's all totally overwhelming at first.

Unusual Games

We discuss seven different casino games in Part One, but as you walk through the casinos, you'll see other games, too. Almost every place has a **Wheel of Fortune**, sometimes called a **Big Six** or a **Parimutuel Wheel**. Numbers on the wheel match currency displayed on a table. Under a sheet of glass are $1, $2, $5, $10, and $20 bills, plus a joker or the casino's logo. The payoff is the same as the denomination of the bill on which you place your money. (There are more $1 spaces on the wheel than anything else.) If you're feeling lucky, put your money on the joker/logo; it pays 40 to 1. The dealer spins the upright wheel—you don't. (It's not like the TV show.) The game is simple and requires no thought—the amount shown is the amount you win—and you may find it's an easy way to get acquainted with the casino and talk to a dealer. (Just don't ask if he lives there!)

Some Nevada casinos have introduced a number of other imaginative games. One is called **Pan**, a combination of poker, gin rummy, pinochle, and bridge. It uses eight decks of cards with all the 8s, 9s, and 10s removed. Then there's **Poker Bingo**, a blend of poker, bingo, and keno using ping pong-like balls marked with card symbols. The object is to make a winning poker hand out of the balls. **Aquarius**, similar to roulette, uses astrological symbols instead of numbers. So if you're into astrology, and Venus is aligned with Mars...

You may be familiar with **Red Dog**. Remember "Acey-Deucy" in college? You put your money in the betting square, the dealer deals two cards face up, then each player bets that the value of the third card dealt will fall somewhere between the value of the two face-up cards. The ace is always high. After the first two cards, you can raise your bet. If the third card drawn is the same as one of the first two, you lose. When the first two cards are a pair, you can't raise your bet, but if the third card drawn matches, you win 11 to 1. If not, you *push*, meaning neither you nor the dealer wins. Sounds easy—except the odds are overwhelmingly in favor of the house.

Pyramid Dice combines different aspects of roulette and craps with one-roll bets. The top payoff can be $250,000, but before you rush off to play, consider that the big payoff is for a shooter playing alone and rolling all 21 dice combinations without repeating any. The odds of that happening are a little better than your being hit by a falling elephant at 2:00pm on Thursday. Still, you never know.

Baccarat was borrowed from the Europeans—you've seen it

Baccarat Rules

When the Player's first two cards total	Player's hand
1, 2, 3, 4, 5, or 0	Draws a card
6 or 7	Stands
8 or 9	Natural/Stands

When the Banker's first two cards total	Banker's hand always draws on a two-card total of	Banker stands when player's third card is
0, 1, or 2	0, 1, 2	
3	1, 2, 3, 4, 5, 6, 7, 9, 0	8
4	2, 3, 4, 5, 6, 7	1, 8, 9, 0
5	4, 5, 6, 7	1, 2, 3, 8, 9, 0
6	6 or 7	1, 2, 3, 4, 5, 8, 9, 0
7	STANDS	
8 or 9	NATURAL/STANDS	

If the **Player's** hand does not draw a third card, then the **Banker's** hand stands on a point total of six or more.

in James Bond movies—and some casinos offer separate baccarat rooms that are open only certain hours, unlike the rest of the casino, which never closes except in a national emergency. (All casinos were closed for the first and only time the day of President Kennedy's funeral.) Many places now have a smaller version, called **Mini-Baccarat**—same game, but played in the main casino on a table smaller than the original.

In the elegant baccarat rooms, the dealers wear tuxedos, and a host seats you at the table. The magic number is 9. The dealer handles everything, and you bet on either your hand or the bank's hand. You're dealt one card face down, and the dealer takes a face-down card. Then you get a second card, face down. The bank, which can be either the house or a player, turns his hand. The object is to get as close to 9 as possible without going over. The face cards and 10s have no value, and the ace counts as 1. The player's hand is played first, then the bank's, and the hand closest to 9 wins even money. The bank's hand wins more often (the casino is usually the bank), and a bet on the bank's hand in baccarat is the second best bet in the casino. (Only the odds bets on the craps table are better.) That's why you must pay a 5% commission when you win a bet on the bank's hand. The dealer keeps track and will ask you for the amount you owe when you're ready to leave the game. That amount is the house percentage on your winnings.

Nevada has betting parlors called **Sports Books**, where you can bet on a variety of major sporting events, including college and professional football, major league baseball, and college and professional basketball, plus special events like the Indy 500, tennis matches, the Kentucky Derby, and major prize fights. Odds on the event are posted. Players receive a receipt for their bets, which they must present to the cashier to collect winnings. Racing fans can bet on races at all major tracks across the U.S.

Betting on team sports involves a *point spread*. For example, if oddsmakers think Miami can beat Notre Dame by 4 points, the point spread will be "plus 4 1/2" for Notre Dame and "minus 4 1/2" for Miami. In other words, the favored team starts out behind, while the underdog starts out ahead. With this system, your team can lose the game, and you can still win your bet. The half-point is in case of a tie. Each casino uses a different system to figure the *line*, which can change from hour to hour. Wise bettors look for games where they think the line is way off and then bet enough on one team to move the line. Then they turn

The Olympiad Race Book at Caesars Palace.

around and bet on the other team at improved odds. That's big-time betting, though, and not for most.

At one of the newest sports books in Las Vegas, the Imperial Palace, there are 106 seats, each with its own 8-inch color TV. You can watch your own event, instead of whatever is on the big screens. There are big screens, too, of course: the Imperial Palace has two 10-foot screens and nine 5-foot screens, plus nine betting windows and a 24-hour payout window.

Fun Books

Almost every Nevada casino offers coupons, or "fun books," which might be good for a free roll of nickels, a $1 steak dinner, a two-for-one bet on a table game (called a "two-fer"), or a pass to a nightclub show. Sometimes the coupons will be in your room, sometimes you must ask at the hotel desk, but always use them wherever possible. They can add up to quite a bit of money.

Casinos, Resorts, and Attractions

Part Two of the book is a guide to the casinos in the large gaming areas of Nevada. If you're driving, you'll see slot machines everywhere the minute you cross the state lines. Grocery stores, service stations, restaurants—all give you a chance to play. All the small towns have casinos, and some have good places to stay.

But the major resorts and glamor spots are found in two parts of the state: The northern area encompasses Reno, Sparks, Carson City, and Lake Tahoe. The southern resorts are in Las Vegas, along the Boulder Highway, in Henderson, and the newest hot spot, Laughlin, on the Colorado River.

The listings tell you what kind of accommodations to expect and what games are offered, along with house rules and table limits. Nevada has a wider variety of price and luxury than most places. You can actually find good hotels for as little as $19 a night. Or consider The Mirage in Las Vegas, where bungalows cost $1,200 a night and come with private pools, gardens, wet bars, and sunken living rooms. (Rooms are provided for your maid and butler, too, of course.) Most of us can only dream of such things, but maybe you'll be like the guy who came to the craps table at the Tropicana recently, plunked down $40 and took home $5,000. (That game lasted an hour and a half, and the biggest winner left with $200,000. It happens.)

Even the "ordinary" rooms at the large hotels can be luxurious, and almost every place has swimming pools, tennis courts, and wonderful restaurants. Hungry? Casinos have the best food bargains anywhere. Their motive is not profit—they just want you to stay inside their building. Some casinos have ten restaurants under one roof, each serving a different kind of food, always good, and always inexpensive. You can still find a 49-cent breakfast and a prime rib dinner for $3.95. Even the dinner shows are a bargain. You eat an elegant dinner and see top entertainers in a glamorous setting—all for less than you'd pay for a concert ticket anywhere else.

If you're traveling with children, you'll be glad to know that many hotels and casinos have excellent child care facilities. Some casinos have large, supervised centers with movies, video games, and play areas. Or, if you prefer, the desk clerk will arrange for a private sitter.

Part Two also gives directions for reaching spots you'll want to include in your trip. Each major gambling area boasts great nearby attractions. Virginia City, the site of the largest silver strike in Nevada, is high above Reno and only a half-hour's drive away. The Ponderosa Ranch, where TV's *Bonanza* was filmed, is at the north shore of Lake Tahoe. Lake Mead, formed by Hoover Dam, is the state's largest recreation area and minutes from Las Vegas. Maybe your vacation time will allow you a day to explore Oatman (near Laughlin), one of many ghost towns in the West.

But you came to gamble, right? And Nevada casinos have excitement unequaled anywhere. Besides, just one night at the tables will give you enough stories to get you through the next 20 years of Chamber of Commerce lunches back home. For instance, there's one about the drifter who picks up a quarter from the floor, drops it into a slot machine, and gets $50. Is this to be his salvation? A night spent sleeping in a bed instead of under the stars? Maybe a hot meal for a change? Not in Nevada! He takes his $50 to the blackjack table, where he runs it up to $135, and decides to go for $200. The drinks are on the house, and free sandwiches are served on graveyard shift, so he sits there all night, betting $2 a hand. By 6:00am he's flat broke, but hey, he had a good time, didn't he? And it didn't cost him a cent. It wasn't his money.

When you walk through the door of the casino, you'll forget the time, the weather, and all about tomorrow. Your imagination will come alive, your heart will beat a little faster. A casino needn't be a strange place at all. Sometimes it's a place where dreams come true.

Disclaimer

Although the information in this book was as accurate as possible at publication, please remember that things change over time. Always call ahead to confirm hours, prices, etc. Neither we nor the publisher can assume responsibility for any problems you incur as a result of an inaccuracy in this book.

We welcome your comments, criticisms, and suggestions. If we use your advice in an updated edition, we'll send you a free copy. Write to us in care of Mustang Publishing, P.O. Box 3004, Memphis, TN 38173, USA.

There are two great pleasures in gambling: that of winning and that of losing. —French proverb

PART ONE

CASINO GAMES

Blackjack

Roulette

Keno

Slot Machines

Pai Gow & the Asian Games

Poker

Craps

No wife can endure a gambling husband unless he is a steady winner. —Lord Dewar (1864-1930)

Blackjack

The blackjack table is empty. I'm standing there, people-watching, trying to look pleasant. A tired-looking man, clad in a rumpled suit with his tie hanging from his coat pocket and a damp cigar clenched in his teeth, dumps a handful of chips on the layout next to third base and collapses on the stool.

"Good morning, sir," I say, smiling. He looks up with blood-shot eyes. "Shut up and deal," he says.

I sigh and pick up the deck. It's going to be another one of those days.

When the blackjack table is full, it's likely to contain an odd assortment of people. Housewives from Indiana with $20 to play, millionaires wearing diamonds the size of Texas, bums off the street playing their last $2—all play together with a camaraderie impossible under other circumstances. This mingling makes for some strange doings, but these people all share a common purpose: *beat the dealer.*

Questions Players Ask

Players are forever asking why dealers don't smile. We do, honest. We even laugh out loud at times. But hey, nobody smiles eight hours a day, and remember, this is a *job.* I'm working. You're the one who's supposed to be having fun. And sometimes there's a good reason why a dealer isn't smiling. Maybe the boss just yelled at her for no good reason, maybe a player has been rude, maybe one of her kids has the flu, maybe the car payment is due and the tips haven't been good. Or maybe someone just took a shot at her. Literally. That happened to me one night on a grave-yard shift when a player decided it was my fault he'd lost too much money. The security guards took him away, and I didn't smile for a week!

"Why don't you smile?" is just one of the questions blackjack dealers hear all shift, every shift.

Another is "Are you going to be nice to me?" Of course, this really means "Are you going to give me all winning hands?" The answer is I'm going to give you whatever comes off the deck when I get to your hand. Maybe you'll win. If that happens, you'll think what a good player you are, and maybe you'll toss me a dollar when you leave the table. If you lose, it will be because I wasn't "nice."

Some players have a bad habit of acting as if the dealer's not there. "Is she being nice?" and "Does she ever smile?" make me wonder if I look like I'm not able to speak or answer for myself. Sometimes the comments are personal. Now, I believe most people don't mean to be rude, but dealers have feelings, too, and comments about someone's personal appearance aren't in good taste anywhere—not in an office, not in a store, and not in a gambling casino.

Players do ask many legitimate questions, however, and before we talk about playing the game, here are the answers to a few things you may be wondering about. Dealer's aprons, for instance. The practice of wearing aprons may go back to the time when aprons were meant to cover pockets—a place for dishonest dealers to hide stolen chips. That was before fish-eye cameras, Gaming Boards, and pit bosses with eyes in the backs of their heads. Today, dealers wear an apron to prevent their clothes from being worn to shreds where they rub against the table. (Anyway, I've never known a dealer dumb enough to risk a career for a $5 chip.)

Many people wonder if you go to school to be a dealer. It certainly helps. In the old days, casinos gave manual dexterity and math tests, and every casino had its own dealer's school. You knew exactly what was expected of you when you were finally put on a game. Today, some casinos will let people come in during a slow time and learn on the game, but usually they must be an employee of the casino, and they must come in before or after their regular shift or on their days off. Reno and Las Vegas both have dealer's schools where you can learn the basics. These schools will try to place you in a job, too.

As with anything, how fast you learn is up to you. You can learn blackjack quickly, but it takes about a year before you really know what you're doing on a game, and about three years before you're considered a good dealer.

Have you wondered why they change dealers just when you're finally on a winning streak? It has nothing to do with you, and that's the truth. In most casinos, dealers work for an hour, and then get a 20-minute break. Depending on the club, the dealer may return to the table or go to a different table after the break. Again, this has nothing to do with the players. After an hour spent in intense concentration, entertaining and placating players, answering a million questions and obeying a million rules, you'd be ready for a break, too. And when we leave the table and clap our hands together, it's because we have to show everyone, including the hidden cameras, that we haven't palmed any chips. (A player once asked me if I was clapping because I was so happy to leave!)

Casinos do have a lot of rules that may seem silly, and it's up to the dealers to tell players about those rules. New players often don't understand, and so they think they're being picked on. But the rules are there to protect everyone, and a dealer can lose her job if she doesn't follow them. No one expects new players to understand everything all at once, but if a dealer tells you not to do something, don't do it again.

Can a dealer lose her job if she loses too much money? Probably not. The old-time pit bosses told dealers they'd better win—or else. Some bosses had favorite "lucky" dealers, used whenever the house started losing heavily. Clubs kept track of a dealer's winnings, and her average for the month had to be a certain percentage, but those days are gone. If a dealer is competent and pleasant, she's probably in no danger of being fired because of a losing shift.

How to Bet

Blackjack is the most popular game in any casino. Many people think they only need to know how to count to 21 to play, and it's partly true: the object of the game is to have your cards total 21 or as near 21 as possible without going over (or "busting"). But of course, there's more to it than that. All cards are face value (face cards count as 10), and the suits don't matter. It's not a group game; it's you and only you against the dealer. You'll see tables that use a single deck of cards, and tables where as many as eight decks are dealt from a box called a "shoe."

Suppose you have a $20 bill clutched in your hand, and you've found a table where you can play a minimum bet and where the dealer and the players seem to be enjoying themselves. (Try to find a table where you can play at a spot other than "third base," at the dealer's immediate right. Superstitious players sometimes moan out loud when a new player sits in that space, since that player is the last to receive cards before the dealer. Some gamblers are positive the whole table will immediately lose if a novice plays that spot.) Step up to the empty spot and put your bill on the layout in front of you, *not in the circle or square where the bet goes.* If you want to bet the whole $20 on one hand, put it in the square and say "Money plays." Otherwise, lay your money down and tell the dealer you want change. The dealer cannot take the money from your hand. The bosses and the cameras must see the denomination of the bill. (If you're changing a $100 bill, the dealer will call out "Changing a hundred" or something similar. This is to prevent cheating by the player and the dealer.)

The dealer will, in most cases, give you ten $1 chips and two $5 chips for a $20 bill. A dealer cannot give you cash in change; if you want cash, you must change your bill at the cashier's cage. After you get the chips, the dealer will wait for you to place a bet before he deals the next hand. Pull your chips in front of where you're standing or sitting, and place your bet in the little circle (or square) in front of you. (There will be a small sign on the table telling you the minimum and maximum bets and other house rules.)

Once the cards are dealt, *don't touch the bet again,* under any circumstances. This rule is to prevent you from adding to or subtracting from your bet after you see your hand. If you win, the dealer will pay you in chips, and you can pick up the bet and the winnings. If you lose, the money belongs to the house—and people have gone to jail for picking up a losing bet and trying to run.

Playing the Game

Your cards must remain over the table at all times, in full view of the dealer. I know, I know—you just want to show your cards to your buddy standing behind you. Well, the guy next to you just wants to switch the ace up his sleeve for the three in his hand. You aren't allowed to touch anyone else's cards, either, for the same reasons.

You'll receive two cards, face down, one at a time. (If you're playing at a "shoe" game, the cards may be dealt face up, and you never touch them at all.) The dealer also gets two cards, one up, one down. Her "up" card will determine how you play your hand. Pick up your cards *in one hand without bending them or touching your money.* Look at the dealer's top card. Always play as if the dealer's "down" card is a 10. If she has an 8 showing, assume she has 18. If your cards total 17 or more, smile, and lay

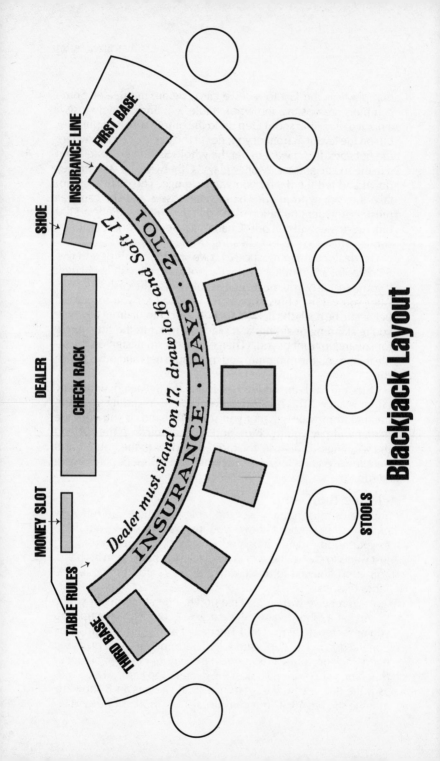

Blackjack Layout

FIRST BASE
INSURANCE LINE
SHOE
DEALER
CHECK RACK
MONEY SLOT
TABLE RULES
THIRD BASE
STOOLS

Dealer must stand on 17, draw to 16 and Soft 17

INSURANCE · PAYS · 2 TO 1

them back on the table, face down, no matter what card the dealer is showing.

If you have a total of 11 or less in your hand, you can ask for another card without any worry of "busting" (going over 21). The dealer will point to your hand. If you want another card (a "hit"), scratch on the table with the two cards. This is important: *Don't ever touch any card except the original two given you by the dealer.* When your cards total 17 or more, tuck them under your bet and *leave them there.*

Once your hand is down, don't touch it again. There are many eyes watching a blackjack game, and visual signals are necessary. Your scratching tells the boss and the cameras you want another card, and when you put your cards down, they know you've finished. A dealer can't go to the next player until you've laid your hand down.

The hands that will break if you hit them with a 10—12, 13, 14, 15, 16—are called "stiff" hands. (It seems like these are the hands you receive most often.) And this is where the dealer's up card becomes important. If her up card is a 2 through 6, she must take a card. Since she could bust and pay the table, tuck your cards under your money and "stand." (That is, let her take the breaking card instead of trying to improve your own hand.) If the dealer's card is 7 or higher, her hand is probably a "pat" hand (she probably has 17 or more), so you should hit your "stiff" (take another card). If you bust, lay your cards face up on the table immediately. The dealer will take your cards and your bet.

Many experts say to hit a 12 when the dealer shows a 2. After 20 years as a dealer, I agree. If I have a 2 showing, I will invariably make a hand, unless a smart player takes my card and leaves me with nothing but a breaking card.

Those same experts will tell you to stand on a 16 even if the dealer shows a 10 or an ace. But I don't agree with that. After all, there are 20 cards of 5 and under in a deck, and depending on what's already been dealt, you do have a chance to catch a small card. And I probably already have your 16 beat, anyway, without a hit. Hitting 16 can cause bitter battles in a game. I've even had a boss turn my hand to show the player I have 19, and the player *still* stood on his 16, afraid of breaking his hand! That's really dumb. Take a chance—that's why they call it gambling.

Probably the most confusing thing for a new player is trying to count a hand containing an ace. An ace counts as 1 or 11. The easiest way is the way dealers are taught: *Always count the ace as a 1, and then add 10 to it.* It's easier than trying to add 11 to 2, 5, and 2, for instance.

Any hand with an ace is called a "soft" hand. In most casinos, dealers must hit a "soft 17" (any combination of cards, with an ace, that you can still call 7). Example: ace-4-2, or ace-6, or 3-3-ace. The odds are in your favor to improve any soft hand under 18—which is why most clubs have their dealers hit a soft 17. It gives the club an extra 0.2% advantage. (Some casinos, especially in Las Vegas, stand on soft 17. Play in these clubs if you can; they are noted in the casino listings in Part Two.) If you have an ace-8 or an ace-9, you already have 19 or 20, and you can ruin a potential winning hand by hitting it with a 5, for instance, and thereby turning it into 14 or 15.

Hit only soft hands that total 18 or less. When you've hit and turned a soft hand into a "hard" hand (one you can count only one way), hit or stand according to the basic strategy. Of course, the best soft hand is a **blackjack**—any face card or 10 and an ace. Always turn this hand up immediately and slide a corner of the cards under your bet. The dealer will pay you 1.5 to 1 ($7.50 for a $5 bet, for instance).

Other Blackjack Plays

Many casinos allow you to turn your cards face up and double your bet when your first two cards total 10 or 11. This is called a **double down**. (If you're not sure how much you've bet, let the dealer count the chips. *Don't touch the bet.*) You'll receive only one card, face down. Of course, you hope it will be a 10 or 11. (Some players will tell you never to look at your double down hit card because you'll change the spots. If you'll excuse the expression, such people are not playing with a full deck.)

Always double with an 11; double on 10 only when the dealer is not showing an ace or 10. Many clubs in southern Nevada allow you to double on any first two cards, but that's not a smart play. It only increases the odds in favor of the house.

You can **split** any pair you're dealt. That is, you can play two hands, but, of course, you must double your bet. If you get a pair of aces, always split. You'll receive one card, face down, for each ace. On other splits, you can get as many cards as you want, face up, until you have a good hand. (In some casinos, you can double down on a 10 or 11 after you split, also. Example: You split a pair of 6s and get a 4, making 10. You can then double on that 10.) **Always split a pair of aces or 8s.** Split 6s only when the dealer shows a 5. Never split 4s, 5s, or 10s, including face cards. (Two 4s hit with a 10 make 18, and that's better than two 14s any time.) Some experts will split 10s, but with a pair of 10s you already have 20, and that's usually a winner.

The question of **insurance** comes up often. If a dealer's top card is an ace and the club offers insurance, she will ask for insurance bets before she looks at her hole card to see if she has a blackjack. If you want to insure your hand, place 1/2 of the amount of your original bet in front of your betting square. Insurance pays 2 to 1, so if the dealer has a blackjack and you've insured your hand, she will take your original bet and then pay your insurance bet. Thus you don't win anything, but you don't lose, either.

Some experts say never take insurance under any circumstances, but again, I disagree. If you have a blackjack and you take insurance, you'll win either way. When the dealer has a blackjack, she must pay the insurance money, which is 2 to 1.

Example: Your bet is $5, so insurance will cost $2.50. Both you and the dealer have a blackjack. You don't insure. You get a "push," meaning you don't lose, but you don't win, either. If you had insured, she would have pushed the blackjack and paid the insurance, giving you $5. On the other hand, if the dealer does not have the blackjack, she'll take your $2.50 insurance bet, and pay your blackjack $7.50, leaving you with a profit of $5. If you take insurance, you will receive the original amount of your bet no matter what the dealer's hand is, and that's all you receive on every other hand, anyway. It's the only sure bet in blackjack. **Always take insurance when you have a blackjack. Otherwise, never take it.**

Some casinos have introduced a gimmick called **no peek**. It means that when a dealer has an ace as her top card, she won't look under it until all the players' hands are completed. If the dealer discovers she has a blackjack, she'll take only your original bet, not the part that was doubled or split. However, this makes it important that you strictly follow the insurance rules. The "no peek" policy was put into effect to keep a dealer from inadvertently letting the players know the value of her down card by her body language or facial expression. It slows up the game and many don't like it, but most of the larger casinos now have this rule, so be prepared.

Shuffling and Card-Counting

When the dealer runs out of cards, she'll stop and shuffle. This won't happen in the middle of a hand, since dealers watch their decks and know when to shuffle. After the shuffle, the dealer will give the deck to a player to cut. A player simply takes a portion of the deck and sets the cut-off portion on the table. The dealer then completes the cut and "burns" the top card by putting it face up on the bottom of the deck. When more than one deck is used, the dealer hands a player a card, and the player cuts by inserting the card into the decks. Players can refuse to cut (some think it's unlucky). If everyone at the table refuses, the dealer must cut the deck herself.

You'll hear a lot about card-counting. It can increase your chances of winning, but only if you're extremely proficient. By the time you become that skillful, the clubs will know who you are, and they'll politely ask you to leave. And yes, they *can* ask you to leave. You're on private property, and they have the right to protect their interests.

Managing Your Money

You can increase your odds of winning at blackjack just by learning to play properly. Managing your money helps, too. The best rule is to take some and leave some: If you start by playing $2 and win, make your next bet $3, not $4. Then if you win again, you'll have $6, and you'll be playing with house money. Don't let the entire bet ride; the dealer *will* win a hand eventually, and you'll be back to betting your own money. You'll rarely win more than three hands in a row. It's possible, and I've even seen 15 in a row, but that's unusual.

Never double your bet when you're losing, just to catch up. That's called "chasing your money," and it's the quickest way I know to go broke. I remember the day a man walked up to the game with a fistful of $100 bills and played them all, a few at a time, losing $15,000 simply because he was determined to beat me. He'd had a bad day at the craps tables and was trying to get his money back. Some players bet more and more money on each hand, trying to beat a particular dealer. That's stupid. You must play the usual patterns; win a couple, lose a couple.

Here's a basic money strategy:

Original bet: $2. Win $2. Profit $2.
Second hand: bet $3. Win $3. Profit $5.
Third hand: bet $4. Win $4. Profit $9—or *lose* $4 and you're still $5 ahead. **Any time you lose a hand, go immediately back to your original bet.**

If you win the third hand:
Fourth hand: bet $6. Win $6. Profit $15.
Fifth hand: bet $10. Win $10. Profit $25.

After winning five hands in a row, drop back to your original bet.

You can play two hands instead of one by betting twice the table minimum on each hand. If you do this, you must completely finish the first hand before you can look at the second. While playing two hands may sound like a good idea, don't do it. What usually happens is you lose one hand and win one. While you're learning, stick to one hand, play correctly, and use good sense with your money.

Pit Bosses

Pit bosses are those stern looking men or women lurking behind the dealer, making what are supposed to be unobtrusive phone calls, signing drink tabs, and bringing money to the games. They're not as bad as they look. (I think the idea is to intimidate the dealers, and in that they've succeeded very well.)

A story that's been circulating for 30 years will tell you how most dealers feel about pit bosses: A dealer dies and goes to heaven, and St. Peter is showing her around. They enter a peaceful room. "Here's the casino," St. Peter says. "No pit bosses, no drunks, and no grouchy players." Beautiful music is playing, there aren't any slot machine bells, and all the players are smiling and tipping the dealers. "This really *is* heaven!" the dealer thinks. Suddenly, a door opens, and in walks a man with a cigar in his mouth, carrying a cup of coffee. He is wearing a plaid sports coat with a loud tie, and he starts yelling at the dealers. "Hey," the dealer says, "I thought you said there weren't any pit bosses in heaven." "Oh, that's not a pit boss," St. Peter says. "That's God. He just *thinks* He's a pit boss."

Actually, the bosses are a strategic part of the casino's management team. There are different levels: The *floor boss* is the person you'll see in the pit behind the dealers. His responsibilities include watching the games to prevent cheating by a dealer or a customer, seeing that dealers get their breaks on time, and assigning dealers to the tables after each break. The *shift boss* is in charge of an entire shift: day, swing, or graveyard. Above him is an assistant casino manager, and above him, the casino manager. All bosses know all the games and can step in and deal in an emergency.

A boss must know how much each table is winning or losing. In the old days, when pit bosses were a lot more colorful, it was not uncommon to see a boss lose his temper when a table was losing. (Some bosses threw money racks and swore at the dealers just loud enough so no one else could hear. I once had a boss who blew a thick cloud of cigar smoke in my face every time I broke a hand.) Then there were the superstitious bosses, like the one who burned a piece of string or sprinkled salt around the table to change the luck. Some bosses could cut a deck in two and tell you the exact number of cards in each stack. The graveyard bosses used to play tricks on new dealers, like sending them over to another club for a "wheel wrench" to tighten the roulette wheel. Of course, the bosses at the other club would oblige by sending back some sort of bent screwdriver or a broken croupier's stick.

Being a boss is a tough job; keeping the dealers *and* the public happy is not easy. Today's pit boss is the link between the customer and the casino. He's there to see that a player enjoys himself and to supervise the games. A boss is always courteous to a player and may even buy you dinner—if you win (or lose) enough money.

The Dealers

Don't forget to tip the dealer if you win. Dealers don't expect you to tip if you're losing, but when you win you've won casino money, and you can afford to give that nice dealer a few dollars when you leave the table.

Some players bet for the dealer while they're playing, and some players always take the extra 1/2 won on a blackjack and bet it for the dealer on the next hand. To do this, put the dealer's bet directly in front of yours, in the betting square. If you win, don't ask the dealer if she wants to let her bet ride. The rules forbid her telling you, but in most clubs, she must take her money immediately. If you're having a lucky streak, you could simply put a couple of dollars atop your own bet, and then if you win, give the $4 to the dealer.

Despite what you may hear, dealers are not well paid. They make barely over minimum wage, and they depend on tips. And if a dealer has entertained you, ordered free drinks for you, and you've won a little money, then you've had a good time, and she deserves a few dollars as thanks.

I know what you're thinking. How can those dealers afford the diamond rings and the fancy watches and the emerald earrings if they make minimum wage? Well, you'd be surprised how many players forget the basic rule: Never bet more than you can afford to lose. Some people play every penny in their pockets, write their checkbook balances down to nothing—and then wonder how they're going to get home. No bus money, no gas money. But they usually have an expensive watch or a piece of jewelry, and guess who they want to sell it to? Tires, cameras, fur coats, diamonds—they'll offer anything you can think of to the dealers for bus fare home. Once I loaned a man $20 for bus fare, never expecting to see it again. But he'd been playing at my table for hours, and he was desperate. A few days later I received his check in the mail, with a nice thank-you note.

Do dealers gamble? Just as in any other societal group, some do and some don't. A few always have to take a "draw" on their paychecks. There's a basic rule in most casinos that an employee can't play where he works. That doesn't stop some dealers from running across the street on a break to play a few hands.

A lot depends on the shift. Day shift dealers often smell of baby powder, not $50-an-ounce perfume, and they usually go home after work to fix dinner for the kids. Graveyard dealers are too tired to do much but go home and sleep. It's the swing shift dealers, the younger ones, who like to stay late after shift, have a drink, and play a few hands.

Of course, that's a generalization. Most dealers come to work, put in their time, and go home again, just as you do with your job. (Of course, when the in-laws come to town for a holiday, we feel obligated to go out with them and play a few hands.)

Casinos and Cheating

Many people assume casinos cheat naïve players. Years ago, when the clubs were run by the mob, some dealers *were* expected to manipulate the cards so the house always won. The Nevada Gaming Commission put a stop to all that, and today everyone connected to a casino has been through a background check that makes the C.I.A. look like Cub Scouts.

When gambling first started in Nevada, it was run by people named Bugsy and Lucky and Legs. Many of those who opened clubs on The Strip in Las Vegas had been operating in places like Chicago and Detroit and Hot Springs, where the games were illegal and controlled by gangsters. There they had to pay protection money, and of course, when players discovered they were being cheated, they stayed away. Then Meyer Lansky (immortalized as "Hyman Roth" in *The Godfather*) discovered that house percentages took care of the winnings and that it was possible to run an honest game and still come out ahead. And an honest operation doesn't have to pay protection money.

Nevada is proud of its clean image, and no casino today would risk losing its license and the millions it makes every year just to scam a few dollars from a player. You can play with absolute certainty that the game is honest. You may not win, but you won't be cheated.

Blackjack Terms

Action: The play, or bets.

Break or Bust: When the total of a hand is more than 21. A **breaking hand** is one that can go over 21 with the next card.

Capping a Bet: Illegally adding to the top of an original bet, or a dealer paying a bet by putting the payoff on top of the original bet.

Casing the deck: Counting the deck.

Double Down: The doubling of a bet on the first two cards. Some casinos allow you to double after a split.

Eye in the Sky: The observation platform behind two-way mirrors above the games.

First Base: The first seat at the dealer's left.

Hard Hand: Any hand containing a 10 that you ordinarily do not hit.

Hit or Draw: To take another card.

Hole Card: The dealer's unexposed card.

Insurance: A side bet offered when the dealer shows an ace.

Limits: The minimum and maximum bet allowed at each table.

Marker: An I.O.U. in lieu of chips.

Natural: A two-card 21, a blackjack.

Parlay: A system where all the money remains bet on the next hand.

Pit: A section of the casino where the table games are set up.

Pit Boss: The supervisor in charge of the games.

Press: Adding money illegally to the size of the bet.

Push: A tie between a dealer and a player.

Snapper: A blackjack.

Soft Hand: Any hand containing an ace.

Stand: The decision not to take any more cards.

Stiff: A hard hand between 12 and 16. A hand with which you can "bust" with one more card.

Third Base: The last seat on the dealer's right.

Toke: The tip given to the dealer.

Basic Blackjack Strategy

Regardless of the dealer's card, **always hit** 11 or less and soft 17 or less.

Regardless of the dealer's card, **never hit** 17, 18, 19, 20 and soft 19 or 20.

Hit 12, 13, 14, 15, 16 if the dealer shows 7 or higher.

Hit 12 if the dealer has a 2.

Hit soft 18 if the dealer has a 10 or an ace showing.

Always double down on 11.

Double down on 10 unless the dealer shows 10 or ace.

Always split aces and 8s.

Split 6s only when the dealer shows a 5.

Never split 2s, 3s, 4s, 5s, 7s, 9s, or 10s.

Always insure when you have a blackjack.

Never insure any other hand.

Roulette

About 30 years ago, an eccentric millionaire lived near Reno. His castle-like house prompted ridiculous tales, but everyone knew the man was a miser. You could drive past at night and see a single light bulb hanging from a wire—no fancy fixtures at this house—and it was rumored he kept his money in tin cans, buried in the dirt floor of the garage. His car was a 1939 Hudson, in showroom condition because he walked all over town. He wore bib overalls and plaid shirts, and people who didn't know him thought he was just a poor, old man.

Playing roulette was his one weakness. Each casino in town kept a supply of roulette chips monogrammed with his initials, for his use only. About once a month he would walk downtown and sit for the entire afternoon at the roulette wheel. He always carried a supply of straight pins and a piece of white paper. He'd sit for a few hours and watch the wheel spin. After each spin, he'd stick pins in the paper and, after two hours or so, he'd start playing, still keeping track of the numbers with his paper and pins.

We all knew this was a "system" of some sort, but no one ever figured out just what the system was. And, of course, it didn't work any better than any other system. Some days he'd win several thousand dollars, and his fellow players thought he must be some sort of genius. They didn't see the many other days when he lost.

Casinos are accustomed to seeing "system" roulette players with their little pads of paper and pencils. Some European casinos even provide their players with stationery supplies—which should tell you something. American casinos aren't as accommodating, but as long as your record-keeping doesn't slow the game, no one will object.

However, systems are a complete waste of time. Roulette has been around since the 17th century, when a French math teacher invented the wheel as an offshoot of a perpetual motion device.

The game has not changed at all since then. Systems players have tried to beat the wheel for four centuries, and supposedly the inventor lost his mind trying to develop his own system.

Roulette is the most popular game in Europe's famous gambling houses, like the Monte Carlo Casino in Monaco. There, a pit boss sits on a very high chair—sort of like the judge at a tennis match—and watches every move. The roulette rooms are plush, with the dealers and floormen dressed in tuxedos with carnations in their lapels. There are three dealers; one does nothing but collect the tips. (Every time the ball goes around, there's a tip for the dealers. This is the kind of job Nevada dealers dream about!)

In U.S. casinos, where roulette is an addition to the blackjack games, the wheel is usually located at the end of a blackjack pit and is handled by one dealer who hopes someone will win—and be generous.

How to Bet

In roulette, you bet the same way as in other games: place your cash on the table, not on the numbers, and ask for change. However, roulette chips are different from chips at other games; they have no monetary value. You can't take them away from the roulette table; they're worthless anywhere else, except as a tip for the cocktail waitress while you're playing. You must cash the chips when you leave the table.

Chips range in value, usually starting at 25 cents, and come in stacks of 20 from the dealer. Each player receives a different color chip and decides its value when he buys them. For example, if you want your chips to be worth $1 each, then your stack would cost you $20. If you want your chips to be worth 25 cents each, then you would get four stacks for a $20 bill. The dealer will take a chip of your color, set it aside, and mark it with a coin. (If you want your chips valued at 25 cents, the dealer will take a quarter from the money tray and place it on top of your color chip next to the wheel.) You can play paper money instead of chips, if you wish. Table minimums are posted at each table.

The Wheel and the Layout

The roulette wheel has 38 numbers: 1 to 36, plus 0 and 00. The numbers are colored red and black, and the 0 and 00 are green. On the layout, the numbers are set up in numerical order, in three columns of twelve, with the 0 and 00 at one end. On the wheel however, the numbers are not in order.

Place your bet on the *layout*, which is simply a table with

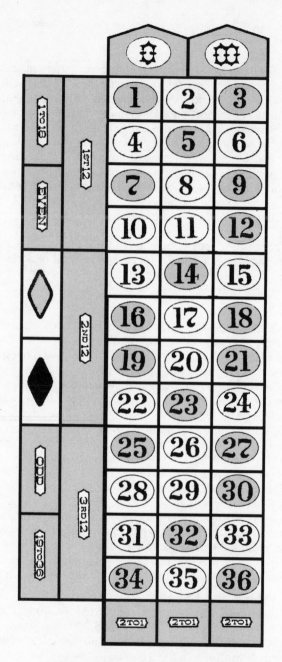

Roulette Layout

squares matching the numbers on the wheel. The squares in the upper part of the layout are numbered 1 to 36, plus 0 and 00. Below these numbers are spaces for betting on Red or Black, Odd or Even, the first, second, or third group of 12 numbers, or numbers between 1 and 18 or between 19 and 36. At the end of the layout, there are three squares where you can bet on the numbers running horizontally across the layout from 3 to 36, 2 to 35, and 1 to 34.

How to Play

Play begins when players have placed most of their bets, and the dealer spins the wheel. The ball is spun in the opposite direction of the wheel. You can continue placing bets until the dealer says "no more bets" as the ball begins to drop. When the ball falls into a number on the wheel, the dealer points to the winning number on the layout or places a marker on that number. The losing bets are taken, and the winning bets are paid. When you win, the dealer will push all your chips to you, so there are no bets left on the layout.

You can bet many ways, and payoffs vary according to where you place the bet. A *straight up* bet—one chip played on one number—pays 35 to 1. If you place a bet on the line dividing two numbers, it's called a *split*, and if either number comes up, the payoff is 17 to 1. Betting three numbers across pays 11 to 1 when any of the three numbers wins. To bet three numbers, place your bet on the line next to the smallest of the three numbers. Example: To bet on 4, 5, and 6, put your chips on the line next to the 4.

Betting four numbers is called a *corner* and pays 8 to 1 when any one of the four numbers comes up. To bet a corner, place your chips where the lines of the four numbers intersect. Example: Place your bet on the corner where the lines intersect 23, 24, 26, and 27.

You can bet five numbers only one way: at the end of the layout, next to the wheel. The numbers are 1, 2, 3, 0, and 00, and it's called *betting the basket*. The bet pays 6 to 1, and you place it at the corner where 1 and 0 intersect.

Betting six numbers across pays 5 to 1. Place your bet on the front line dividing the smallest number and the fourth number, such as 31 and 34 if you're betting 31, 32, 33, 34, 35, 36. On 10 through 15, you would place your bet on the outside line between 10 and 13.

A *section* is comprised of 12 numbers, so the layout is divided into three sections: 1-12, 13-24, and 25-36. You may bet on any section or on two sections (or on all three, which is silly) by placing your bet on the layout marked "1st 12," "2nd 12," or "3rd 12." A *section bet* pays 2 to 1, so a bet placed on all three sections would break even. People do bet this way, though—a sure way to drive the dealer to the bar after work.

The layout also has three columns of 12 numbers. The columns begin with 1, 2, and 3, but the numbers are not in succession. The column closest to you starts with 1 and ends with 34. The middle column begins with 2 and ends with 35, and the top column begins with 3 and ends with 36. A *column bet* pays 2 to 1, and you place it at the right end of the column where you see the designation "2 to 1."

Betting all the numbers from 1-18 or from 19-36 pays even money (you're paid the same amount you bet). Place this bet on the layout where it says either "1-18" or "19-36."

The simplest bets are Odd or Even and Red or Black. Each of these pays even money, and there are spaces in which to place these bets at the front of the layout. Of course, if you bet on one of these spaces and 0 or 00 comes up, you lose.

You'd be surprised at the number of people who think they can't lose if they bet *both* Red and Black, or Odd and Even at the same time. That's not roulette—it's Russian roulette. Nothing ever seems to happen, but when it does, it's always bad. With every spin you are simply trading money—until 0 or 00 comes up, and then it's all over except the swearing.

The *courtesy line* is for players who want to bet 0 and 00, the green. It's placed on the line dividing the second 12 numbers and the third 12 numbers. It's a split and pays 17 to 1.

Any time you wish to place a bet at the opposite end of the layout from where you're standing, or if you just can't reach the number you want, hand your chips to the dealer and ask him to place the bet for you.

We mentioned above that the numbers on the wheel are not in order, although they're in numerical order on the layout. Many people like to play sections of the wheel because they think the ball is landing in a certain section regularly. If you want to play a section of the wheel, and the ball is continually falling in the area of 24, for instance, you might want to bet on 13, 36, 24, 3, and 15, which are neighboring numbers to 24.

Don't forget that your chips are valued at your purchase price. If you have designated them to be worth 25 cents and you bet 11 chips straight up on a number, you aren't going to win $385. You'll win 385 x 25 cents, which is $96.25.

Single Number Payoffs	Double Number Payoffs
1 chip pays $35	1 chip pays $17
2 chips pay $70	2 chips pay $34
3 chips pay $105	3 chips pay $51
4 chips pay $140	4 chips pay $68
5 chips pay $175	5 chips pay $85
6 chips pay $210	6 chips pay $102
7 chips pay $245	7 chips pay $119
8 chips pay $280	8 chips pay $136
9 chips pay $315	9 chips pay $153
10 chips pay $350	10 chips pay $170
11 chips pay $385	11 chips pay $187
12 chips pay $420	12 chips pay $204
13 chips pay $455	13 chips pay $221
14 chips pay $490	14 chips pay $238
15 chips pay $525	15 chips pay $255
16 chips pay $560	16 chips pay $272
17 chips pay $595	17 chips pay $289
18 chips pay $630	18 chips pay $306
19 chips pay $665	19 chips pay $323
20 chips pay $700	20 chips pay $340

Roulette Systems

Several years ago, some guys from M.I.T. spent two weeks in the casino researching roulette for a thesis on the law of probability. They had worked out the perfect system, they said. The town waited to see what would happen. They lost.

One of the most popular systems for roulette dates to the late 1800's and is called the "cancellation system." A player writes down a row of four numbers, such a 5, 6, 7, 8. It doesn't matter what numbers he uses, although everyone who uses this system is convinced there is something magical about his four numbers. On the first bet, you wager the number of chips equal to the total of the first and last numbers in the row (in this case, 13). Each time the bet loses, the player writes the amount of that bet at the end of the row. Each time the bet wins, the player crosses out the first and last numbers. The next bet is always the total of the first and last uncancelled numbers in the row. When he succeeds in crossing out all the numbers, he has a net profit equaling the total of the original row of numbers; in this case, 26 chips. At that point he starts over with a new row of numbers.

Neighboring Wheel Numbers

The number in the middle is the number on the wheel, and to either side of it are its neighboring numbers. Reading from left to right:

9 - 28	**0**	2 - 14
10 - 27	**00**	1 - 13
27 - 00	**1**	13 - 36
28 - 0	**2**	14 - 35
36 - 24	**3**	15 - 34
35 - 23	**4**	16 - 33
34 - 22	**5**	17 - 32
33 - 21	**6**	18 - 31
32 - 20	**7**	11 - 30
31 - 19	**8**	12 - 29
30 - 26	**9**	28 - 0
29 - 25	**10**	27 - 00
20 - 7	**11**	30 - 26
19 - 8	**12**	29 - 25
00 - 1	**13**	36 - 24
0 - 2	**14**	35 - 23
24 - 3	**15**	34 - 22
23 - 4	**16**	33 - 21
22 - 5	**17**	32 - 20
21 - 6	**18**	31 - 19
18 - 31	**19**	8 - 12
17 - 32	**20**	7 - 11
16 - 33	**21**	6 - 18
15 - 34	**22**	5 - 17
14 - 35	**23**	4 - 16
13 - 36	**24**	3 - 15
12 - 29	**25**	10 - 27
11 - 30	**26**	9 - 28
24 - 10	**27**	00 - 1
26 - 9	**28**	0 - 2
8 - 12	**29**	25 - 10
7 - 11	**30**	26 - 9
6 - 18	**31**	19 - 8
5 - 17	**32**	20 - 7
4 - 16	**33**	21 - 6
3 - 15	**34**	22 - 5
2 - 14	**35**	23 - 4
1 - 13	**36**	24 - 3

A believer in this system will tell you that you will always succeed, because you cancel two numbers each time you win and add only one number when you lose. You can therefore lose more than half your bets and still come out a winner.

What they don't anticipate is a run of bad luck, so you keep getting more losers than winners. Your bets will steadily grow, until your required bet will exceed the table limit, leaving you with a long row of numbers, a stubby pencil, a wastebasket full of paper—and no money.

Those who sell systems love to talk about "computer tested" programs. Don't believe it! While computers have developed good blackjack card-counting systems, so far no one has devised a successful computer ploy to beat the roulette wheel. You'll win just as much betting your mother's birthday or the day you graduated from grade school.

Remember the millionaire at the beginning of this chapter? Well, he died recently. They found the money he buried in the garage, stuffed into tin cans. His grieving widow immediately remodeled the house, adding new light fixtures and an indoor swimming pool. Nobody knows what has happened to the monogrammed roulette chips.

Keno

Everyone who's played a keno ticket has a story about the one that got away, the ticket they didn't play in time, for one reason or another. Including us. We played our first ticket ever while sitting at the bar after work one night. We marked an 8 spot and decided to finish our drinks before we went to the keno counter. Of course, all 8 numbers came up, and we would have won $25,000. In all the years since, we've never seen those numbers come up again.

Keno is kind of like roulette and the state lottery. You simply pick your lucky numbers and hope. Some swear that the law of probability comes into play somewhere along the line and, as with roulette, you'll see people sitting in the keno lounges with pads of paper and pencils, marking the numbers that come up on each game.

Casino employees play "freeno" while working. Most have a set of numbers they know by heart. You'll often see dealers standing at a dead game watching the keno board. Many times one number will come up game after game. What happens when the dealer goes on break and plays that one number? You know.

Keno payoffs are the biggest in the casino, because the odds against winning are the highest. It's still a very popular game, though, probably for the same reason people fly from Germany to play the Florida state lottery when it reaches $30,000,000. They figure somebody's going to win, and it could be them.

Keno originated in China over 2,000 years ago and was called *pak kop piu* ("white pigeon game") because carrier pigeons carried the tickets. Today, keno runners pick up your tickets from anywhere in the casino: at the bar, the blackjack table, in the dining room. Every bar and gambling table has keno tickets, and you should have your ticket marked before the runner arrives. Keno runners carry change, too. Some people like to have the runners choose the numbers for them. Once, a man playing blackjack asked the runner to choose eight numbers and promised that if the numbers came up, he'd divide the winnings with her. Well, they all came up, and the runner got over $11,000.

Keno Basics

A keno ticket is a piece of paper divided into 80 squares matching the keno boards displayed throughout the casino. As the game ("race") is called, the winning numbers light up on the boards. You begin by marking your ticket with a black crayon, supplied by the club. Mark any number of spots, from one to 80. You can play all tickets for any multiple of the minimum bet allowed.

Take your ticket to the keno counter. Most clubs have a large lounge set aside for keno players, so they can sit and watch the games come up—game after game after game.

At the counter, a keno writer will copy your ticket and return the copy while keeping your original. The ticket you give to the writer is called an *inside ticket*. The ticket you receive is an *outside ticket*, and it's marked with your numbers and the number of the game. It's your responsibility to see that this ticket is marked exactly the way you want it. If it isn't and you don't correct it, the inside copy will be considered correct in case of a dispute. Your copy is your receipt, and you'll need it to claim your winnings.

When the game begins, 80 numbered ping pong-like balls are mixed by air pressure in the keno bowl. Twenty balls are ejected at random into tubes, and those become the winning numbers. The order the numbers come up makes no difference. The amount you win depends on the number of spots you play and the amount of money you bet. The casinos have little pamphlets at the keno counters explaining the payoffs and bets, and every club is different, so read before you write your ticket.

How to Play

Most players simply mark eight numbers and pay whatever the going rate is. Example: Mark eight spots (numbers), bet $3, and if five of those eight come up, you'll win $27. Six spots pays $276, seven pays $4,440, and all eight pays $50,000.

Dedicated keno players often play something called a *way ticket*, which allows you to play several tickets on one, using groups of numbers combined in different ways to form larger groups. You can bet on all the possible combinations of the groups you've chosen. You separate the groups by drawing circles around them. Way tickets can be very complicated, but you can win more with

Keno Ticket

them than if you play a straight spot ticket. Even a single number can be circled and combined with other numbers to be counted as a "group." This is called a *king*. On a 10-spot ticket, you could have three groups of three, and a king.

Let's say you want to play an eight-spot. By marking 12 numbers, you can play a way ticket: a three-way eight, and a three-way four-spot, all on one ticket. Example: Mark 61, 62, 71, 72 and circle those numbers. Now mark 24, 34, 45, and 56 and circle those. The last four numbers could be 10, 20, 30, and 40. Circle those. If each group costs $2.50 per way, and you have three eight-spots and three four-spots, the ticket will cost $15 ($2.50 x 6). If three numbers in each of two groups comes up, you'll win $180. Here's how your way ticket would pay in groups of 4-4-4:

If you catch	you'll win
3-0-0	$10
3-1-0	$10
3-1-1	$10
3-2-0	$24
3-2-1	$24
3-2-2	$38
3-3-0	$180
3-3-1	$180
3-3-2	$208
3-3-3	$510
4-0-0	$450
4-1-0	$464
4-1-1	$478
4-2-0	$610
4-2-1	$624
4-2-2	$770
4-3-0	$4,060
4-3-1	$4,074
4-3-2	$4,234
4-3-3	$7,830
4-4-0	$100,000
4-4-1	$100,000
4-4-2	$100,000
4-4-3	$100,000
4-4-4	$100,000

If you catch three from one group and one from the other group, you'll lose money, but if you catch three from one group and two from another, you'll be ahead. Any keno writer can figure how many possible combinations you have on your ticket.

You can even mark all 80 numbers on a ticket, for 20 groups of four. Each group of four combines with each other group of four to form an eight-spot. There are 190 ways to form an eight-spot, giving you 190 ways to win.

The Payouts
In most casinos, you must claim your winnings immediately after the race. Some of the larger resorts offer variations, however. One is called **multi-race keno**, which lets you play up to 20 consecutive games with one ticket. Your ticket will be checked for winners, automatically replayed, and your winnings paid at the end of your last game. A few places have **Keno-To-Go**, where you

can play as many as 1,000 consecutive games and take up to a year to collect your winnings. There's also **computerized keno**, where a computer picks the numbers for you.

Keno players often don't understand that a payout of $100,000, for example, is an *aggregate* payout; all winning players on a race share that amount. That is, if all your numbers come up, you won't receive the entire $100,000 because others have won lesser amounts.

You should know that the IRS watches the keno game, too, and requires casinos to report all net payoffs of $1,500 or more. Keno players have objected to this for years, arguing that gamblers win $1,500 and more at table games without being reported, but the rule remains. Many times, an IRS agent was in the casino at the time of a big win and insisted that winners pay their taxes on the spot.

Keno Tales

The best way to learn keno is to play. Try a way ticket. You may be surprised at the amount you can win.

Does anyone ever win the really big money? Of course. All it takes is knowing what numbers to mark...

Or maybe there's more to it. Once at Lake Tahoe, around 3:00am, a couple dressed in white robes came through the door and headed straight for the keno counter. They marked an eight-spot, lit two purple candles, and knelt in front of the counter. They prayed the entire time the game was running. And yes, they won $25,000, collected their winnings, and left. True story.

And then there's the couple who came to town for the first time, checked into their hotel, and asked for Fun Books, which included a free ticket at the keno counter. The man went to the counter, asked how to mark his ticket, and watched as $12,500 worth of his numbers came up—and then found that his wife had marked an identical ticket!

That's the fun thing about keno—you don't even have to know what you're doing. Just play a ticket at the bar, at lunch in the coffee shop, or while you're at the blackjack table. You never know.

Slot Machines

Suppose you're playing a slot machine and you're breaking even. Nearby, a man has been pouring money into a similar machine without even one coin falling into the tray. He's grumbling, but he puts his coin cup over the handle of the machine and goes looking for a change person. Should you move to his machine, figuring it's due to "hit?"

No, no, no! Slot players are very possessive. Once a player has pumped money into a machine, that machine is *his*, so don't even think about getting near it. Casinos have seen many fights erupt when someone, inadvertently or not, plays a machine that someone else has marked as his own.

Though this may seem extreme, consider the poor player. After all, he's been sitting at the machine for hours, getting small payoffs now and then and hoping that the jackpot isn't far off. He certainly doesn't want someone else stepping up with one coin and winning the big money. Besides, he left his cup over the handle, which in slot machine parlance says, "This machine is taken. The owner will be right back."

But there's a better reason. Slot machine payoffs are random; each pull of the machine handle is completely independent of the previous pull. Though slots can seem to go on hot and cold streaks, you can only be sure that the next pull may either continue the streak or change it. There's no way to tell. The machines are set to pay a certain percentage of the money dropped into them over a long period of time. When enough people drop enough money, the casino returns the percentage and keeps the rest.

For the player, there's little to it. You just hope you're there when the percentage is right, and the symbols line up across the reels. Some players ask change people which machines are "hot." Forget it! The odds are the same each time you pull the handle, regardless of the machine you play.

Playing Smart

You can, however, be smart about it. Some casinos set their machines for a higher rate of return than others. If you're strictly a slot player, you might as well play at those casinos. A casino may advertise "loose" slots or claim they give a "97% payback." This doesn't mean you're going to win 97% of the time. It means the casino keeps only 3% of the money put into the slot machines.

Another way to gain an edge is to join a "slot club" offered at many casinos. Membership is always free, and members get "bonus points" when they hit a jackpot, free entry into slot tournaments, and free gifts. Some places have monthly drawings for vacations, discounts on food and lodging, free cars and boats, etc.

Slot Payoffs

The payoffs in some casinos can be tremendous; some offer millions in jackpots. For example, **MegaBucks** is a system linking many dollar slots throughout Nevada. As the machines are played, the jackpot grows until someone, in some casino somewhere in the state, hits it. Then it's reset to $3,000,000, and it starts all over again. MegaBucks once paid a $6,800,000 jackpot.

A similar game, called **Quartermania**, is linked to over 30 casinos in the state. In case you believe you can't win by playing just a quarter, consider the couple from Oregon who won $410,654 after playing only $10 in quarters at a Quartermania machine in Harrah's in Laughlin. And at Bally's in Reno, two first-time visitors walked out with more than $116,000 from two rolls of quarters.

Progressive nickel machines offer big payoffs, too—up to $200,000.

Playing the Slots

Progressive machines have a counter at the top, like a cash register, which records each increase as each coin is played. These machines will usually have four or five reels, and you must play more than one coin to hit the jackpot. The first coin pays on the middle line, the second on the line above, and the third on all three visible lines. There's nothing worse than playing only one coin and seeing the winning symbols line up on the row you didn't play. A chart on the machine will tell you how many coins to play for the best payoff.

Many people think that a machine will show a winner on a line they haven't played, just to get them to play more money. Not true. It's illegal for a slot machine manufacturer to build that kind of feature into a machine. So if you play only one line, and the winner comes up on the line you didn't play, it's just bad judgment.

By the way, it doesn't matter how hard you pull the handle or whether you push a button. The handle or button is simply a trigger for an electronic process that spins the reels. Once, casinos had to watch for "rhythm" slot players, who could time the pulls of a handle to bring the symbols to the pay line. There aren't many of these old-time slot machines around anymore, though.

More Slot Machine Etiquette

In addition to not poaching someone's machine, there's more etiquette involved with slots, believe it or not. When you're walking past a row of machines and one whispers "Play me, I'll make you rich," you don't have to go to the change booth. Though you can put a cup over the handle to signify you're playing that machine, it's not smart. If you need change, just push the button on the machine that says "Change," and a change person will quickly appear.

When you hit a payoff, large or small, it's polite to put one more coin in the machine and pull the handle before you walk away. It's annoying to another player to walk up and see that the machine has supposedly just paid 20 coins, but no one is around. He doesn't know if the machine is broken and hasn't paid those 20 coins, or what has happened. Play off your winners.

Television and the movies tend to distort what really occurs in a casino. You know how they always show coins tumbling all over the floor when a jackpot hits? (This goes for book covers, too!) That's only for effect. In reality, a machine drops only a small fraction of the payoff. The ringing of the bell on the machine calls attention to the payoff, and someone will come and pay you the balance in paper money. You must wait until the slot attendant verifies the jackpot before you make any additional plays on that machine. If you don't wait to be paid and continue to play the machine, you'll wipe out all record of the jackpot.

The players around you can be a good show, too. Many older women still wear a white glove to keep their hand clean—nickels make your hand black—and carry stools to sit on, just in case all the chairs are full. The optimists go from row to row, checking the drop trays for abandoned coins and pulling handles hoping to find a "sleeper," a free play on a machine where someone has put in a coin and not pulled the handle.

New Slot Technology

The latest slot machines are entertainment in themselves. Music plays and little characters jump all over the video screen, like the bandit who says "nyah, nyah, nyah" when you miss a payoff, and the gunfighter who falls to the ground with his feet in the air and says "You got me!" when you win.

Video poker machines are the latest in gaming technology. Winning is a matter of chance, but it's also connected to a player's knowledge of poker. When you put your money in a video poker machine, five cards appear on the screen. The object is to make the best poker hand possible with five cards. You have one chance to draw new cards by pushing the "discard" and "hold" buttons, and the buttons beneath each card signify which cards you want to keep. New cards will appear to replace the ones you discarded. Video poker is different from regular poker because you aren't playing against other player's cards. You're only trying to get a hand high enough to get a payoff from the machine. So while a pair of nines could win in a regular game, you won't win with it on a poker machine (most machines pay only on a pair of Jacks or better).

Some casino's machines pay more coins than other's for different hands. You can win eight coins for a flush or only seven, depending on the casino. On some video machines you can win $1,000 from only five coins.

The computers in the machine randomly go through a 52-card deck and select 10 cards. The first five are displayed on the screen, the other five are held in reserve to be used when you push the discard button. If you draw more cards, you'll receive the cards held in reserve. Knowing when to draw can help you win. Trying to draw to an inside straight is harder than drawing to a straight that could be filled from either side. The odds depend on how well you play.

Video poker and blackjack machines can be played with one to eight coins, and in some places you can play on a credit meter. Be careful with this—the play is faster, and you can owe a lot of money in a hurry.

Why Play Slots?
Slot machines have been around for a long time. The reason may be that while some people like to play cards or dice with a real, live person, some are more comfortable facing a machine. The possibility of becoming a millionaire by spending only a dollar is hard to resist, too.

Just don't forget that the odds, as always, are with the casino. You can put $60 a minute into a dollar machine. But then again, it takes only a second to win that million!

Pai Gow
and the Asian Games

Pai Gow (rhymes with "tie cow") is an ancient Chinese game dating back 1,000 years or more. Played throughout Asia for centuries, it is the forerunner of Chemin de Fer, blackjack, and baccarat.

Asian players are big business in Nevada, and the casinos are sensitive to Asian customs. Dealers won't wear jade, for instance, because jade is a symbol of power in the Orient, and Asians won't play against dealers wearing it. Harrah's has a separate section exclusively for Asian games, and the Chinese New Year is a popular event in Reno.

Though gambling is an integral part of Asian culture, it is not considered mere entertainment. You'll notice that most Asians don't drink or even talk while gambling. They don't want to be distracted, since their main goal is to make money.

Dealers at Asian games speak the languages of their players. They also speak English, though, and you don't have to be afraid to play these games. They are fast becoming the most popular games in the casinos.

Translated, Pai Gow means "make nine." It's played with a set of 32 dominoes (tiles), each with 2 to 12 red or white dots. The color of the dots doesn't matter; it simply makes reading the tiles easier. The tile's value is the entire face. It's not divided into top and bottom, as in dominoes.

How to Play

The dealer will shuffle the tiles face down and arrange them, still face down, in stacks of eight. The bank starts the game by rolling three tiny dice, which must bounce off the stacks of tiles. All bets must be made before the dice are thrown. The total on the dice determines which player receives the first set of tiles. (The dealer counts from the bank, counter-clockwise.) The bank decides the order the tiles come off the stack.

Each player arranges his four tiles into two combinations—a high pair and a low pair. A ranking system determines the value of each pair, and the object of the game is to set the tiles into the best ranking combinations. Both hands must be higher than the bank's hands to win.

Place the lower hand in front of the higher hand. If your two rankings are higher than the bank's, you win. If they are lower, the bank wins. When the bank and the player have the same ranking combination, the hand with the highest ranking tile wins, and only the highest ranking tile is considered. If one hand is higher and the other lower, it's a push. If the bank and the player have identical hands, the bank wins.

The players and the dealer take turns being the bank, and the bank changes after each round of play. Each player thus has the opportunity to bank the bets against the other players, including the house. A player must be able to cover all bets to be the banker, but if a player can't cover all the bets, the house, at its option, will bank half. If no player wants to be the bank, the house always will. A disc placed in front of the hand indicates who is the bank.

Incidentally, if you're the bank and the other players lose, don't grab their money. The house dealer handles all money transactions, no matter who's the bank. Payoffs are even money, but the house collects a 5% commission on all winning hands.

Ranking the Combinations

Nine is the highest point, as in baccarat, but there are 20 different combinations of tiles higher than nine. Sixteen of these are pairs; the other four are called Wong and Gong. Each of these combinations has a ranking, and the symbolism of the tile, not the numerical value, determines that ranking.

Each single tile is also ranked according to its symbolic value, and single rankings are used to break ties. A tile with two dots stands for the Earth (one dot represents land, and the other water.) The tile with eight dots stands for the eight Chinese moralities: love, loyalty, honesty, courtesy, sincerity, modesty, grace, and devotion to parents.

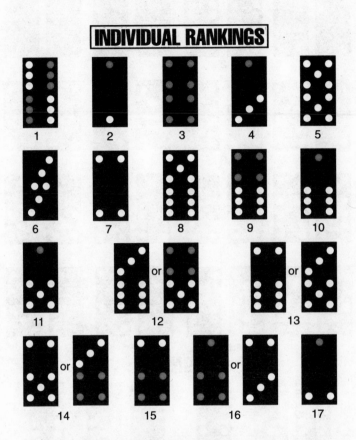

Single Rankings:

#1 ranking: Three red dots vertically and three white dots verti-
cally at the top, plus three white dots and three red dots ver-
tically at the bottom. This is *Teen*, or Heaven.

#2 ranking: One red dot at the top and one white dot at the
bottom. This is *Dey*, or Earth.

#3 ranking: Four red dots at the top and four red dots at the bot-
tom. This is *Yun*, or Man.

#4 ranking: One red dot at the top and three white dots on a
diagonal at the bottom. This is *Gor*, or Goose.

#5 ranking: Five white dots at the top and five white dots at the
bottom. (Four corners and the middle.) This is *Mui*, or Flower.

RANKING COMBINATIONS

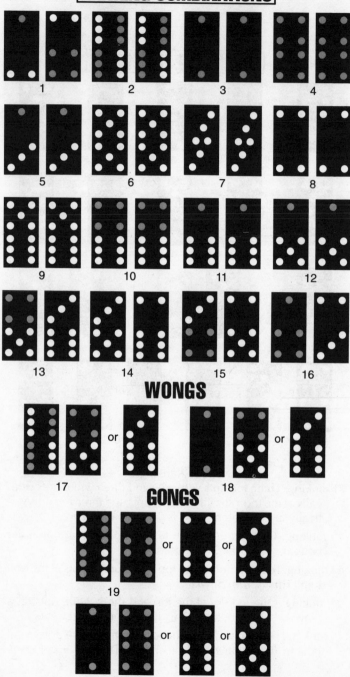

WONGS

GONGS

#6 ranking: All white dots, three diagonally at the top and three diagonally at the bottom. This is *Cheung*, or Long.

#7 ranking: Two horizontal white dots at the top and at the bottom. This is *Barn*, or Board.

#8 ranking: Five white dots at the top and six white dots at the bottom. This is *Foo*, or Hatchet.

#9 ranking: Four red dots at the top and six white dots at the bottom. This is *Ping*, or Partition.

#10 ranking: One red dot at the top and six white dots on the bottom. This is *Chut*, or Long Leg 7.

#11 ranking: One red dot at the top and five white dots at the bottom. This is *Luk*, or Big Head 6.

#12 ranking: Three white dots on a diagonal at the top and six white dots at the bottom, or four red dots at the top and five white dots at the bottom. This is *Jaap Gow*, or Mixed 9.

#13 ranking: Three white dots on a diagonal on top and five white dots on the bottom, or two white dots at the top and six white dots on the bottom. This is *Jaap Bart*, or Mixed 8.

#14 ranking: Two white dots on the top and five white dots on the bottom, or three white diagonal dots on the top and four red dots on the bottom. This is *Jaap Chut*, or Mixed 7.

#15 ranking: Two white dots on top and four red dots on the bottom. This is *Luk*, or Low 6.

#16 ranking: Two white dots at the top and three white diagonal dots on the bottom, or one red dot at the top and four red dots on the bottom. This is *Jaap Ng*, or Mixed 5.

#17 ranking: One red dot at the top and two white dots at the bottom. This is *Saam*, or Low 3. #15 and #17 are the "jokers" and are interchangeable.

Pair Rankings:

(Refer to single rankings for names.)

Pairs #1-16 are called *Bo*, or Precious.

#1 Pair: Called *Gee Joon*, or Supreme. Made up of *Saam* and *Luk*.

#2 Pair: Called *Teen*, or Heaven. Made up of two *Teens*.

#3 Pair: Called *Dey*, or Earth. Made up of two *Deys*.

#4 Pair: Called *Yun*, or Man. Made up of two *Yuns*.

#5 Pair: Called *Gor*, or Goose. Made up of two *Gors*.

#6 Pair: Called *Mui*, or Flower. Made up of two *Muis*.

#7 Pair: Called *Cheung*, or Long. Made up of two *Cheungs*.

#8 Pair: Called *Barn*, or Board. Made up of two *Barns*.

#9 Pair: Called *Foo*, or Hatchet. Made up of two *Foos*.

#10 Pair: Called *Ping*, or Partition. Made up of two *Pings*.

#11 Pair: Called *Chut*, or Long Leg 7. Made up of two *Chuts*.

#12 Pair: Called *Luk*, or Big Head 6. Made up of two *Luks*.

#13 Pair: Called *Jaap Gow*, or Mixed 9. Made up of the #12 single rankings as a pair.

#14 Pair: Called *Jaap Bart*, or Mixed 8. Made up of the #13 single rankings as a pair.

#15 Pair: Called *Jaap Chut*, or Mixed 7. Made up of the #14 single rankings as a pair.

#16 Pair: Called *Jaap Ng*, or Mixed 5. Made up of the #16 single rankings as a pair.

Pairs #17 and #18 are called *Wong*, or King.

#17 Pair: Called *Teen Gow Wong*, or King of Heaven. Two combinations have the same ranking. Made up of *Teen* and either of the *Jaap Gow*, or Mixed 9.

#18 Pair: Called *Dey Gow Wong*, or King of Earth. Made up of *Dey* and either of the *Jaap Gow*, or Mixed 9.

Pairs #19 and #20 are called *Gong*, or Treasure.

#19 Pair: Called *Teen Gong*, or Treasure of Heaven. Made up of *Teen Yun*, or *Teen* and either of the *Jaap Bart*.

#20 Pair: Called *Dey Gong*, or Treasure of Earth. Made up of *Dey Yun*, or *Dey* and either of the *Jaap Bart*.

How to Win

To win a bet, both of a player's pairs—low and high—must beat the bank's pairs. Usually, a pair's value equals the last of the total of dots on the two tiles. Example: A 12-dot tile and a 7-dot tile add up to 19, so their value is 9. However, the 20 special pairs described above rank higher than a nine hand, based on the symbolic values of the pair. Example: Two 12-dot pairs add up to 24, which would give a numerical value of 4. But a pair of 12s is called "double *Teen*," or Heaven—the second highest pair in Pai

Gow. Obviously, you'll need to memorize the ranks of the combinations or have this book when you play.

An unusual situation is that the two lowest ranking single tiles, low 6 and low 3, when combined form the *highest* ranking pair. They also act as wild cards; the six can act as the three, and vice versa.

The 2nd-16th rankings are pairs, called *Bo*; the 13th-16th are mixed pairs called *Chop*. After the pair rankings, the best combination is the *Wong* (King), 12 (Heaven) and any 9. This is followed by 2 (Earth) and 9. Next is 12 (Heaven) and any 8—called *Gong* (Steel)—and any 8, followed by the Earth and any 8.

Basic Rules

There are four basic rules of play:

1. Play the pairs, and be careful. *It's easy to overlook the unmatched pairs.*

2. Play a 2 or a 12 with a 7, 8, or 9. This gives you either a high 9, a *Gong*, or a *Wong*.

3. Play two small tiles that equal 7, 8, or 9.

4. Play the biggest tile with the smallest to make the low hand as high as possible.

Payoffs

The house dealer will push amounts lost by players to the center of the table. (When the house loses, its money goes to the center also.) The house dealer then distributes the winnings, which are paid with the losing bets, and the banker's money. Whatever is left goes to the bank. Don't forget the house gets a 5% commission on your winnings, and *ho choy* (good luck)!

Pai Gow Poker

Pai Gow Poker combines the basic elements of Chinese Pai Gow with American poker. While Pai Gow uses tiles, Pai Gow Poker uses the familiar card deck. Those who have trouble with *Gongs* and *Jaap Gows* will find this game easier.

Pai Gow Poker is a slow game because so many hands push. Although the minimums are higher—$5 in most places—you can play for a long time on a small amount of money.

The deck contains the usual 52 cards, plus a joker. You can use the joker only as an ace or to complete a straight, a flush, or a straight flush. The house dealer shuffles the cards and deals seven cards to each player and himself. These hands are placed face down in front of the money tray, and the leftover cards go in a discard holder. You then place your bets in the betting circle.

The house dealer or any player can be the bank, and all players bet against the bank. If you decide to be the bank, you must have enough money to cover all the player's bets. The bank is offered to each player, who must accept or pass. If no player accepts, the house dealer is the bank. A square of white plastic identifies the bank.

How to Play

The bank rolls a die (or three dice, depending on the casino) to decide who will receive the first hand. The bank's position is always #1, and the dealer counts from that position. The dealer places the cards on the table in a clockwise rotation from the starting point indicated by the die.

Each player arranges his cards into two hands: a two-card low hand and a five-card high hand, ranked just like regular poker hands:

High card—The highest value card when all the rest are unmatched. The 2 is the lowest, and ace is the highest.

One pair—Two cards of the same value.

Two pair—Two sets of pairs.

Three of a kind—Three cards of the same value.

Straight—Five cards of different suits in numerical order.

Flush—Five cards of the same suit, not in any order.

Full house—Three cards of the same value, plus a pair.

Four of a kind—Four cards of the same value.

Straight flush—Five cards of the same suit, in numerical sequence.

Royal flush—The ace, king, queen, jack, and 10, all in the same suit.

Your five-card hand *must* rate higher than your two-card hand. On the table in front of each player are two squares, one marked "L" for low, one marked "H" for high. When all the players have put their hands into the proper spaces, the dealer will turn over the bank's hand and arrange his cards in front of the money tray, face up. He then compares his low hand to each player's low hand, and his high hand to each player's high hand. If *both* your hands are higher than *both* the bank's hands, you win even money, less a 5% house commission.

Remember, you must win both hands to win, so if one of your hands is higher and one lower, you push—which is why there are so many pushes. If both of your hands are lower, you lose. And if you haven't arranged your hand correctly, you'll lose. For instance, if the two-card hand is higher than the five-card hand, you should have been more careful. Or maybe you put three cards in a low hand and four in a high hand. Too bad. (It's possible but unlikely that the bank could arrange his hand wrong. He doesn't lose, however—he just has to set it right.)

The winning hands remain face up. The losing hands go into the discard tray, and the money goes into the center of the table to pay the winning bets.

As with blackjack, *never touch your cards after the bank shows his hand.* Players are not allowed to show their cards to each other or talk to other players until all the hands are up. And it does no good to bluff, as in a traditional poker. Either the cards are there or they aren't.

Sic Bo

Sic Bo, which means "dice pair," is also an old Chinese game. The betting table ("layout") is a board showing all the possible combinations of numbers that can come up when three dice are shaken in a clear plastic container. You bet on two-number combinations, on long shots like three matching numbers, or on whether the total on the dice will be below or above nine.

The object is to select a single number or a combination that appears on the dice after they're shaken. You can put your money on any number; the board will light up under the winner. Payoffs run from even money to 150 to 1 for three-of-a-kind.

Pan Nine

Similar to baccarat, Pan Nine is dealt from a "shoe," a box containing eight decks of cards with all the 7s, 8s, 9s, and 10s removed. Face cards are left in. The object of the game is to have a total as close to nine as possible without going over. (The Chinese seem to have affection for the number 9, don't they?)

The dealer and the players each receive three cards face down. Count the cards at their face value. Face cards have no value, and any combination totaling 10 has no value. With any combination over 10, only the *last digit* is counted. (That is, the value of the hand, if it totals 10 or more, is the total *minus* 10. Example: the three cards 6, 6, and 4 would be counted as 6.)

After you get three cards, you can draw one more card to improve your hand. The house dealer must stand on any hand of 6 or more and must draw on 5 or less.

Remember, you don't have to get 9 to win. As with blackjack, you only need to be *closest* to the winning number, so you should stand on 7, 8, or 9. The dealer stands on 6, and since only an ace, 2, or 3 can better your hand, you should probably stand on 6 as well—unless you're a genius and can account for all the cards in eight decks. A 6 is kind of like getting a 17 in blackjack— not great, but too high to risk a hit. If you have the same total as the dealer, you push.

As with most Asian games, the house takes a 5% commission on all winning hands. Losing bets go to the center, and winning bets are paid after every hand has been determined.

Nines Up

A combination of Pai Gow, poker, and baccarat, Nines Up can be confusing. It's played with just one card deck, and the object is to arrange four cards into two poker hands. Obviously, then, the cards must fit into some kind of ranking. A pair is fine, and pairs are ranked as usual, with a pair of aces high and a pair of 2s low. Four of a kind is the highest possible hand. But let's face it, how often are you dealt four of a kind?

If your hand has only one pair, or no pairs, the next best hand is anything that totals nine. However, some nines are better than other nines. The rankings are as follows:

ace, 8	10, 9
king, 9	7, 2
queen, 9	6, 3
jack, 9	5, 4

As in Pan Nine, face cards have no value, and in any hand totaling more than 10, only the last digit is counted. Example: A hand of 7 and 8 counts as 5.

Each player has the chance to be the bank. (In some casinos, the house dealer is always the bank.) You must have enough money to cover all the bets on the table, including the dealer's bet. You can also ask that the house not play. All players play against the bank.

The dealer shuffles, then the banker rolls two dice to determine how many of the cards will be "burned" from the top of the deck. This is the same as in blackjack—the cards are turned under and are not in play. Each player then receives four cards from the deck. In front of each player are two boxes, one marked "L" and one marked "H" to indicate the high and low hands. Arrange your four cards into the best possible combinations, making one hand high and one hand low. If you don't have a pair, get as close to nine as possible.

If you win one hand and lose the other, it's a push, but if even one of your hands is exactly the same as the bank's, you lose, because the bank wins all ties. If *both* your hands are higher than the bank's, you win even money, minus the 5% commission.

General Comments on Asian Games

While you're looking around the Asian games, you might notice that several people are playing on one hand. This is okay in Pai Gow. If there are no empty spots on the table, two players may bet on the same hand.

Another thing peculiar to Asian players: they pool money for a larger bankroll. You may even see a man with a briefcase stuffed with money—probably an accumulation of bets from everyone in the neighborhood. They trust one person to play for everyone. You can understand why that player doesn't want to be distracted by talk, drinks, or anything else.

The talk around the Asian games used to be all Chinese. Sometimes the pit bosses had to rely on the Chinese dealers to tell them what was going on. In recent months, many of the clubs have trained Asians to be bosses, and the language might be Filipino, Korean, or Vietnamese.

The Asian games can be addictive, too. One regular player showed up on his wedding day in his formal attire, with his bride dressed in white satin on his arm. The casino brought champagne, and the groom played Pai Gow—before and after the ceremony.

Poker

A man's idea of a card game is war—cool, devastating, and piti-less. A lady's idea of it is a combination of larceny, embezzle-ment, and burglary. —Finley Peter Dunne (1867-1936)

Poker has long been the American way to gamble at home. In many families, Grandpa and the uncles always start a game after Thanksgiving dinner, and the ante is pennies, matches, jellybeans, or gum drops. Depending on Grandpa's humor at the end of the game, the youngest player might even get back what he lost. And when that kid gets older, he probably has a Thursday night game with "the boys."

But casinos play differently from "the boys." In the casino, you can't shout or call each other obscene names, and you're not al-lowed to get crumbs from potato chips and sandwiches all over the table.

After a few minutes inside a casino's poker room, you'll un-derstand why poker is also popular away from home. When you enter the room, a host will greet you and make you feel as though the game has been waiting just for you. The host will explain the kinds of games and the limit on each game. If a seat is open in the game of your choice, you'll be seated immediately. If not, your name will go on a list, and you'll be called when your seat is available.

The usual casino poker games are 7-Card Stud, Texas Hold 'Em, Hi-Lo Split, and Omaha. Some clubs offer more obscure games like Pineapple and Razz, too. The amount of chips you must pur-chase to join the game (the "buy-in") varies according to the type of game. There's no time limit on your play; you can play for one hand or sit there for your entire vacation. All games are played with a standard deck—no jokers or wild cards.

Poker Rankings (High to Low)

Royal Flush: Every poker player's dream. The five highest cards in a common suit: ace, king, queen, jack, and 10 in all spades, for example.

Straight Flush: Five cards in sequence in one suit. Example: 4, 5, 6, 7, and 8—all hearts.

Four of a Kind: Four cards of the same value.

Full House: Three cards of one value and two cards of another value. Example: jack, jack, jack and 6, 6.

Flush: Five cards of the same suit. Example: 3, 5, 9, king, and ace—all clubs.

Straight: Five cards of different suits, in numerical order.

Three of a Kind: Three cards of the same value.

Two Pair: Two groups of two cards of the same value. Example: 9, 9 and 5, 5.

One Pair: Two cards of the same value.

High Card: Value of the hand determined by the highest ranking card, from the ace down.

Poker and Its Variations

The fun of poker is bluffing—that is, pretending you have a much better hand than you actually have. One of the best bluffs we've ever seen was by a TV star in the World Championship of Poker some years ago. The pot was $300,000, and only two players were left. People stood six deep behind velvet ropes to watch the play, and everyone was betting that an old, crotchety gambler from Texas would win the pot. The TV star never allowed an expression to cross his face. The old man held only a pair of 4s, and the TV star kept raising. The entire casino waited, and each move was broadcast over loudspeakers. Finally the old man folded, and the TV star won the pot—with a jack-high hand.

7-Card Stud is the most popular poker game in the casinos. Each player gets seven cards: the first two come face down and the third face up, in rotation. Usually, the player with the lowest face-up card opens the betting. Each of the players may then fold, call, or raise. The dealer deals three more cards face up, with a round of betting following each card. The final card comes face down, followed by another round of betting. You can fold or raise any time it's your turn. The best five-card hand from the seven cards wins the pot.

Almost every casino offers **Texas Hold 'Em**, too. Each player gets two cards, face down. Then the dealer places three cards face up in the center of the table that all players use. There's a round of betting, followed by one more card for everyone's use. There's another round of betting, a fifth card comes face up, and there is a final round of betting. When the last round of betting is over, there's a showdown, and the pot goes to the player with the best five-card hand.

In some casinos, the deal passes from player to player, and you might want to observe the players before you join a table. One night, our favorite bartender, "Skinny Mike," decided to play a friendly game of poker after his shift. He slid into a seat just as a hand ended. The man next to him became the dealer. He picked up the deck and cut and shuffled it several times, all with one hand. Skinny Mike looked a second time. Why would anyone shuffle with only one hand? Because that's what you do when you have only one arm. Mike became alarmed. A one-armed dealer? If a man had spent that many hours learning to shuffle with one hand, he was obviously not there for a casual game. Mike pushed his chair back, said "Thanks, but no thanks," scooped up his chips, and almost ran back to the bar. Moral: Some games are friendlier than others. It's up to you to know the difference.

Poker Terms

All-In: A situation where a player receives action on all the money he puts in the pot. The players remaining in the hand form their own pot on the side.

Ante: A small bet from each player, placed to make a pot before the cards are dealt.

Blinds: Term used in Hold 'Em that signifies forced bets in each hand, usually required from players to the left of the dealer when there is no ante, before any cards are bet.

Call: To match the bet of another player.

Check: When a player is the first to bet and decides not to bet, but stays in the pot because no one else bets.

Check and raise: When a player first checks and then raises after another player bets in that same round of betting. Allowed unless posted otherwise at the table.

Community cards: Term used in Hold 'Em referring to the five cards that each player uses with his two hole cards.

Fold: To give up your hand and any claim to the pot.

Hand: The cards a player has at any point during the game.

Hole cards: The cards dealt to each player face down.

Limits: The amount a player can bet or raise during a round of betting.

Pot: All antes, blinds, calls, and bets collected in the middle of the table. The player who wins the hand wins the pot.

Raise: To increase the amount of a bet. Each raise must be at least the amount of the previous bet or the last raise.

Table Stakes: All the chips and/or the cash on the table at the beginning of the hand. Players are not allowed to add chips or cash during a hand. If a player doesn't have enough chips or cash to call a bet, he may go "all-in" for that part of the bet he is able to call.

How to Bet

When you arrive at a table, see who is throwing ("shooting") the dice, and stand to his right if you can, because dice go clockwise from shooter to shooter. It's better to watch for a while before you shoot.

To put your money into action, wait until the dice have been placed in front of the boxman, and everyone begins placing bets. (Never put a bill on the table when someone's shooting.) Place your money on the table directly in front of you, next to the edge of the table. Be sure the money doesn't touch any lines on the layout. Call out to the dealer nearest you "Change only," loud enough for the stickman and boxman to hear. (Unlike a blackjack game, a boss—called a *boxman*—sits at the table and supervises.)

The dealer will pick up your bill, set it in front of the boxman, and say, "Change only, $20." The dealer will take two $5 chips and ten $1 chips from his stack and push them across the table to you. Don't touch them until the dealer says, "Here's your $20 change." Put any chips you are not betting into the wooden railing in front of you.

Now you're ready to bet. There are no secrets at a craps table! Always call out your bets loud and clear so the dealer can hear you. He must repeat your bet so there's no misunderstanding and so the boxman knows exactly what your bet is. The only exception is a *field bet*—a bet made on the section of the layout containing the numbers 2, 3, 4, 9, 10, 11, and 12—which is not called out by you or repeated by the dealer.

Whenever you make a bet, you must always place it *directly* in front of you, never in front of any other player. Otherwise, someone else could try to claim your bet.

Listen to the stickman. He runs the game, and everything he says is important. Each hand starts with a *come-out roll* and will be called out ("advertised") by the stickman. The stickman will tell you the bets you can make. Example: "New shooter coming out, get your bets down or get left out. Bet 7, bet 11, 2, 3, or 12, bet the horn, and hopping hard ways." This might sound like a foreign language to you, but the stickman is actually saying "Now's the time to make a Pass Line bet and prop bets—all one-roll bets."

The Dealer's Lingo

Like jazz musicians of an earlier era, craps dealers have their own language. It's slang set in rhyme, and each dealer learns from his predecessors and eventually coins a few phrases of his own. The stickman is talking to the players, but he knows most don't listen. The patter tells the dealers what to do on each roll of the dice, and it's also to amuse, to make a long shift pass more quickly. You'll probably hear more lingo on a graveyard shift, when the game is likely to be slow, than on a game where the action is heavy and the boxman won't stand for any nonsense.

Some talk is standard. Craps dealers have names for all the numbers. For instance, a 2 is "Aces," 4 is "Little Joe," 6 is "Jimmy Hicks," and 7 is "Skinny Dugan." How about "Skate and Donate" for 8? Ten is known as "Puppy Paws"—and you only have to look at two 5s to know why. Most people know that 11 is "Yo" and 12 is "Boxcars."

Sometimes a die will jump into the money rack, giving the stickman a chance to use some far-out patter. "Too tall to call, y'all," or "One high, one low, no action on the dough." If a die goes on the floor, you're liable to hear "Knock, knock," which refers to the superstition that when a die rolls on the floor, 7 will soon come knocking at the door.

If you hear "The boys are 10 and down, and we thank you," you'll know there was a bet made by a player for the dealers ("the boys") on the hard 8 that just rolled. The dealers can't let a bet ride; it must come down as part of the payoff when it hits.

(By the way, you can make a bet for the dealers any time, and they prefer to bet with you on the Pass Line.)

How to Play

The best way to start is on the Pass Line, sometimes called the *front line*. If you want to bet that the shooter will win, place your bet on the Pass Line before the first roll (the "come out" roll). If the shooter throws a 7 or 11 on the first roll, you'll win even money. If he throws craps (2, 3, or 12) on the first roll, you lose. (If you are the shooter, the stickman will tell you "You lose your money and your friends, but you get to keep the dice. Make another bet and apologize—throw 7 or 11.")

If the shooter throws any other number, that number becomes the *point*. After the point is established, a marker, called a *puck*, will be placed on that number in front of the dealers at each end of the table. You can then increase your bet by *taking odds*. What this means is you can bet additional money that the shooter will "make the point" by rolling the same number before rolling 7. If he does this, you win. No other number has any bearing on whether you win or lose. If he rolls 7, the hand is over, you lose, and the dice move to the next shooter.

(*Warning!* Never say the word "seven" on a craps table. The dice have little ears and can hear you. They immediately come up 7. Everyone will lose, and it will be your fault.)

If you think the shooter will lose (i.e., not make his point), place your bet on the Don't Pass Line (the *back line*) before the come out roll. If the shooter throws 3 or 12 on the first roll, you win. If he throws 2, it's a push and no one wins. If he throws 7 or 11 on the first roll, you lose and must replace your bet. If he throws any other number, that number becomes the point. He must throw 7 before he makes the point for you to win. On Don't Pass Line bets, you can remove your bet any time by asking the dealer. (You can't do this on a Pass Line bet.)

You can make a *come bet* on any roll after the first if a point has been established. Come Line bets are subject to the next roll. If it's a *natural* (7 or 11), you win. If it's craps (2, 3, or 12), you lose and can replace your bet. Any other number becomes your *come point*, and the dealer will move your bet to that number on the layout, corresponding to your position among the players at your end of the table. The bet stays there until your point is rolled and you win or until the shooter throws 7 and you lose. No other number affects the bet. If you think the shooter will throw the Come number before 7, you can take the odds the same as on a Pass Line bet. Come bets pay even money. If you have a bet on the Come Line when the shooter throws 7, the Come bet will be paid, and the stickman will say something like "Seven out, the line is away, pay the don'ts, and the last come gets some." It's the player's responsibility to pick up his last Come bet along with the payoff.

Don't Come bets, placed on the Don't Come Line, are subject to the next roll after a point has been established. You're betting that the Don't Come point will not be thrown again before a 7 rolls. If 2 rolls, it's a push. If 3 or 12 roll, you win. If 7 or 11 roll, you lose, and you can replace your bet. The Don't Come bets also pay even money.

If your bet is on the Pass Line or the Come Line, your money is subject to that roll of the dice, whatever it is. If your bet is on the Don't Pass or the Don't Come Line, you have a choice. If you don't want to bet against that number, tell the dealer "no action," and he'll leave your money there for the next roll of the dice. (Most "Don't" bettors do not want to bet against the 6 or the 8, because there are too many ways to roll those numbers.)

Field bets are a one-roll bet on 2, 3, 4, 9, 10, 11, or 12. Place the bet in front of you, any place in the Field, as it's marked on the layout. If the shooter throws any of the above numbers, except 2 or 12, you win even money. If he throws 2, you win 2-1. If he rolls 12, you win 3-1. After the bet is paid, you must decide to leave all your money, leave some of it, or take it all before the next roll of the dice.

If you want to bet the shooter will throw 6 or 8 before he throws 7, place your bet on the Big Red Six or Big Red Eight on the corner of the table at the end of the Field. You control these bets. (That is, you can bet them or take them away any time.) They pay even money. Dealers tend to forget these bets, so pay attention and make sure the dealer pays you.

Let's say you've got a hunch, or, in craps talk, "you got a phone call." You make a bet, and it rolls immediately. To make this bet, give your money to the stickman, tell him which one-roll bet you want to play, and he'll place it for you. Any craps pays 7-1. Bets on 3 or 11 pay 15-1. Bets on 2 or 12 pay 30-1, and on any 7 pay 4-1.

If you want to bet the shooter will throw 2, 3, 11, or 12, make a *horn high* bet. If any of these numbers rolls, you win. You must make these bets in units of five, because your bet is divided among the four numbers with an extra unit on the high number. Example: Your "phone call" told you 12 was going to roll, but to increase your chances you decide to bet the other three numbers also. You have $1 on 2, $1 on 3, $1 on 11, and $2 on 12. The phone call was "close and almost"—a 2 comes up, which pays 30-1. After you subtract your losing bets ($4 spread among the other three numbers), you'll find you won $26.

You can also make a split bet; half your bet on any craps, half on 11. This is called a *C and E* bet. If any craps rolls (any 2, 3, or 12), you're paid 3-1, and 11 pays 7-1.

The numbers 4, 6, 8, and 10 can be thrown the "easy way" and the "hard way." Since there's only one way to throw a hard way, it has high odds. One-roll hard ways (two 2s, two 3s, two 4s, or two 5s) pay 30-1. "All-day" hard ways pay less; hard 6 and 8 pay 9-1, hard 4 and 10 pay 7-1. These bets will lose if an easy way (3 & 1, 4 & 2, 5 & 1, 6 & 2, 5 & 3, 6 & 4) or any 7 rolls. The stickman controls any one-roll bet (also called a *proposition bet* or "prop" bet).

If you want to bet that the shooter will throw 4, 5, 6, 8, 9, or 10 before he throws 7, tell the dealer you want to make a *place bet*. You can bet any or all of these numbers. The dealer will take your money and put it on the number you request. Place bets pay different odds according to the number. For example, you must bet the 4 and 10 and the 5 and 9 in units of five. Four and 10 (remember, when one is up, the other is down) pay 9-5; the 5 and 9 pay 7-5. You must bet 6 and 8 in units of six. They pay 7-6.

You can stop a place bet any time by telling the dealer, "No action on my place bets this roll." Your money remains on the layout. On the next roll, your money is back in action again. Of course, if you can call a bet off, you can also take it down (remove it from the layout) any time by asking the dealer.

Playing the Odds

After a point is established, if you feel the shooter will roll the point before he rolls 7, you can increase your return by taking odds. Place the *odds bet* directly behind your original bet.

Different points pay different odds based on the combinations that produce a number. There are six ways—more than any other number—to throw 7. There are five ways to throw 6 or 8, four ways to throw 5 or 9, and three ways to throw 4 or 10. Odds are computed against the six ways you can throw 7. So, 6 and 8 pay 6-5, because the odds are 6-5 that you'll throw 7 before you throw 6 or 8. (The reason the payoff is the same for 6 and 8 is because when 6 is showing, 8 is on the opposite side of the dice. The same is true for 5 and 9, and 4 and 10.)

On 6 and 8, you can take 2.5 times your original bet if the casino offers double odds. Example: Your original bet is $2. You're allowed $5 odds ($2 x 2.5=$5.) Place $5 on the table directly behind the $2 bet. Your point rolls. You are paid $2 on your original bet, and $6 on your odds bet. On 5 and 9, you can take two times your original bet, if the casino offers double odds. Example: A $2 original bet pays $2, and the $4 odds bet pays $6, or 3-2.

A few casinos offers triple odds. On 4 and 10, you can take three times your original bet. Example: A $2 original bet will pay $2, and the $6 odds bet will pay $12, or 2-1.

Listen to the Dealer

Once we were standing around on a dead game, telling war stories. An elderly woman approached the table with three young men. In broken English she asked, "How do I win this game?"—a question guaranteed to get the attention of any craps dealer. We all know from past experience that she will do one of two things: either "shoot up a hand" (make the point hand after hand) or make a point, roll 7 immediately, and walk away.

The stickman explained she had to make a minimum Pass Line bet to shoot, so she put $1 on the Pass Line and proceeded to make point after point for the next hour. Along the way, she repeatedly threw all the hard ways, every horn bet, and Field roll after Field roll. We begged her to put $1 on the hard ways, but she was afraid to bet more than her $1 Line bet. The three guys with her didn't know any more about the game than she did. They trusted us to tell them how to bet, but they were a little scared, too.

Finally, they started betting the all-day hard ways. The entire time she was shooting, no one else came near the table. When she finally sevened-out, she had won $9, and each of the guys with her had won over $100. If they had bet the way they should have, they'd have gone home with thousands.

Moral: If the dealers tell you—or beg you!—to bet when the dice are "passing," listen up. You could win your own casino.

Craps Basics

There are basic rules to craps that you must understand. First, your Pass Line bet and your Come bets are *contract bets* once a point has been established. That means you can add to them, you can take odds on them, but you cannot subtract from or pick up those bets.

Second, you can call off place bets, odds bets, and prop bets, and you can pick up the Big Red Six and Eight bets any time.

Third, make your bets when the dice are in the middle of the table (that is, in front of the stickman). A quick way to make yourself extremely unpopular is to have the dice hit your hand while you're making a late bet.

Good manners are crucial in craps. Don't push your way through the crowd just so you can stand next to the guy with all the chips, even if you do think that's a lucky spot. The dealer pays all bets in rotation, so don't yell at him. He'll get to you, and then you can tell him what you want done with your money.

Always keep your drink on the shelf under the money railing. Never set your drink on the layout or the money rail.

Beware of "rail thieves"—people who help themselves to your chips in the railing while you're leaning over the table placing a bet. Or they may offer to help you learn the game by placing and picking up your bets for you. "Thanks, but I'd rather do it myself," applies here. Watch out!

And while we're on the subject, never let anyone cash your chips for you, even if he is wearing a suit. Just because a man is wearing a suit doesn't mean he's a nice guy. Look for the name tag. It's always there.

Also, watch for the "claimers," who like to claim your bet as theirs. This is the why you always place your bet directly in front of you, so the dealer is positive whom the bet belongs to.

Superstitions

Do you notice the difference in the clothes of the younger and older bosses? The young men could be insurance salesmen or stock brokers, with their expensive suits, pastel shirts, striped ties, and pocket squares. The older bosses look like the stereotype of used car salesmen: plaid pants and sports coat, a bright shirt, a necktie that may be a gift from Christmas 1963, and, almost always, cowboy boots—and not by accident. The older bosses still believe the old superstitions. The boots are usually a size too large for good reason—a kick at the table to "change the luck" doesn't hurt if the boots are too big. The older bosses have been known to burn a piece of string under the table to change the luck or take a salt shaker from the coffee shop and surreptitiously walk around the table sprinkling salt on the floor.

I remember a game when the dice had been passing for 20 minutes, long enough for the table to have lost a bundle. I looked up to see my boss walking behind the players, salt shaker in hand. Just as he passed the shooter, the man sevened-out, and I heard my boss mumble, "Should've done that a long time ago."

One of the most ridiculous superstitions is that of "the lucky stance." This is the way a boss stands or leans against the podium, legs crossed at a specific angle. The lucky stance is guaranteed to change a player's luck for the worse. Writing "seven out" on a piece of paper at the podium works, too. Sure.

Even casino owners have odd beliefs. I worked for a man who never let players eat peanuts near a game, and no dealer was allowed to wear a bandage of any sort on his fingers. (It meant you were wounded and not at full strength to combat the players.)

Players have silly superstitions, too. For instance, some believe that if you throw a penny under the table, the dice continue to pass. That's because, as a player explained, the copper in the penny reacts to the metallic paint in the little white dots on the dice. Ain't science grand?

Of course, certain people can make you lose. Did you know a woman is very bad luck near a craps game? (This one was probably hatched by a man who didn't want his wife around while he was gambling.) This belief often causes problems for female pit bosses, and some old-time gamblers refuse to play if a woman is anywhere around the table.

And be careful how you pick up the dice! They always come back and show the same number they were showing when you touched them.

Plus, you should know that when a shooter throws the dice

off the table, it's time to call off your bets. The dice always know when they hit the floor. Since they don't like it one bit, they come up 7 on the next roll. Every time.

Just as on a blackjack game, a strange assortment of people sometimes crowds around a craps table. There's the guy who comes in each afternoon precisely at three to play a $5 bill, never more and never less. There are the honeymooners who spend more time looking at each other than at the game. There's the "railbird" who leans on the rails all day watching the dice go from end to end without ever making a bet. There's the housewife, the college kid, and the high roller with the gold chains. But when the dice are passing and the shouting begins, no one cares who's standing next to whom. As each player will tell you, the only bad bet on a craps game is a losing bet.

Craps Terminology

Ace: The 1-spot on a die.

Any Craps: The numbers 2, 3, or 12, individually or as a group.

Bet the dice to win: You bet the shooter will pass.

Bet the Horn: A single bet made in units of five, covering 2, 3, 11, and 12.

Big Six and Big Eight: A section of the layout on the corners where you bet 6 or 8 will roll before 7.

Book: To accept a bet.

Boys: Craps dealers of both sexes.

Boxcars: Two dice, each showing six.

Boxman: Supervisor who sits at the table.

Chip or Check: The token used in place of money.

Come Bet: The same as a Pass Line bet, after a point has been established.

Come-Out Roll: The first roll that establishes the point.

Cold Dice: Dice that don't pass.

Deuce: The 2-spot on a die.

Don't Pass or Don't Come: A bet that the shooter will not make a pass.

Field: The section of the layout containing numbers 2, 3, 4, 9, 10, 11, and 12.

Front Line or Pass Line: The section on the layout where you bet the dice will pass.

Hard Way: The numbers 4, 6, 8, or 10, thrown in duplicates.

Hopping Hard Way: A one-roll bet that the designated hard way will roll.

Hot Dice: When the dice are passing.

Layout: All sections of the table where bets are made.

Line Away or Line In: When a shooter sevens-out.

Natural: A 7 or 11 thrown on the come-out roll.

One-Roll Bet: Any bet that has action for a single roll of the dice.

Pass: A natural on the first roll, or to make an established point.

Phone Call: A bet made on a hunch that pays off.

Point: Any 4, 5, 6, 8, 9, or 10 thrown on the come-out roll.

Proposition Bet: One-roll bets paying high odds.

Seven-Out: When 7 rolls after a point has been established.

Shooter: The player who throws the dice.

Snake Eyes: Two dice, each showing one spot.

Stick: The croupier's stick used to send and retrieve the dice.

Stickman: The dealer who controls the dice and books prop bets.

Two-Way Bet: A bet made by a player to be split with the dealers.

World Bet: A bet on the horn that also includes any 7.

Yo Bet: A bet that 11 will roll.

PART TWO

HOTELS, CASINOS & ATTRACTIONS

Carson City

Lake Tahoe

Reno

Sparks

Henderson & the Boulder Highway

Las Vegas

Laughlin

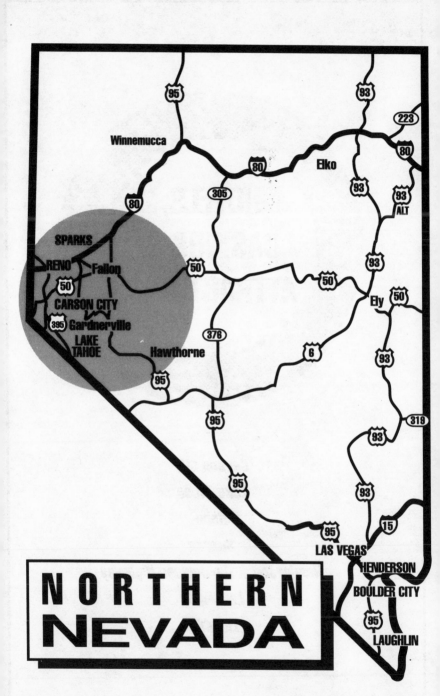

Carson City

Carson City, named for adventurer Kit Carson, blends the area's colorful past with modern entertainment. In the heart of the Old West, the town lies in a beautiful valley at the foot of the Sierras. There's plenty of gambling, plus snow skiing and water sports nearby.

Carson City was founded in 1851 as a trading post for miners who had not struck it rich in the California gold rush, and it would have become a ghost town were it not for the silver strike of the nearby Comstock in 1859. When Nevada was admitted to the Union in 1864, Carson City became its capital, and for over 100 years the legislature met in the sandstone building in the center of town.

In addition to gambling and sports, there are numerous historic activities in town. For example, the old Pony Express Trail runs through the city, and each June the ride from Fort Sutter (near Sacramento, CA) to St. Joseph, MO is reenacted. Also, the old Carson Mint, which made over $50 million in silver and gold coins until 1893, is now home to the Nevada State Museum.

Area Attractions

The Nevada State Museum: Considered one of the West's top museums, Carson City's mint-turned-museum is a lot of fun. Kids will love the replica of a silver mine beneath the building, as well as the coin press from the old mint and a display of Carson City silver dollars. There's great Nevada history, too, and a special gallery honors women who made major contributions to the state. Other displays showcase willow baskets made by Washoe Indians, arrowheads, guns, antique gaming devices, and cowboy memorabilia. Open daily 8:30am-4:30pm. Admission: $1.50 for adults, children under 18 free. Tours by appointment. Address: 600 North Carson St. (702-885-4810).

Nevada State Railroad Museum: The V&T (Virginia and Truckee) Railroad Museum, a branch of the State Museum, features four

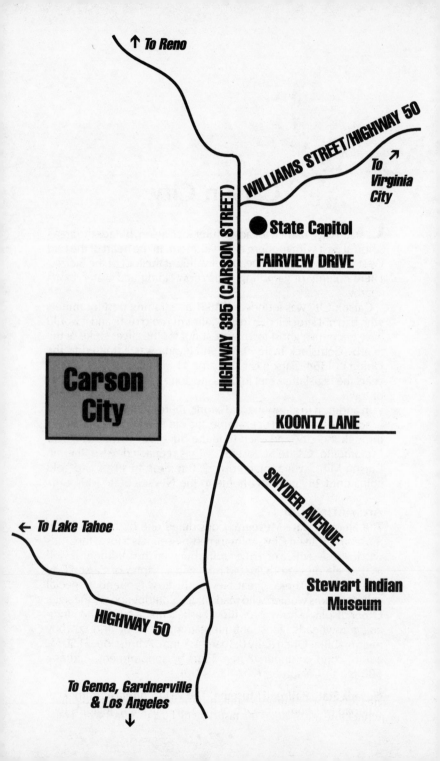

old locomotives and an assortment of restored freight and passenger cars. A steam locomotive pulls covered observation cars on holiday weekends ($2.50 for adults and $1.00 for children). Open June-Oct 8:30am-4:30pm Fri, Sat, Sun, and holidays. Admission: adults $1.00, children free. Address: Highway 395 South at Fairview Drive (702-687-6953).

Carson & Mills Park Railroad: This park features a mile-long train ride plus picnic areas, tennis, swimming, and a playground. The main station has a ticket office, gift shop, and a model railroad. Open 11:00am-4:00pm weekends. All rides are $1 (children under 2 free). Address: Mills Park, Williams St. (Highway 50 East), Carson City (702-885-8578).

State Capitol Building: Restored in 1971 to its original grandeur, the capitol is lovely, and visitors may peek into the old Senate and Assembly chambers. The legislature now meets in a new building a few blocks away, and you're welcome to watch the lawmakers in action there. For information and admission, call 702-885-5030.

Genoa: A few miles south of Carson City on Highway 395, Genoa was Nevada's first settlement, and it still evokes a feeling of the Old West. Attractions include Mormon Station, where pioneers first settled, the courthouse built in 1865, and the oldest bar in the state, still serving thirsty visitors. Also, **Wally's Hot Springs** has pampered travelers for 127 years with its hot mineral waters. You can enjoy six mineral pools, a fresh-water pool, a fitness center, and a world-class restaurant, and you can stay overnight in a private cabin. For more information on Wally's, call 702-782-8155 or 702-883-6556.

Carson Hot Springs: For a soothing treat after a hard day at the casino, try Carson Springs at the north edge of town. Address: 1500 Hot Springs Rd. (702-882-9863).

Bowers Mansion: Built in 1864 by Nevada's first millionaire for $250,000, the mansion has been restored to its original state and is fun to tour. You'll see many fine European furnishings, and the lovely grounds have picnic facilities and a swimming pool. A guided tour costs $2 for adults, $1 for children under 12. Open daily May-Nov, 11:00am-4:30pm. Address: off Highway 395 North (702-849-0201).

The Governor's Mansion: Built in 1908, this is a gem of colonial architecture and reflects the tastes of the First Families who lived there. Guided tours highlight state rooms, the family areas, dining rooms, parlors, and salons. Oriental and American antiques blend with Venetian and Czech works of art. Free admission. Tours by appointment only; call 702-882-2333.

Dayton: One of the most colorful old towns from Nevada's mining days, Dayton lies 10 miles east of Carson City on Highway 50. Some of the oldest buildings in the state are there, including **Ogden Hall**, one of Nevada's first saloons, built in 1862.

Gold Display: The **Carson Nugget** downtown displays perhaps the rarest collection of natural gold formations in the world. The collection, which took 70 years to accumulate, includes leaf gold, wire gold, thread gold, and crystallized gold, just as they are found in nature. Open 24 hours.

Stewart Indian Museum: This museum and trading post was established in 1982 on the former campus of the Stewart Indian Boarding School. Changing exhibits feature Indian history and culture, baskets, artifacts, and photos. The trading post offers jewelry, artwork, pottery, rugs, and beadwork. Located three miles south of town at 5366 Snyder Ave. (702-882-1808). Open 9:00am-4:00pm daily. The annual powwow and arts festival runs the third weekend in June.

Virginia City: The wildest town of the Old West was at one time the largest city between Denver and San Francisco, with a population of 30,000. Once called the richest place on earth, the town poured $400 million in silver and gold into the economy. At its peak, Virginia City was a wide-open, 24-hour boomtown, with opium dens, newspapers (including Mark Twains' *Territorial Enterprise*, still operating), operas, a red light district, and the first miner's union in the U.S. The great fire of 1875 nearly destroyed Virginia City, but in a year the town was rebuilt, and most of the present buildings date to that time. Over 750 miles of tunnels wind beneath the town, and boardwalks line the streets in front of saloons and museums. Old cemeteries, schools, and mansions are all open to the public. You can ride the V&T steam train, take an underground mine tour, watch a camel race, or eat homemade fudge. Virginia City is 14 miles from Carson City via Highway 50 East. It's a must.

Fishing: The **Carson River** is a favorite trout stream in the area, and **Washoe Lake**, 15 miles north of Carson City on Highway 395, is known for white bass and catfish. A 10-day permit costs $25 for non-residents.

Eagle Valley Golf Course: Two courses, both par 72 and open all year. East course costs $12, West course $17.50, for 18 holes. Restaurant, bar, putting green, driving range. Address: 3999 Centennial Park Dr. (702-887-2380).

Ophir Creek Hiking Trail: This path leads to two lakes, Rock and Price, located at the base of Slide Mountain. Five miles long, the trail is difficult due to the continuous uphill grade. It starts at Davis Creek, 13 miles north of Carson City on Highway 395. Call the Forest Service at 702-882-2766 for more information.

Centennial Park: At Highway 50 East. Tennis courts, ballparks, an outdoor handball court, and a rifle and trap range.

Weddings
Carson City Courthouse, Clerk's Office, 198 North Carson St., Carson City, NV 89701 (702-887-2084). Hours: 8:00am-midnight daily. Fee: $32.

Climate and Dress
See Reno.

Air Services
Carson City has a small airport for private planes. Most tourists fly to Reno International Airport, 27 miles north. There's also an airport on the south shore of Lake Tahoe, an hour's drive away.

Driving Distance from Major Cities
San Francisco—251 miles Seattle—772 miles
Las Vegas—420 miles   Salt Lake City—500 miles
Portland—597 miles   Los Angeles—440 miles

RV Parks & Campgrounds
Next to gambling, northern Nevada's natural beauty is its top draw. The area has mountains, desert, forests, spectacular lakes, and abundant outdoor sports.

Davis Creek State Park: 11 miles north of Carson City on Highway 395. Picnic sites, nature trails, camping sites for tents and trailers to 26 ft., sewage dump, restrooms, showers, swimming pool, fishing, and drinking water. Open all year. Phone 702-849-0684.

Washoe Lake State Park: 12 miles north of Carson City in a sand dune environment with terrific views of the Sierra Nevada Mountains. 25 sites for tents, and trailers to 30 ft. Sewage dump, equestrian area, picnic sites, boat ramp, docking facilities, water sports. Phone 702-885-4379.

Bed & Breakfast Accommodations

Chollar Mansion, 565 South D St., Virginia City, NV 89440 (702-847-9777).

Edith Palmer's Country Inn, South B St., Virginia City, NV 89440 (702-847-0707).

Edward's House, 204 N. Minnesota St., Carson City, NV 89703 (702-882-4844).

Genoa House Inn, Box 141, Genoa, NV 89411 (702-782-7075).

Hardwicke House, Box 96, Silver City, NV 89429 (702-847-0215).

House on the Hill, Sky Lane—Gold Hill Nevada, Virginia City, NV 89440 (702-847-0193).

Sierra Spirit Ranch, 3000 Pinenut Rd., Gardnerville, NV 89410 (702-782-7011).

Wild Rose Inn, 2332 Main St., Genoa, NV 89411 (702-782-5697).

Winters Creek Ranch, 1201 Highway 395 North, Carson City, NV 89701 (702-849-1020).

Casinos, Hotels, Resorts, & Games

Cactus Jack's Casino, 420 North Carson St., Carson City, NV 89701 (702-882-8770).

The friendliest place in town—and a fine place for beginners— Cactus Jack's emphasizes personal service and old-fashioned Western hospitality. More of a social club, Cactus Jack's has a great Slot Club where players can earn credits for cash or prizes. (This place is the local leader in new and innovative slot machines, and most machines are tied to a progressive machine.) There's also a restaurant featuring a 99-cent breakfast and a steak dinner for $2.99 (open 6:00am-4:00am).

Games

Blackjack: Three tables, $2-$50, two tables single-deck games, one table six-deck shoe, dealer hits soft 17, Insurance offered. Double on 10 or 11.

Slots: 210 slot machines, penny-$1 slots, MegaBucks pays millions, video poker, blackjack.

Poker: Two tables (the only poker room in Carson City), Hold 'Em, Omaha Hi/Lo (player's choice), and pot limit available. Buy-in $20.

Carson Horseshoe, 402 North Carson, Carson City, NV 89701 (702-883-2211).

Strictly a slot club, the Horseshoe has 178 machines, 22 progressive machines, and 160 poker machines. Complimentary drinks for players.

The Carson Nugget, 507 North Carson St., Carson City, NV 89701 (702-882-1626 or 800-426-5239).

Although the Nugget bills itself as "The Happiest Casino in the World," the casino and its dealers have an indifferent attitude. The largest casino in the capital, it's famous for its inexpensive, generous restaurants. There's elegant dining in the Steak House, fresh seafood in the Oyster Bar, fast food in the Garden Coffee Shop, and a huge Bonanza Buffet. A children's lounge is fully staffed, you'll find a gift shop and the world's rarest gold collection. The maximum keno payout is $50,000, you can enjoy 21, craps, roulette, slots, and progressive poker machines, plus live music every night in the Theatre Lounge.

The **City Center Motel** offers a Nugget Fun Pack for two for $33 that includes two buffet dinners, four 50-cent keno credits, four cocktails, four Lucky Bucks for the table games, and a room for one night.

Carson Station, 900 South Carson St., Carson City, NV 89701 (702-883-0900 or 800-528-1234). Rates: $35-$85.

This Best Western hotel has 90 rooms, a gift shop, and two restaurants. Its tiny casino is a good place to learn craps. The Station Restaurant is open Sun-Thurs 6:00am-11:00pm, and on weekends until 1:00am. The Sportsbook Snack Bar is open 24 hours. There's also a Cabaret Lounge with live entertainment nightly and no cover charge.

Games

Blackjack: Seven tables, $2-$100, single-deck games, dealer hits soft 17, Insurance offered, double on 10 or 11.

Craps: One table, 25 cents-$100, double odds available.

Keno: Minimum 50 cents, way tickets, $25,000 max. payout.

Slots: 250 machines from 5 cents-$5, progressive machines, poker machines.

Race & Sports Book: 100 seats, four TVs.

Carson Valley Inn, 1627 Highway 395 South, Minden, NV 89423 (702-782-9711 or 800-321-6983). Rates: $39 midweek & winter, $69 weekends & summer.

Situated in a beautiful valley at the foot of the mountains surrounding Lake Tahoe, the Carson Valley Inn is a lovely hotel with friendly service and a nice, small casino. The Inn features 160 rooms, two glass-enclosed spas, a 60-site RV resort, a free, supervised children's fun center, game arcade, a Cabaret Lounge with entertainment and dancing nightly, a wedding chapel, and two restaurants. Katie's Restaurant is open 24 hours, and Fiona's is open for lunch Mon-Fri, brunch on Sunday, and dinner every night.

Games

Blackjack: Nine tables, $2-$200, one single-deck game, four-deck shoes, dealer hits soft 17, Insurance offered, split any pair, double on 10 and 11.

Craps: One table, $2-$100, full double odds.

Roulette: One table, 25 cents-$10 on straight-up bets.

Keno: $1 ticket, $1 minimum way tickets, $25,000 max. payout.

Slots: 370 machines, 5 cents-$1, many progressive machines, MegaBucks meter, poker and 21 machines.

Ormsby House, 600 South Carson St., Carson City, NV 89701 (702-882-1890 or 800-648-0920). Rates: $45-$130.

This small hotel and casino is not overly friendly, but it is centrally located in downtown Carson City. Built in the style of the Old

West, the Ormsby House has 200 rooms, a seasonal swimming pool, a gift shop, and a child care center. It's also well-known for its fine Basque cooking.

Restaurants & Lounges

Woody's: Gourmet dining with rack of lamb a specialty.

Coffee Shop: open 24 hours with burgers, sandwiches, and ice cream delights. Breakfast served around-the-clock.

Curry Street Buffet: Freshly baked breads, daily theme menus, Sunday champagne brunch.

Games

Blackjack: 12 tables, all single-deck. $2-$200 and $5-$200. Dealer hits soft 17, Insurance offered, double on 10 or 11 only.

Craps: One table, 25 cents-$200, double odds available.

Roulette: One table, 25 cents-$1, $25 straight up.

Keno: 50-cent minimum ticket, $50,000 maximum payout.

Slots: 385 machines, 5 cents-$1, progressive machines, poker and 21 machines.

Pai Gow: $5-$100, played with cards, bank passes.

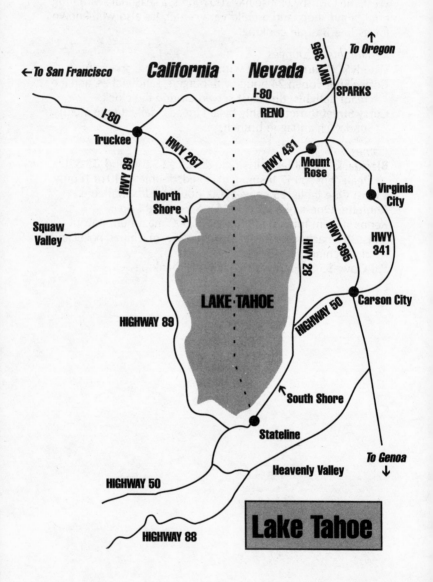

Lake Tahoe

The Washoe Indians lived in the Lake Tahoe Basin for hundreds of years, undisturbed by the outside world. In 1844, John Fremont and Kit Carson discovered the lake, and nothing's been the same since. The gold rush of 1849 brought hordes of miners to the foothills, and many stumbled upon Lake Tahoe. As the silver of Virginia City's Comstock Lode was discovered, more people arrived, and the area provided lumber for homes, fuel, and support beams for the mines. By 1890, almost all the trees were gone from the Tahoe Basin.

After the mining boom, the area was largely abandoned. A few roads were paved in the 1930's, but things stayed quiet through the 1940's, when the gaming industry discovered the lake. In 1950, there were about 2,500 residents. In 1960, when the Olympic Games were held at Squaw Valley, the world rediscovered the Tahoe Basin, and today, Tahoe is synonymous with recreation and beauty. Millions visit each year, in every season. About 80,000 people live there today, and in peak season over 100,000 visitors arrive every weekend.

Lake Tahoe is the largest alpine lake in North America: 12 miles wide, 22 miles long, with a shoreline over 72 miles. With an average depth of 989 feet (the deepest part is 1,645 feet), the lake is cold. Below 700 feet, the temperature stays 39° year-round. During the summer, only the surface (top 12 feet) gets up to 68°.

Skiing is a major activity during the winter. There are more ski resorts in the Lake Tahoe area than anywhere on earth, with runs accommodating everyone from beginners to the most advanced expert. The lake receives an average of 215 inches of snow a year, and the higher elevations can get 500 inches in a winter.

Tahoe boasts several world-famous attractions: The North Shore is home to the Ponderosa Ranch, where the TV series *Bonanza* was filmed. Emerald Bay, on the California side of the lake, is one of the most-photographed spots in America. And the South Shore is lined with some of Nevada's most beautiful resorts and casinos.

When Mark Twain first saw Lake Tahoe, he wrote: "As it lay there, with the shadows of the mountains brilliantly photographed upon its still surface, I thought it must surely be the fairest picture the whole earth affords." Few who see the lake today would disagree.

Area Attractions

Ehrman Mansion, Bliss State Park: Site for the filming of *The Godfather, Part II*, the building is an outstanding example of the architecture at the turn-of-the-century at the lake. Open 11:00am-4:00pm, July-Sept, with tours on the hour. Highway 89, Tahoma, CA (916-525-7232).

Vikingsholm Castle, Emerald Bay State Park: At the head of Emerald Bay, near Eagle Falls, this 39-room castle, complete with turrets and towers, is one of the best examples of Swedish architecture in the nation. Tours run June-Labor Day, 10:00am-4:00pm ($1 for adults, 50 cents for children under 17, kids under 6 free). Highway 89, South Lake Tahoe (916-541-3030).

Emerald Bay State Park: One of the world's most beautiful and most-photographed spots, with terrific views of the lake and mountains. Hiking trails, boating, and camping, plus Tahoe's only island. Lookouts and plenty of parking. Picnic area. Highway 89, West Lake Tahoe (916-525-7232).

U.S. Forest Service Visitor's Center: The area near Taylor Creek has a self-guided tour on the flora of Lake Tahoe. Something else to see is the **Stream Profile Chamber**, where you can watch the annual run of kokanee salmon through the windows of an underground chamber in October. There is an amphitheater and nature talks by the rangers. Open June-Sept, 8:00am-6:00pm. Highway 89, South Lake Tahoe (916-573-2600).

Donner State Park: This park memorializes the members of the ill-fated Donner expedition of 1846-47. Museum open all year, park open May-Oct, weather permitting. Admission to the museum is $1 for adults, 50 cents for children under 17. Open 10:00am-noon and 1:00pm-4:00pm, except holidays. Highway 40, Truckee, CA (916-587-3841).

The Ponderosa Ranch: The location of the *Bonanza* TV series, featuring the Cartwright house (now filled with show memorabilia), shooting galleries, antique autos and ranch equipment, a petting farm, and an authentic western town complete with shops. Open May-Oct. Admission: $6.50 for adults, $4.50 for children 5-11, under 5 free. Don't miss the hayride breakfast, a specialty at the Ponderosa. Passengers ride through tall pines to a high plateau for a gorgeous view of the lake, and they finish with an all-you-can-eat pancake breakfast. Highway 28, Incline Village, North Shore, Lake Tahoe (702-831-0691).

River Rafting: Rent equipment at Fanny Bridge (named for the people who hang over the bridge to watch the trout swimming below) in Tahoe City at the lake's only outlet (and the source of the Truckee River). Ride from the North Shore and float four miles downstream to the River Ranch. The ride takes about 2½ hours, and there's a restaurant at the River Ranch, where you can relax over a drink afterwards. **Truckee River Raft Rentals** (916-583-9724) or **Fanny Bridge Raft Rentals** (916-583-3021).

Golf Courses:

Incline Village Golf Course—Executive course: par 58, 3,508 yds, open Memorial Day-Oct 1, $45. Championship course: par 72, 7,138 yds, open May 1-Oct 15, $55-$65. Both courses 18 holes. Carts mandatory. Driving range, restaurant, snack bar, bar and lounge. 955 Fairway Blvd., Incline Village, NV (702-832-1144).

Edgewood at Tahoe—Par 72, 7,491 yds., 18 holes, open May-Oct, $75. Carts mandatory. Restaurant, driving range, putting green. Rated one of the top 100 courses in the country. Stateline, NV (702-588-3042).

Lake Tahoe Country Club—Par 71, 6,700 yds., 18 holes, open May 1-October 30, $23. Carts optional. Restaurant, driving range, putting green. South Lake Tahoe, CA (916-577-0788).

Glenbrook—Par 34, 3,200 yds., 9 holes, open April 15-Oct 15, $25 (twilight fee $18). Pro shop, restaurant, bar. Glenbrook, NV (702-749-5201).

Northstar-at-Tahoe—Par 72, 6,890 yds., 18 holes, open May-Oct, $30. Carts mandatory. Restaurant, driving range, putting green, snack bar, bar. Truckee, CA (916-587-0290).

Plumas Pines—Par 72, 6,365 yds., 18 holes, open April-Oct, $26. Cart mandatory. Restaurant, driving range, putting green. Blairsden, CA (916-836-1420).

Scenic Rides:

Heavenly Valley Tram—Ride the tram at Heavenly Valley Ski Resort year-round for spectacular views of the lake and surrounding country. $9 fee for adults, $5 for children 12 and under. Open 10:00am-4:00pm daily. There's a gourmet restaurant at the top where you can sit and enjoy the view. Winter hours: 11:00am-2:30pm. Summer: 10:00am-10:00pm daily. Wedding and banquet facilities, Sunday brunch. South shore, Lake Tahoe (916-541-7544).

Squaw Valley Tram—The lake's most spectacular aerial cable car takes you to 8,200 feet. Open daily 10:00am-4:00pm in summer (until Oct 1). Cost for adults is $8, children under 13, $5. At Squaw Valley, north shore of Lake Tahoe (916-583-6985).

Truckee: A small mountain town on the river, Truckee was a booming logging town 100 years ago. It's been restored to a village catering to tourists, with many shops, terrific restaurants, and stores featuring unique crafts. Truckee is 35 miles west of Reno and 15 miles north of Tahoe City, CA.

Lake Tahoe is a paradise for water sports enthusiasts and fishermen. Boats, water skis, scuba gear, and windsurfers are all available for rent at various shops around the lake. The lake is known for rainbow trout and kokanee salmon. Non-resident fishing permits are available at sporting goods stores. A year-round license costs $35; a 10-day license is $20. For fishing party information, contact the following:

The Color System, Zephyr Cove Marina, South Shore (702-588-4102).

Fishing Magician, Tahoe Vista, North Shore (916-546-8248).

Hooker for Hire Sportfishing, Tahoe City, North Shore (916-525-5654).

Tahoe Sportfishing, Ski Run Blvd., South Shore (916-541-5448).

Zephyr Cove Marina, Zephyr Cove, South Shore (702-588-3833).

For boating information, contact

Anchorage Marina, Camp Richardson, West Shore (916-541-1777). Boat rentals and launching, fishing, swimming, horseback riding, restaurant, bar, lodging.

North Shore Sailing, Tahoe Vista, North Shore (916-546-4333).

North Tahoe Marina, Hwy 28 on the North Shore in Tahoe Vista (916-546-8248). Food, gas, supplies, repairs, launching, and rentals.

Sand Harbor State Park, Hwy 28, East Shore (702-831-0494). The best beach on the lake, boat launching, fishing, picnicking.

Tahoe Boating Company, in the Roundhouse Mall at Tahoe City, North Shore (916-583-5567). Boat launching, travel lift and fork services, power boat rental, repair shop, restoration, gas.

Zephyr Cove Sailing Center and Marina, Zephyr Cove, South Shore (702-588-3833). Skiing, party boats, pedal boats, jet skis, boat launching, swimming, and fishing.

Hiking Trails:

East Shore, from Stateline to Tahoe City:

Marlette Lake Trail—A moderate hike of five miles to a lovely little mountain lake surrounded by pines. Spectacular view of Lake Tahoe. The trail begins at Spooner Lake Park on Hwy 28, north of the junction with Hwy 50.

Hobart Reservoir—A continuation of the Marlette Trail on fire roads, good for mountain biking. Eight miles. The same trailhead as Marlette.

Northstar-at-Tahoe—Mountain bike rentals, trail system around Mt. Pluto and Watson Lake (916-562-1010).

Tahoe Rim Trail—Spooner Summit trailhead goes two ways: south for eight miles or north for four miles. There is another trailhead at Tahoe City on the North Shore (marker is on Hwy 89 at Fairview Drive). This trail covers seven miles. For information, call 916-577-0676.

West Shore from South Lake Tahoe to Tahoe City (*Note*: Many of these hikes are in the Desolation Wilderness Area and require a permit from the ranger stations):

Eagle Falls Trail—Some of the most beautiful views in the lake basin. Steep climb through the wilderness to Eagle Lake. Trailhead at Emerald Bay. 1 mile, 45 minutes.

Fallen Leaf Trail—A leisurely trail near Fallen Leaf Campground. Meadows and a lake. 1.25-mile loop, 1.5 hours.

Granite Chief Scenic Area—Back-country area for hikers and horses. No bikes. Alpine terrain. Several good lakes for fishing.

Meeks Bay Trail—The most popular entry into Desolation Wilderness. Many lakes, trailhead at Meeks Bay on the West Shore. 4.6 miles, all day.

Squaw Valley—Mountain bike tours weekends and holidays. Tour includes cable car ride, lunch, mountain bike and helmet rental, guided tour. $30. Phone 916-583-6985.

Twin Peaks Trail—Along Ward Creek to Twin Peaks. Great lake views. Trailhead at Pineland-Twin Peaks Drive. For information ask at William Kent Campground on the North Shore. 5 miles, all day.

Horseback Riding:

Camp Richardson Corral, West Shore on Hwy 89 (916-541-3113).

Cascade Stables, off Hwy 89 between Baldwin Beach and Cascade Lake (916-541-2055).

Northstar Stables, on Hwy 267 between Kings Beach and Truckee (916-562-1230). Reservations required. $14 an hour. Guided trips.

Ponderosa Stables, at Incline Village on the North Shore (702-831-2154).

Squaw Valley, between Tahoe City and Truckee off Hwy 89 (916-583-7433). Lessons by reservation.

Zephyr Cove Stables, 4 miles north of Stateline on Hwy 50 (702-588-5664). Open 8:00am-6:00pm. Guided trail rides by reservation.

Lake Cruises: If you're not a sailor and you're not in shape to row your own boat, you can still see the lake close-up. The *M.S. Dixie*, an old sternwheeler, and Woodwind Sailing Cruises leave Zephyr Cove for half-day or full-day tours of the lake, April 26-Nov 2. The *Dixie* is a glass-bottomed boat.

There are sunset cruises with live entertainment, too. The *Tahoe Queen*, another sternwheeler, leaves from South Shore. The *Queen* offers narrated Emerald Bay cruises, sunset dinner-dance cruises, and live entertainment. Weddings and group charters are available. Also, the *Sunrunner* leaves from the North Shore.

For more information, call: *M.S. Dixie* (702-588-3508), *Sunrunner* (916-583-0141), *Tahoe Queen* (916-541-3364), Woodwind Sailing Cruises (702-588-3000).

Tennis:

Kirkwood Tennis Facility, off Hwy 88 at Kirkwood. 4 courts, no lights.

Lakeside Tennis Club, Hwy 28, Incline Village (702-831-5258). 12 courts, no lights.

North Tahoe Regional Park, end of National Avenue in Tahoe Vista (916-546-5043). 5 courts, lighted.

Squaw Valley Tennis Club, end of Squaw Valley Road. 6 courts, no lights.

Truckee Regional Park, off Hwy 267, ½ mile south of Truckee. 2 courts, no lights.

Winter Sports

The Tahoe area is famous for the abundant snow it receives each winter. Combine this with the spectacular beauty of the High Sierra, major alpine resorts, and some of the best touring trails in the country, and you understand why Lake Tahoe is rated #1 by Rand McNally for winter sports in the United States.

Downhill Skiing:

Alpine Meadows: 11 chair lifts, 2 surface lifts, 25% beginning runs, 40% intermediate, 35% advanced. Summit elevation 8,637 feet, vertical drop 1,800 feet. (916-583-4232).

Boreal Ridge: 9 lifts, 30% beginning runs, 60% intermediate, 10% advanced. Summit elevation 7,800 feet, vertical drop 600 feet. Night skiing available. (916-426-3666).

Diamond Peak, Ski Incline: 7 lifts, 18% beginning runs, 49% intermediate, 33% advanced. Summit elevation 8,540 feet, vertical drop 1,840 feet. (702-832-1177).

Donner Ski Ranch: 4 chair lifts, 25% beginning runs, 50% intermediate, 25% advanced. Summit elevation 7,751 feet, vertical drop 825 feet. (916-426-3635).

Echo Summit: 3 lifts, 40% beginning runs, 40% intermediate, 20% advanced. Summit elevation 7,400 feet, vertical drop 550 feet. (916-659-7154).

Granlibakken: 2 surface lifts, 40% beginning runs, 60% intermediate. Summit elevation 6,500 feet, vertical drop 300 feet. (916-583-9896).

Heavenly Valley: 1 tram, 16 chair lifts, 9 surface lifts. 25% beginning runs, 50% intermediate, 25% advanced. Summit elevation 10,100 feet, vertical drop 3,600 Nevada, 2,900 California. Heavenly Valley is the site of the John Denver Celebrity Ski Classic each February. (916-541-1330).

Homewood: 5 chair lifts, 5 surface lifts, 15% beginning runs, 25% intermediate, 35% advanced, 25% expert. Summit elevation 7,880 feet, vertical drop 1,650 feet. (916-525-7256).

Kirkwood: 10 chair lifts, 1 surface lift, 15% beginning runs, 50% intermediate, 35% advanced. Summit elevation 9,800 feet, vertical drop 2,000 feet. (209-258-6000).

Mt. Rose: 5 chair lifts, 30% beginning runs, 35% intermediate, 35% advanced. Summit elevation 9,700 feet, vertical drop 1,450 feet. (702-849-0704).

Northstar-at-Tahoe: 1 gondola, 8 chair lifts, 2 surface lifts. 25% beginning runs, 50% intermediate, 25% advanced. Summit elevation 8,600 feet, vertical drop 2,220 feet. (916-587-0290).

Sierra Ski Ranch: 10 chair lifts, 20% beginning runs, 60% intermediate, 20% advanced. Summit elevation 8,852 feet, vertical drop 2,212 feet. (916-659-7453).

Soda Springs: 3 chair lifts, 30% beginning runs, 50% intermediate, 20% advanced. Summit elevation 7,350 feet, vertical drop 650 feet. (916-426-3666).

Squaw Valley USA: 1 gondola, 1 tram, 27 chair lifts, 4 surface lifts. 25% beginning runs, 45% intermediate, 30% advanced. Summit elevation 9,050 feet, vertical drop 2,850 feet. (916-583-6985).

Sugar Bowl: 1 gondola, 7 chair lifts, 20% beginning runs, 30% intermediate, 50% advanced. Summit elevation 8,383 feet, vertical drop 1,502 feet. (916-426-3651).

Tahoe Donner: 2 chair lifts, 1 surface lift, 50% beginning runs, 50% intermediate. Summit elevation 7,350 feet, vertical drop 600 feet. (916-587-9444).

Cross-country Skiing:
Experienced Nordic skiers will find thousands of acres available for ski touring. Check with the U.S. Forest Service before setting out for the latest snow conditions and/or avalanche warnings (916-587-3558). Developed areas are listed below:

Cross Country at Galena: On the Mt. Rose Hwy 431, across from the Mt. Rose ski area. About 20 kilometers of groomed trails. Rental equipment available. (702-849-2513).

Diamond Peak Cross Country: On Mt. Rose Hwy above Incline Village. 20 kilometers of marked trails, miles of open terrain. (702-832-1177).

Kirkwood Cross Country: On Hwy 88 near Carson Pass. 75 kilometers of groomed trails with 20% advanced, 60% intermediate, and 20% beginning tracks. (209-258-7248).

Northstar-at-Tahoe: On Hwy 267 between Truckee and Kings Beach. 45 kilometers of groomed trails. Telemark skiing available. (916-562-1010).

Royal Gorge: On the old Donner Pass Road in Soda Springs. 77 trails, 317 kilometers of marked trails. (916-426-3871).

Squaw Valley: 12 trails on 50 kilometers of groomed track. (916-583-8951).

Tahoe Nordic Center: 2 miles east of Tahoe City. 60 kilometers of groomed trails. They also offer moonlight cross country ski tours. The full moon illuminates the trails through the Sierras, and the tour ends with a bonfire, hot wine, and cider (916-583-0484).

Snowboarding:
Boreal Ridge: Rentals, lessons, night events. (916-426-3666).
Diamond Peak at Ski Incline: Rentals, lessons. (702-832-1177).
Donner Ski Ranch: Rentals, lessons. (916-426-3635).
Heavenly Valley: Nevada side only. (916-541-1330).
Soda Springs: Rentals, lessons, sales. (916-426-3666).
Squaw Valley: Rentals, lessons, sales. (916-583-6985).

Snowmobiling:
There are many trails in the Sierras, and you can rent machines at several outlets.

Mt. Lake Adventure: At Incline Village. 100 miles of guided tours through the wilderness. (702-831-4202).
Snowmobiling Unlimited: At North Lake Tahoe. (916-583-5858).
Reindeer Lodge Snowmobile Rental: On the Mt. Rose Hwy. (702-849-9902).
Zephyr Cove Snowmobiles: On Hwy 50 at Zephyr Cove, South Shore. Track and wilderness tours. (702-588-3833).

Tobagganing and **sledding** are popular, too. An area about eight miles up the Mt. Rose Hwy has provided fun for Reno residents for many years. The Granlibakken Ski Area has a hill just for saucers. And at the Tahoe Regional Park on the North Shore at Tahoe Vista, there's a hill for tobaggans, saucers, and inner tubes. Equipment rentals are also available.

Sleigh Rides: How about a Christmas card ride through the backcountry pulled by Belgian horses adorned with tinkling bells? Call *Tahoe-Donner Cross Country* (916-587-9484), and they'll make the arrangements.

Weddings:
Civil marriages at the lake are performed at Incline Village by the Justice of the Peace (865 Tahoe Blvd., Suite 301, 702-832-4100). Weekdays only, hours vary. Fee $20. Wedding chapels include:

Cal-Neva Lodge at Crystal Bay, North Shore (702-832-4000).
Church of the Ponderosa, North Shore (702-831-0691).
The Dream Maker, 907 Tahoe Blvd., Incline Village (702-831-6419).

Climate & Dress
The weather at the lake is somewhat cooler than in the Reno area. You'll almost always need a light sweater or jacket in the evening. The lake enjoys warm, dry days in the summer and cold, crisp, sunny days in winter. (Beware of sunburn while skiing!) Heavy winter clothing is not necessary, and ski clothes are ap-

propriate anywhere. For dinner shows, you'll want something dressy, and men should plan on wearing a jacket (tie optional).

RV Parks & Campgrounds

You can make reservations for most campgrounds through Ticketron.

Camp Richardson Campground: On Hwy 89 West, two miles north of the South Shore. 230 sites for tents and trailers, hookups, flush toilets, showers, dump station, lodge, cabins, convenience store, restaurant and bar on the beach, gas station, boat ramp. $12 nightly fee. Open May to mid-Sept. (916-541-1801).

Bliss State Park: Between Meeks Bay and Emerald Bay off Hwy 89. 168 tent sites, trailers under 21 feet, flush toilets, water, showers. Reservations. Open Memorial Day to mid-Sept. (916-525-7277).

Donner Memorial Park: At Donner Lake off I-80 near Truckee. 125 tent sites, trailers under 28 feet, water, flush toilets, showers, boat ramp, beach. Reservations. $10 nightly fee. Open Memorial Day-Sept. (916-587-3841).

Fallen Leaf Campground: On Fallen Leaf Lake Road, one mile off Hwy 89 on the West Shore. 205 tent sites, trailers to 24 feet, water, toilets, boat ramp. Reservations. $10 nightly fee. Open Memorial Day-Sept. (916-573-2600).

General Creek Campground: In Sugar Pine State Park, one mile south of Tahoma on the West Shore. 175 tent sites, trailers to 30 feet, water, toilets, showers, swimming. Reservations. $10 nightly fee. Open all year. (916-525-7982).

Granite Flat Campground: On Hwy 89, north of Tahoe City on the Truckee River. 75 sites, tents and trailers, no water. Open mid-May to mid-Sept. No fee. (916-587-3558).

Meeks Bay Campground: South of Tahoe City at Meeks Bay. 40 sites for tents only, toilets, water, boat ramp, swimming. $8 nightly fee. Open Memorial Day-Oct. (916-573-2600).

Nevada Beach: One mile north of Stateline. 54 sites, tents and trailers to 24 feet, water, toilets, picnic sites. $10 nightly fee. Open May-Oct. (916-573-2600).

El Dorado Campground: Two miles south of Stateline. 170 sites, tents and trailers to 22 feet, motor homes, water, toilets, dump station, showers, boat ramp, swimming. $12 nightly fee. Open May-Oct. (916-583-2059).

Tahoe State Recreation Area: One mile north of Tahoe City. 39 sites, tents, and trailers under 21 feet, water, toilets, showers, boat ramp. Reservations. $10 nightly fee. Open Memorial Day-Labor Day. (916-583-3074).

Tahoe Valley Recreation Campground: West of the South Y Center on the South Shore. 300 sites, tents and trailers, hookups, water, showers, toilets. $13 nightly fee. Open all year. (916-541-2222).

William Kent Campground: South of Tahoe City in Nevada. 95 sites, tents and trailers to 24 feet, water, dump station, toilets. $8 nightly fee. Open late May-Oct. (916-544-6420).

Zephyr Cove Campground: In Nevada on Hwy. 50 at Zephyr Cove. 70 tent sites, 120 hookups, trailers to 40 feet, cabins, water, showers, toilets, convenience store, laundry, restaurant, rental boats, boat ramp. Shuttle to casinos. $17.75 nightly for full hookup, $12 nightly for tent site. (702-588-6644).

Casinos, Resorts, Hotels, and Games
North Shore

Cal-Neva Lodge, Stateline Road, Crystal Bay, NV 89402 (702-832-4000 or 800-225-6382). Rates: $59-$249.

Though its casino caters to big-money players, the legendary Cal-Neva Lodge, a.k.a. "The Lady of the Lake," is a homey, friendly hotel at the edge of Lake Tahoe, right on the California/Nevada line (which actually runs through the middle of the fireplace in the Indian Room). During Prohibition, mobsters like "Pretty Boy" Floyd and "Baby Face" Nelson often visited. The famous Indian Room Lounge, decorated with bear skins and wildcats, launched the careers of Pearl Bailey and Spike Jones. The Celebrity Showroom features big-name entertainment, and the Circle Bar and restaurant provide unforgettable views of the lake.

In addition to 190 rooms, 14 cabins, and 13 chalets, three wedding chapels are on the grounds. The Lady of the Lake Chapel seats 120 guests, while the smaller Lakeview Chapel accommodates 50. For a large wedding, the lodge provides a white lattice gazebo. The Cal-Neva has a staff of wedding consultants to help with all aspects of the ceremony, plus a wedding boutique, a gift shop, and a flower shop. Some rooms are furnished with heart-shaped beds and tubs, and mirrored ceilings.

An expansion plan calls for 200 more rooms, a convention center, and a complete health club.

Restaurants & Lounges
Sir Charles Fine Dining: Open 5:00pm-10:00pm daily. Gourmet food, beautiful lake and mountain views.
Lakeview Coffee Shop: Open 24 hours.

Games

Blackjack: ten tables, $3-$200, single-deck games, dealer hits soft 17, Insurance offered, double on 10 or 11.

Craps: one table, $2-$200, double odds to $100, none to $200.

Roulette: two tables, 50 cents-$500

Slots: 350 machines, MegaBucks.

Poker: 7-card Stud, Hold 'Em, $20 buy-in. Great new poker room with old-fashioned card room appearance.

Crystal Bay Club, Crystal Bay, NV 89402 (702-831-0512).

A small casino, the Crystal Bay Club offers casual games and could be more accommodating. The coffee shop is open 24 hours, and the steak and lobster house, open 6:00pm-10:00pm, is known for excellent dinners. There's a small dance floor in the lounge, with rock music every night except Monday. The lounge is open 9:00pm-2:00am. You'll also find an arcade for children open 8:00am-midnight.

Games

Blackjack: ten tables, single-deck games, one six-deck shoe, $2-$200, dealer hits soft 17, no Insurance offered, double on 10 or 11 on single deck, any two cards on shoe game.

Craps: one table, $2-$100, double odds, $100 max. field bet.

Roulette: one table, 25 cents-$10 straight up.

Keno: 50 cents on way tickets, $1 minimum ticket, $25,000 maximum payout.

Slots: 100 machines, 5 cents-$1, progressive machines $10,000 maximum payoff, poker machines.

Hyatt Regency Lake Tahoe Resort and Casino, Country Club Drive and Lakeshore, Incline Village, NV 89450 (702-831-1111 or 800-233-1234). Rates: $69-$209, lakeside cottages $450-$875.

The Hyatt Regency, a luxury resort with high-limit games and a big-money atmosphere, is built among the tall pines near Incline Village on the North Shore, away from the crowds and the noise of the South Shore's casino strip. It's a complete resort, with a health club (free for guests), Jacuzzi, 24-hour heated pool, two tennis courts, sports shop, and two gift shops, plus a child care center and the popular Camp Hyatt program for kids.

Restaurants & Lounges

Sierra Cafe: Buffets and limited menu. Open 24 hours.

Ciao Mein Trattoria: Oriental and Italian cuisine. Open Sun-Wed 6:00pm-10:00pm.

Hugo's: Spit-roasted duck, steak, seafood. Open daily, 6:00pm-11:00pm.

Wurst Place: Deli, open every day.

Cabaret Stage Bar: In casino. Entertainment nightly except Mondays.

Hugo's Lounge: Piano bar/vocals.

Games

Blackjack: 23 tables, $3-$3,000, single-deck games, six-deck shoe games, dealer hits soft 17, Insurance offered, double on 10 or 11 only on single decks, first two cards on shoe games.

Craps: three tables, $2 min., $1000 max., double odds.

Roulette: 25-cent game with $875 maximum payoff.

Keno: $2 minimum ticket, way tickets, $25,000 maximum payout.

Slots: 411 machines, 5 cents-$25. MegaBucks, Quartermania, $157,550 on progressive machines, 21 and poker machines.

Race & Sports Book: six screens, 26 inches.

Poker: Texas Hold 'Em, Crazy Pineapple, Hi-Lo Split, 7-card Stud, $20 buy-in. Five tables, weekly tournaments.

Also: **Red Dog**.

Tahoe Biltmore Lodge, Crystal Bay, NV 89402 (702-831-0660). Rates: $39-$59.

A small lodge with a small casino and indifferent dealers, the Biltmore offers 44 hotel rooms and 42 cottages, a gift shop, clothing store, and a souvenir/sundries shop. The coffee shop is open 24 hours, and there's a lounge with entertainment and dancing, plus a children's arcade.

Games

Blackjack: ten tables, all single-deck games, $2-$200, dealer hits soft 17, Insurance offered, double on 10 or 11.

Craps: one table, $2-$200, double odds up to $100, then single odds.

Roulette: one table, 25 cents-$25 straight up, $75 maximum payoff.

Keno: $1 tickets, way tickets, $25,000 payout.

Slots: Video poker.

Pai Gow Poker: $5-$200.

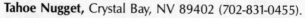

Tahoe Nugget, Crystal Bay, NV 89402 (702-831-0455).

Jim Kelley's Tahoe Nugget, which offers slots only, is the sole casino allowed to close its doors at any time during the year. A seasonal operation, open late May to early January, the Nugget has established itself as the casino with the friendliest employees on the North Shore and for serving great 14-ounce well drinks. The snack bar has daily, innovative specials. Beer connoisseurs will want to try the new Draft Beer Bar, specializing in quality imported beers. The other bar features award-winning wines, and both bars have video poker machines.

The casino has no table games but is known for its "loose" slot machines. There are 34 video poker machines, 23 video bar poker machines, six video Keno machines, and 115 other slot machines, including Quartermania. Double jackpot time comes along every 15 minutes, and players get free drinks and sandwiches.

South Shore

Caesars Tahoe, Highway 50, South Lake Tahoe, NV 89449 (702-588-3515 or 800-648-3353). Rates: Rooms $95-$125, suites $275-$950.

Caesars Tahoe, a world-class resort with a casino for high-rollers, calls itself "the gem of the Sierra Nevada." The 440-room resort, situated on 27 acres in the heart of Lake Tahoe's South Shore, has deluxe rooms and suites, 40,000 square feet of casino, eight restaurants, two lounges, a first class showroom, a health spa, and a convention center.

Most of Caesars' rooms are quite elegant, featuring Roman tubs, king-sized beds, and two TVs. The suites include a master bedroom, a furnished living area with large-screen TV, a dining area with wet bar, a Jacuzzi, and a steam room. One entire floor offers non-smoking rooms, and eight rooms are especially designed for handicapped guests. Caesars Spa has an award-winning, lagoon-style swimming pool with islands and waterfalls, a weight training room, racquetball courts, saunas, tanning beds, outdoor tennis courts, massages, and a beauty and barber shop. The Shopping Galleria includes a specialty boutique called Caesars Exclusively, and Caesars Tahoe Gift Shop has unique gifts and everyday necessities. Plus, Cartier, Ciro, and Gucci are there. A games arcade is open to children of all ages, and there's a 5,500-seat outdoor sports arena. Caesars also provides free "chariot service" throughout the South Shore.

Restaurants & Lounges

Le Posh: Recognized as one of northern Nevada's most elegant restaurants, specializing in French gourmet cooking and fine wines, served in an atmosphere of crystal, etched glass, and candlelight.

The Empress Court: Features delicacies from various regions of China in an exotic, oriental setting.

The Broiler Room: Traditional steakhouse. Prime rib, seafood, and Cajun specialties.

Primavera: Italian gourmet cuisine. Canopied tables reminiscent of European outdoor cafes.

Cafe Roma: Natural rock and wood setting. Informal meals, open 24 hours. All-American favorites for breakfast, daily specials.

Post-Time Deli: In the Sports Book. Pizza, hot dogs, burritos, clam chowder, apple pie, and the Colossal Sandwich (sold by the inch).

The Yogurt Palace: Honey Hill Farms yogurt with gourmet toppings, fresh fruit smoothies, espresso, and cappuccino.

Emperors Lounge: Seats 200, large screen TV and nightly entertainment.

Spooner Lounge: Serves appetizers nightly.

Caesars Cabaret: 300-seat show lounge, entertainment includes comedy, magic, and revues.

Circus Maximus: A 1,600-seat show room, top name entertainment and sporting events such as professional boxing and tennis.

Games

40,000-square-foot casino with non-smoking areas. 45 blackjack tables, six crap tables, five roulette wheels, one French roulette wheel.

Keno: One main counter, two outstations. Can purchase 5 games in advance and collect after fifth game. $50,000 maximum payout.

Slots: Over 1,000 machines, 5 cents-$100 machines. Progressive slots, MegaBucks, Quartermania, million-dollar payoffs.

Poker Room: A host will greet you. Deluxe tables and TV. Minimum buy-in is $20 for 7-card Stud and Texas Hold 'Em. Buy-ins are 10 times the minimum betting limit. Superstars of Poker Tournament.

Sports Book: 12 giant TVs and seating for over 100.

Also: **Baccarat** and **Mini-Baccarat, Big Six Wheels, Pai Gow**, and **Pai Gow Poker**.

Harrah's Lake Tahoe Resort and Casino, Highway 50, Stateline, NV 89449 (702-588-6606 or 800-648-3773). Rates: $100-$450 and up.

Harrah's Lake Tahoe Resort, an 18-story, 540-room hotel, is the only hotel casino in the world to receive both the Mobile Five-Star and AAA Five-Diamond Awards—and Harrah's has received both awards for 11 consecutive years. Clearly, it's a world-class resort. There's plenty of big-money play, no low-limit tables, and dealers have an attitude problem.

Each hotel room has over 500 square feet of space, two baths (each with its own TV and phone), and an in-room beverage valet—a computerized beverage dispenser that serves everything from a martini to the finest wines. Angled windows allow guests to enjoy magnificent views of the Sierras and Lake Tahoe. In addition to the rooms, Harrah's has 64 suites and 17 luxury suites with butler service. Convention facilities include 12 meeting rooms and a 17,000-square-foot special events center. An arcade is open from 9:00am-midnight with over 100 video games. Child supervision is available for 6- to 14-year-olds for $5 per child (up to five hours).

The shops are innumerable, and the health club offers an indoor pool, gym, spa, tanning salon, and a masseuse. Complimentary Tahoe airport shuttle.

Restaurants & Lounges

Summit Restaurant: Rooftop restaurant, one of Nevada's premier dining spots. Gourmet dining on stepped levels for an uninterrupted view of the lake.

Friday's Station Steak and Seafood Grill: Open for lunch and dinner from 11:30am, serving American dishes.

Forest Restaurant: Breakfast, lunch, and dinner. Sunday brunch from 9:00am.

Cafe Andreotti: Italian food served for lunch and dinner, plus a special late-night menu from 11:30pm-2:00am.

Corner Deli: Continental breakfast and New York-style deli sandwiches, soups, salads, and pastries.

Stateline Cabaret: Lounge with live entertainment.

South Shore Room: 1,000-seat show room with top-name entertainment. Dinner is served before the show; the cocktail show menu offers wines, dessert, and an international coffee bar.

Games

Blackjack: 98 tables, $3-$5,000 per hand, single-deck games, six-deck shoe games, dealer hits soft 17, Insurance offered, double on 10 or 11 on single decks, double on anything on shoe games.

Craps: 11 tables, $3-$5,000, double odds available.

Roulette: six tables, 50 cents-$100 minimum. No maximum.

Keno: $2 minimum ticket, way tickets, $250,000 payout.

Slots: 1,851 machines, 5 cents-$100, unlimited progressive machines, video poker and 21 machines. Harrah's Tahoe has also created the state's first Asian slot machine, using mahjong symbols on the reels. The $1 machines have brilliant red and gold colors and Asian art designs. The symbols are the same the Chinese use for luck, and the symbol for the $10,000 jackpot means "instant fame and fortune."

Bingo: 93-seat room, 3 cards per board, 3 min. and 8 max. boards, maximum payout $1,199.

Baccarat: $5-$10,000, bank does not pass, separate room, varying hours.

Pai Gow: $5-$500, tiles, bank passes.

Race & Sports Book: 102 seats, 25-inch screens, during football season the special events center adds 200 seats.

Poker: $20 buy-in, 12 tables, tournaments and contests.

Also: **Sic Bo Poker, Pai Gow Poker, Red Dog, Super Pan 9, 9's Up.**

Harvey's Resort Hotel/Casino, Highway 50 at Stateline Ave., Stateline, NV 89449 (702-588-2411 or 800-648-3361). Rates: $75-$450.

A beautiful hotel with an extremely friendly staff and casino, this is a great place to learn how to play. Harvey's is a AAA Four-

Diamond Hotel with 15,000 square feet of convention space and the most slot machines in northern Nevada. There are 717 rooms, 36 suites, a health club, pool, wedding chapel, a barber, and a beauty salon. The shopping arcade includes a jewelry store, clothing stores, and gift shops.

Harvey's is located directly on the shoreline of the lake, so nothing stands in the way of the incredible view from your room or from the Top of the Wheel restaurant. Guests receive a free breakfast at the Garden Buffet, complete with pancakes, hash browns, fruits, eggs, breakfast meats, and a sinful array of cakes, muffins, puddings, and pastries.

Restaurants & Lounges

Sage Room: Authentic Western atmosphere, seafood, poultry, veal dishes. Extensive wine list.

Top of the Wheel: A glass elevator takes you to the top floor for a spectacular view of the lake and the Sierras. Gourmet Continental, American, and Polynesian specialties. Dancing and a romantic atmosphere.

Seafood Grotto: Chinese and seafood favorites, Maine lobster, crab and shrimp.

Garden Buffet: Wednesday night is Basta Pasta night, Friday night seafood buffet, weekend brunch, scrumptious salad bar.

El Vaquero: Mexican food, garden courtyard setting. Lounge.

Carriage House: Snacks and full meals 24 hours. Steaks, seafood, sandwiches, pasta, hamburgers, salads.

Classic Burgers: Hamburgers, curly fries, milkshakes, other snack bar favorites.

Winners Deli: Deli with sandwiches and desserts.

The Emerald Theater: Classic bands and name entertainment.

Games

Blackjack: 80 tables, $2-$2,000, single-deck games, six-deck shoe games, dealer hits soft 17, Insurance offered.

Craps: eight tables, $2-$2,000, double odds available.

Roulette: six tables, 25 cents-$25 straight up.

Keno: $1 min., way tickets, $50,000 payout.

Slots: 2,300 machines, 5 cents-$25, 47 progressive carousels, poker and 21 machines, Black Gold $5 Slots with $25,000 jackpots.

Baccarat: $5-$5,000, separate room, open 7:00pm daily.

Poker: $20 buy-in, Stud and Hold 'Em, 14 tables, TV's, prizes for accumulated hourly play, breakfast served to morning players.

Pai Gow: $5-$1,000, tiles.
Race & Sports Book: 78 seats, 12 TVs.
Also: **Pai Gow Poker, Red Dog, Big Six Wheel**.

Harvey's has a "Party Ace" gaming instructor who teaches you how to play craps, baccarat, blackjack, poker, Pai Gow, and roulette. Classes run noon-6:00pm daily, starting on the hour. At the end of the lesson, you receive a $2 token—so you can make your first bet—and a pin that reads "Party Ace Graduate—Harvey's/Lake Tahoe."

Lake Tahoe Horizon Casino/Resort, Highway 50, Stateline, NV 89449 (702-588-6211 or 800-648-3322). Rates: $80-$320.

Luxury resort. Recently re-opened under new management. Friendly casino, okay for learning.

Formerly the High Sierra, the Lake Tahoe Horizon was renovated in 1990 and now has 537 rooms and 20 suites. You'll find three outdoor hot tubs, a pool, children's arcade, gift shops, a beauty and barber shop, and souvenirs. Rental car desks and tour company connections are located in the lobby. The convention center has 22,000 square feet, and there are six restaurants. The bars feature premium beers of the world.

Restaurants & Lounges
Four Seasons Coffee Shop: Open 24 hours, with breakfast, lunch, and dinner menus.
Gregory's: Open nightly. Serving ribs and chicken with all the trimmings.
Le Grande Buffet: Open for brunch and dinner, daily. The Lake's best buffet, with live entertainment.
Beaumont's: Gourmet dining with mesquite-broiled steaks and wild game. Open nightly.
Sugar Pine Bistro: French-style bistro. Coffees and teas, quiches, fresh pastries.
Snack Bar: Open 24 hours.
High Sierra Theater: For many years northern Nevada's premier showroom. Big name entertainment, 1,200 seats, luxurious. Dinner and cocktail shows.
There are also four lounges, one with entertainment, one with dancing.

Games

Blackjack: 55 tables, $3-$1000. Dealer hits soft 17, Insurance offered, double on any two cards, split any pair.

Craps: five tables, $1-$1,000, double odds available.

Roulette: four tables, 25 cents-$50 straight up.

Keno: $1 ticket, 50-cent way tickets, multi-race with one ticket, top and bottom tickets, $50,000 payout.

Slots: Lots! 5 cents-$5, progressives, super progressives, poker carousels, 21 and video poker machines.

Poker Room: 7-card Stud, Texas Hold 'Em, Low Ball. $10 buy-in, five tables, tournaments.

Also: Race & Sports Book, Big Six, Pai Gow Poker.

Reno

Reno was once called Lake's Crossing, which was simply a one-man ferry service across the Truckee River. In 1861, Myron Lake purchased a crude bridge across the Truckee River, obtained a franchise from the Nevada Territorial government, and built a toll road and an inn.

Thanks to the silver strike in Virginia City, business was good, and when the Central Pacific Railroad began building its way across the state, Mr. Lake offered 80 free acres to the railroad if they would develop a town site and deed half the lots back to him. The railroad agreed and named the new town Reno, after a Union officer killed during the Civil War. Almost overnight, the inn and the few buildings turned into hundreds more. The path of the wagon trains headed for the California gold country led through the valley, and the city was a trading post on the trail.

Today, the old toll road is Virginia Street, and Reno, in a part of Nevada that includes alpine mountains, green valleys, and high desert, remains rich in the history and customs of the Old West. Long before white explorers found the Sierras, the Washoe and Paiute Indians hunted, fished, and roamed through the area. The traditional home of the Paiute tribe, Pyramid Lake (northeast of town), is considered one of the most beautiful high desert lakes in America. It's still an Indian reservation, and modern powwows continue traditions of dancing, feasting, and trading.

Reno is one of the last places you can experience the true American West. Just outside the glittering city, cowboys still ride the open range. The hills are full of wildlife: deer roam through the mountains, game birds like pheasant, quail, and sage hen are abundant, and wild horses run free. Trout fill the streams in the canyons, lakes are plentiful for boating and swimming, and there are endless opportunities for hiking and camping.

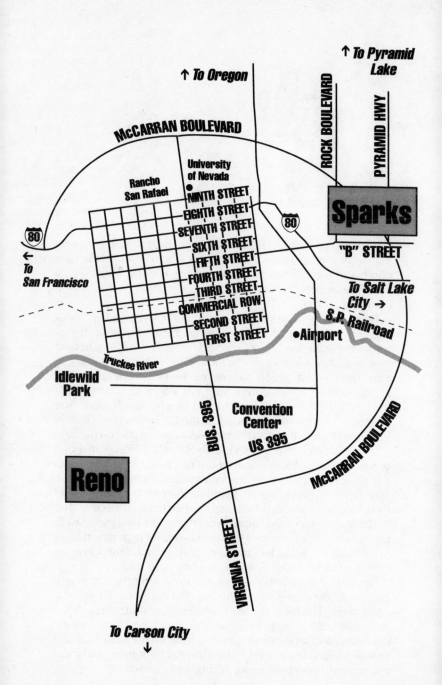

The famous Reno arch spanning Virginia Street with the words "The Biggest Little City in the World" was first built in 1927, and the original arch stood for 40 years. The slogan encapsulates the small town friendliness and big city amenities you'll find in Reno—a special sophistication blended with mountain hospitality.

Area Attractions

Fleischmann Planetarium: For anyone interested in space travel and the secrets of the universe, the Fleischmann Planetarium offers daily films and star shows, along with scheduled telescope viewing. Located at the north edge of the Univ. of Nevada/Reno campus on North Virginia St. Admission is $4 for adults, $2.50 for children under 13 and senior citizens. For information and show schedules, call 702-784-4811.

Harolds Club Gun Collection and Museum: A unique collection of antique firearms, including Samuel Colt's first patented revolver and 30 Winchester rifles. Open 24 hours, free admission. Address: Harolds Club, 250 North Virginia St. (3rd floor). Phone: 702-329-0881.

The William F. Harrah Automobile Museum: Over 200 antique, classic, and unique cars are on display downtown at Mill and Lake Streets in this large museum. Included in the tour is a presentation about the automobile's impact on our culture. Admission is $9.50 for adults, $8.50 for seniors, and $2.50 for children 6-15 (kids under 5 free). Phone: 702-333-9300.

Slot Machine Collection: The Liberty Belle of 1898, the first three-reeler slot machine, is among the many early slots displayed at the Liberty Belle Saloon, 4250 South Virginia. There's also Nevada memorabilia and a horse-drawn vehicle collection. Open 11:00am-11:00pm daily. Phone 702-825-1776.

Virginia Lake: This beautiful, 32-acre, tree-shaded lake and bird refuge has a fitness station, jogging trail, picnic area, and playground equipment. Fishing is permitted, and feeding the ducks is a must. Take Virginia Street south to Plumb Lane, turn right, and then left on Lakeside Drive. Turn left at the "Caution—Duck Crossing" sign.

May Great Basin Adventure: This theme park in San Rafael Park features a petting zoo, mining exhibits, dinosaurs to climb on, gold panning, and a log flume ride. Call 702-785-4319 for current hours and fees. Also in San Rafael Park, there's a museum of memorabilia collected by Wilbur May, son of the department store magnate, who led the life of a movie adventurer. An adjoining arboretum specializes in flora representative of the surrounding high desert (open daily 8:00am-sunset, free). The museum is open 10:00am-5:00pm Tues-Sun in summer, Wed-Sun the rest of the year. $2 for adults, $1 for children. Guided tours are available. 1502 Washington St. (702-785-5961).

Lake Mansion: The home of Myron Lake, Reno's founder, has been restored completely and is a treasure of early Nevada history. Open 8:00am-5:00pm Mon-Fri. The house is on South Virginia St. at the Reno Convention Center grounds. Free admission.

Pyramid Lake: When you first come over the ridge and see Pyramid Lake, you may think it's a mirage. The water is a brilliant blue, lying between low, brown mountains and surrounded on all sides by high desert. The shoreline is a jumble of strange rock formations, the last remnants of a prehistoric sea that covered parts of California and Nevada. The lake, home to the prehistoric cui-ui fish and one of two pelican rookeries in the country, is also known for its giant cutthroat trout, and you can tour the hatchery where the cui-ui and trout are raised. Open daily from 9:00am-11:00am and 1:00pm-3:00pm. Call 702-673-6335 for more information. Pyramid Lake Charters (702-476-0160) will take you fishing, or you can rent a boat from them. The lake is owned by the Paiute Indian Tribe, and Native American crafts are sold at stores in Sutcliffe and on the Pyramid Highway.

Verdi: Once a sawmill town at the foot of the Sierras, Verdi is now a quaint community with guest ranches, old homes, and fruit trees. You'll find many antique shops, some outstanding restaurants, and nice picnic grounds alongside the Truckee River. Crystal Peak Park, outside Verdi on Old Hwy. 40, has large picnic areas, fishing, and, if you're lucky, a beautiful, natural crystal waiting for you to find.

Reno Tahoe Gaming Academy: Reno's only accredited casino dealer's school is open to the public. You'll learn how to play each game from student dealers, plus you get a peek into the one-way mirrors above the gaming pits in the Cal-Neva Casino. Tours (at 12:30pm and 2:00pm Mon-Fri) cost $5 and include a free drink. Phone 702-348-7788.

Ballooning: For a spectacular view of the city and the surrounding countryside, try **Aerovision Balloons** (702-747-4144), **Balloon Adventure Company** (702-826-5858), or **Zephyr Balloons** (702-329-1700).

Bicycling: Whether you prefer mountain biking or cruising around Virginia Lake, you'll find many places to rent a bicycle. And since Reno is home to Greg Lemond, three-time winner of the Tour de France, biking is quite popular. Try **Citation Cycles** (702-322-3038), **College Cyclery** (702-323-1809), or **Reno Bicycle Center** (702-323-1221).

Golf: Reno has four public golf courses:

Lakeridge—18 holes, par 72, 6,717 yards, rolling terrain. Open all year. Carts mandatory, $29 green fee, pro shop, restaurant. 1200 Razor Back Rd. (702-825-2200).

Northgate—18 holes, par 72, 6,966 yards, rolling desert terrain. Open all year. Carts mandatory, $32 green fee, pro shop, bar, snack bar, teachings pros available daily. 1111 Clubhouse Dr. (702-747-7577).

Sierra Sage—18 holes, par 71, 6,600 yards, rolling and flat terrain. Open all year. $10 green fee, restaurant, driving range, putting green. Highway 395 North, Stead. (702-972-1564).

Washoe County—18 holes, par 72, 6,695 yards, rolling terrain. Open all year, $10.50 green fee, driving range, putting green. 2601 Arlington Ave. South. (702-785-4286).

Horseback Riding:

Bull Creek Ranch—On Old Hwy. 40 near Verdi, 10 miles west of Reno. (702-345-7500).

Rancho San Rafael—In San Rafael Park. One-hour, two-hour, and half-day guided trips daily. Group rates available. (702-329-7433).

Western Riding Stables—Off I-80, Clark Station exit, 18 miles east of Reno. $8 first hour, $7.50 thereafter. Open 8:00am-6:00pm daily. (702-343-0104).

Hiking: Many trails in the Sierras provide breathtaking views of the valley. For more information, call the U.S. Forest Service at 702-882-2766.

Big Meadows—A 16-mile hike along the Mt. Rose trail and then to Verdi. This trail is excellent for mountain bikes, also.

Galena Creek—A five-mile trail up Jones Creek Canyon to the headwaters of White's Creek and a small lake. Rated difficult.

Mt. Rose—Through meadows to the top of Mt. Rose (elevation

10,000 feet). Five miles long, rated difficult. The trailhead is at the summit of the Mt. Rose Highway, on the right next to the maintenance building.

Swimming Pools: Idlewild Park (702-785-2267), Moana Swimming Pool (702-785-2268), Northwest Pool (702-785-2203), Traner Pool (702-785-2269).

Tennis:
Bally's Reno—5 indoor courts, 3 outdoor, lighted. Reservations required. 2500 East 2nd St. (702-789-2145).
Lakeridge Tennis Club—4 indoor courts, 12 outdoor courts, 3 lighted. 6000 Plumas St. (702-827-4500).
Reno Y.M.C.A.—2 courts, no lights. 1300 Foster Dr. (702-329-1311).
Univ. of Nevada—6 courts, no lights. North & Evans (702-784-4879).
Washoe County—6 courts, 2 lighted. 2335 West Moana Lane (702-785-6133).

Soaring: Thanks to optimal air currents and favorable temperatures, Reno is one of the best places in the country to soar. Call **Soar Reno** at 702-972-7627 for glider rates, which start at $45. Open 11:00am-5:00pm daily except Monday.

Special Events
The Reno area is famous for three special events. In June, the **Reno Rodeo**—"The Wildest, Richest Rodeo in America"—offers over $300,000 in prize money for rodeo contests. The world's top cowboys compete at the Nevada State Fairgrounds, a few minutes from downtown. Mid-September brings the **Reno National Championship Air Races**. Everything from midget planes to World War II P-51's and British Spitfires fly over the Nevada desert at Stead Airport north of downtown. Stunt flying demonstrations and other aerobatics add to the thrills. The **Great Reno Balloon Race** also occurs in September, with pilots competing in races for prize money and a new car.

Weddings
Reno does not require a blood test or a waiting period for marriage, and the license is valid anywhere in the state. You must be 18 or older, and both must appear before the county clerk. The fee is $27, and you can get the license at the Marriage Bureau in the courthouse. Legal ID required. Contact: **Commissioner of Civil Marriages**, 195 Sierra St. South (702-328-3275). Open Mon-Fri 8:00am-5:00pm. Fee $27. On weekends and holidays, also

open 5:00pm-midnight ($30).

Wedding chapels include **Bally's Wedding Chapel** (702-322-5353), **Chapel of the Bells** (702-323-1375), **Heart of Reno Chapel** (702-786-6882), **Park Wedding Chapel** (702-323-1770), and **Silver Bells Chapel** (702-322-0420).

Climate & Dress

Reno offers warm, sunny, dry days year-round. The high altitude and low humidity make every season comfortable. Winters can be cold, but the days are sunny and crisp. In the summer, nights are almost always cool. The altitude is 4,400 feet, the average precipitation only 7 inches, and the average humidity 32%.

You'll need a sweater or jacket most evenings. Dress casually for daytime and evening, but if you're attending a dinner show, you'll want something a little dressier. Men should plan on a jacket, with tie optional, for dinner shows. In the winter, ski clothes are acceptable in all restaurants and casinos.

Air Services

Nine major airlines serve Reno International Airport, and charter service is also available. During peak periods in the airport, you'll find "ambassadors" who can answer your questions and give directions. They wear red sweaters and an "Ask Me" button. Airlines include:

America West—702-348-2777 or 800-247-5692.
American Airlines—702-329-9217 or 800-443-7300.
Canadian Air International (charter)—702-826-6822.
Continental Airlines—702-322-9075 or 800-525-0280.
Delta Airlines—702-323-1661 or 800-221-1212.
Great American Airways (charter)—702-786-7373.
Northwest Airlines—800-225-2525.
Sky West—702-785-2888 or 800-453-9417.
United Airlines—702-329-1020 or 800-241-6522.
United Express—800-241-6522.
USAir—702-329-9365 or 800-428-4322.

Some of the hotels and motels have free courtesy buses on call for airport transportation, or you can call the limousine service (702-786-3700). The service charges $2.45 to downtown Reno or $1.90 to Bally's. Taxis are plentiful, and there are 18 car rental companies at the airport.

Amtrak

Amtrak serves the old Reno depot in the heart of the downtown casino district. The *California Zephyr* has daily service to San Francisco each morning and to Chicago each evening. Call 800-USA-RAIL for reservations and information.

Driving Distances to Major Cities

San Francisco—221 miles   Seattle—742 miles
Las Vegas—450 miles   Salt Lake City—530 miles
Portland—567 miles   Los Angeles—470 miles

Sightseeing Companies

Hardy & Associates (702-329-3114). Daily narrated tours to Truckee, Lake Tahoe, Carson City, and Virginia City. Complimentary pick-up and return to all hotels and motels.

Gray Line of Reno & Lake Tahoe (702-329-2877). Daily tours year-round to Virginia City, Lake Tahoe, the Ponderosa Ranch, and Heavenly Valley.

Virginia City-Lake Tahoe Tours (702-826-6888). Daily narrated tours to Virginia City, Lake Tahoe, and Carson City. Complimentary pick-up and return to all hotels and motels.

Ski Shuttle Service

Diamond Peak at Ski Incline (702-832-1177). Free shuttle service throughout the North Shore and Incline Village. Call for information.

Mt. Rose Ski Area (702-849-0704).

Gray Line of Reno (702-329-2877). Reno to Squaw Valley, Alpine Meadows, Northstar, Diamond Peak at Incline, and Mt. Rose.

Squaw Valley (800-545-4350). Daily shuttles from the airport in Reno to Truckee and Squaw Valley. Reservations required. $20 per person, one way, in ski season only.

RV Parks & Campgrounds

Lookout Campground: 10 miles west of Reno off I-80 on the California border. 21 sites, water, 14-day limit, no fee. Open June-October.

Warrior Point Park: At Pyramid Lake on SR 445. 40 sites, water, restrooms, hot showers, BBQs, fishing, swimming, boating.

Casinos, Resorts, Hotels, and Games

Bally's, 2500 East 2nd St., Reno, NV 89501 (702-789-2000 or 800-648-5080). Rates: $69-$99.

This huge, world-class resort hotel has over 2,000 rooms and a crowded casino that caters to the high-stakes player. The hotel features a health club with an Olympic-size pool, a bowling alley with 50 lanes, indoor and outdoor tennis courts, and twin movie theaters. A gallery of over 40 shops lines the main floor with apparel, jewelry, souvenirs, and a beauty and barber shop.

Restaurants & Lounges
Cafe Gigi: Gourmet French dining. Open 5:00pm-midnight.
Caruso's: Superb Italian food and atmosphere. Opens at 5:00pm.
The Steak House: Fine steaks and prime rib. Open 5:00pm-11:00pm.
China Seas: Oriental cuisine. Open for dinner.
The Bounty: Seafood specialties for lunch and dinner.
Patio Room Coffee Shop: Open 24 hours.
Ziegfeld Room: Sunday champagne brunch with over 50 items, 10:00am-3:00pm.
Catch a Rising Star Comedy Club: Top comedians perform Tues-Sun at 8:30pm and 11:00pm. $7 weekdays, $9 weekends.
Lion's Den Lounge: Top lounge acts nightly 7:30pm-2:00am.
Leo's Lair: Cocktail lounge with dancing.

Games
Blackjack: 75 tables, $2-$10 minimums, single-deck and six-deck shoe games, dealer hits soft 17, Insurance offered, double on 10 or 11.
Craps: six tables, $2-$10 minimums, double odds available.
Roulette: four tables, $1-$5.
Keno: separate lounge with 250 seats, $1 ticket, way tickets, $50,000 maximum payout.
Slots: over 800 machines, 5 cents-$1, progressive machines, MegaBucks, poker and 21 machines.
Pai Gow: $2-$500, bank passes.
Race & Sports Book: 100 seats, six screens at 57".
Poker: separate room, buy-in $10, 7-Card Stud, Texas Hold 'Em.
Also: **Red Dog**.

Boomtown Hotel & Casino, Interstate 80/Garson Exit, Verdi, NV 89439 (702-345-6000 or 800-648-3790). Rates: $34.95-$39.95 for rooms, $65-$70 for suites.

This former truck stop on the California/Nevada border has grown into a major resort, complete with a children's arcade that's open 24 hours. The Boomtown is an extremely friendly complex, with a good casino for beginners.

The hotel has 120 rooms, an indoor pool, and two spas. There's also a large RV park with full hook-ups and a laundromat. Truckers still get some priority here: they have their own lounge and restaurant. Plus, you'll find a gift shop, a 24-hour mini-mart, gas stations, and one of the best restaurants in the area for Western food. The buffet, open 10:00am-11:00pm, features a different specialty each day, and there's a 24-hour menu as well. The Red Eye Lounge is a comfortable spot for drinks.

Games
Blackjack: 36 tables, $2-$500, single-deck games only, dealer hits soft 17, Insurance offered, double on 10 or 11 only.
Craps: three tables, $1-$1,000, double odds available.
Roulette: two tables, 25 cents-$25.
Keno: $1 minimum ticket, way tickets 50 cents per way, $50,000 payout.
Slots: 1,000 machines, 5 cents-$5, progressive machines, 21 and poker machines.
Poker: $20 buy-in, 7-Card Stud, Texas Hold 'Em.

Circus Circus, 500 North Virginia, Reno, NV 89503 (702-329-0711 or 800-648-5010). Rates: $38-$44.

Like it's sister in Las Vegas, Circus Circus is a hotel/casino complex built around a circus theme. Clowns and jugglers roam the building, trapeze acts perform directly above your head as you play the games, and the whole affair is a great time for the entire family.

The crowded, large casino offers friendly dealers and is good for beginners. The hotel, with its pink-and white-striped roof made to look like a circus tent, has 1,651 reasonably priced rooms. There's a 24-hour coffee shop and a gourmet steak house open 5:00pm-11:00pm. As you might expect, Circus Circus is extremely popular; you need to make reservations at least a month in advance.

Games

Blackjack: 60 tables, $2-$500, single-deck and six-deck shoe games, dealer hits soft 17, Insurance offered, double on 10 and 11.

Craps: four tables, $1-$500, double odds available.

Roulette: three tables, 25 cents-$100.

Keno: $1 ticket, way tickets, $50,000 maximum payout.

Slots: 2,500 machines, 5 cents-$1, MegaBucks, poker and 21 machines.

Pai Gow Poker: $1-$500, bank passes.

Race & Sports Book: Part of the lounge, six 27" screens.

Poker: Buy-in $10, 7-Card Stud, Texas Hold 'Em.

Also: **Red Dog**.

Clarion Hotel Casino, 3800 South Virginia St., Reno, NV 89502 (702-825-4700 or 800-762-5190). Rates: $79-$125.

Directly across from the Convention Center, this hotel has 303 gorgeous rooms and suites, plus northern Nevada's only 30-foot indoor waterfall. Each room features a private spa, wet bar, and in-room keno. Courtesy airport and downtown shuttle available, and there's a complete health club, a gift shop, and an arcade. Two exceptional dining rooms are in the Clarion: the Pizza Cafe and the Purple Parrot Restaurant, with an all-you-can-eat soup and salad bar. The Center Stage Cabaret offers dancing and live entertainment until dawn. The Clarion's $30 Fun Book includes free cocktails, free pizza, half-priced dinner, free keno credits and blackjack bucks, and a free night's stay.

Games

The Clarion has single-deck 21 games, and you can double down on the first two cards. (The dealers here still peek under their 10s, too.) Slots advertise a 100% payback, and there are 25-cent and $1 video poker machines at all bars, plus weekly slot tournaments. The Clarion also has roulette, craps, poker, keno, and a sports book, all with standard rules and procedures.

Club Cal-Neva, 38 East 2nd St., Reno, NV 89501 (702-323-1046).

For a large casino, the Club Cal-Neva is unusually casual, and it's a good place for beginning craps players. The Club offers seven restaurants, all open 24 hours. The Top Deck features a 99-cent ham and egg breakfast. For fine dining, try the Copper Ledge, known for its $4.95 prime rib and $5.95 steak and lobster dinners. At the Hofbrau, chefs prepare your food at your table, and there are numerous snack bars throughout the casino.

Games

Blackjack: 30 tables, $2-$1,000, single-deck games only, dealer hits soft 17, Insurance offered, double on 9, 10, or 11.

Craps: four tables, 25 cents-$1,000, triple odds available.

Roulette: two single-0 tables, three 00 tables, 10 cents-$30.

Keno: 10-cent way tickets, multi-race tickets, $250,000 payout.

Slots: 1,200 machines, 5 cents-$5, progressive machines to $500,000, $3,000,000 on MegaBucks, 340 poker machines.

Pai Gow Poker: $5-$500.

Race & Sports Book: 250 seats, over 75 TVs.

Poker: $10 and $20 buy-ins, 7-Card Stud, Pan, Texas Hold 'Em.

The Colonial, 250 N. Arlington, Reno, NV 89501 (702-322-3838). Rates: $45-$75.

This small hotel offers a tiny casino with only blackjack and slots. Three blocks from busy Virginia Street, the Colonial has 168 rooms and a 24-hour restaurant. There are four blackjack tables, $2-$500. All games are single-deck, the dealer does **not** hit soft 17, and Insurance is offered—it's a good place for beginning blackjack players. There are also 60 slot machines (5 cents-$1), plus 21 and video poker machines.

Comstock Hotel Casino, 200 West 2nd St., Reno, NV 89501 (702-329-1880 or 800-648-4866). Rates: $35-$85.

Two blocks from all the noise of Virginia Street, the Comstock is another modest hotel with a small, friendly casino good for beginning blackjack play. This Western-style hotel has 309 rooms and six suites. Its Specialty Room restaurant is famous for rainbow trout and steak dinners, just $5.99. The Miner's Cafe is open 24 hours, and the Comstock Dinner House has gourmet dining (open 5:00pm-11:00pm, reservations suggested). There's also a gift shop and a health club.

Games
Blackjack: six tables, $1-$500, all single-deck games, dealer does **not** hit soft 17, Insurance offered, double on 10 or 11.
Craps: one table, $1-$500, double odds available.
Keno: $1 ticket, way tickets, $50,000 maximum payout.
Slots: 500 machines, 5 cents-$1, MegaBucks, poker and 21 machines.

♡ ♠ ◇ ♣

El Dorado Hotel & Casino, 345 North Virginia St., Reno, NV 89503 (702-786-5700 or 800-648-5966). Rates: $26-$150.

This luxury hotel in downtown Reno has a huge casino and dealers who can be impatient with beginners. The hotel offers a new 25-story tower, 800 rooms and suites, Jacuzzi, pool, 12,000 square feet of convention and meeting facilities, gift shop, boutique, and bakery. With seven restaurants, the El Dorado provides some of the best food in town, plus Reno's hottest cabaret with top-name lounge entertainment.

Restaurants & Lounges
La Strada: "The World's Greatest Italian Restaurant," with a wood-burning pizza oven from Italy. Open for dinner from 5:00pm.
Mardi Gras: Chinese food. Open 24 hours.
Market Place Buffet: Huge selection of salads, vegetables, the hotel bakery's pastries and breads, and a variety of hot entrees. Open for lunch and dinner daily.
Choices Express Food Cafe: Nine food and beverage stops, grilled meats and poultry. Sidewalk cafe with street lamps, silk trees, and hanging plants.
The Vintage Room: Continental cuisine and fine wines. Open for dinner from 5:00pm daily.

Games
Blackjack: 65 tables, $2-$1,000, 27 single-deck games, six-deck shoe games, dealer hits soft 17, Insurance offered, double on 10 or 11.
Craps: four tables, $2-$500, double odds available.
Roulette: four tables, 25 cents-$25 straight up.

Keno: $1 minimum ticket, 50 cents per way on four ways or more, $100,000 payout.
Slots: 1,544 machines, 5 cents-$25, MegaBucks, progressives, no limit to payoff, poker and 21 machines.
Baccarat: $2-$1,000, no separate room, bank does not pass.
Pai Gow: $5-$500, tiles, bank passes.
Race & Sports Book: 26 seats, plus a sports bar seating 23.
Pai Gow Poker: $5 minimum, $500 maximum, no buy-in, bank passes.
Also: **Over/Under 13, Red Dog, Big Six Wheel**.

Fitzgerald's Hotel Casino, 255 North Virginia St., Reno, NV 89501 (702-785-3300 or 800-648-5022). Rates: $32-$65 weekdays, $78-$100 weekends.

If you're superstitious and need to see some lucky talismans, stay here. Fitzgerald's, built on an Irish theme, features a collection of good-luck charms from around the world, including the only Blarney Castle stone ever to leave Ireland, an echoing wishing well, and a leprechaun cave filled with pots of gold.

Next to the Reno Arch, Fitzgerald's has 345 rooms and a friendly casino. Mollie's Garden Restaurant is open 24 hours for light snacks and entrees from pancakes to steaks, and the Emerald Room serves a buffet daily from 7:30am-10:00pm. There's also live entertainment nightly in the lounge.

Games
Blackjack: ten tables, $2-$1,000, only single-deck games, dealer does **not** hit soft 17, Insurance offered, double on 10 or 11.
Craps: two tables, $1-$1,000, double odds available.
Roulette: one table, 25 cents.
Keno: $1 ticket, way tickets, $50,000 maximum payout.
Slots: 2,500 machines, 5 cents-$1, MegaBucks, $50,000 dollar machine, poker and 21 machines. 97% payback on $1 slots.

Flamingo Hilton, 255 North Sierra, Reno, NV 89501 (702-785-7000 or 800-950-2946). Rates: $59-$159.

The Flamingo is a standard Hilton with a crowded casino that caters to high-limit play. There are 605 rooms, a games arcade, and a gift shop. Restaurants include Paco's, serving Mexican food (with "thunderstorms" every half-hour); Sierra Crossing, a deli/coffee shop open 24 hours with a buffet at each meal; and Top of the Hilton, open 4:00pm-11:00pm with gourmet food, a fine wine list, and a terrific view of the city. The Showspot lounge features local bands nightly, and the showroom has a Comedy Club.

Games
Blackjack: 36 tables, $2-$5,000, single-deck games and six-deck shoe games, dealer does **not** hit soft 17, Insurance offered, double on 10 or 11.
Craps: three tables, $2-$2,000, double odds available.
Roulette: three tables, $1-$3,000 outside.
Keno: $1 ticket, 50-cent way tickets, $50,000 maximum payout.
Slots: 904 machines, 5 cents-$100, progressive machines, over $1,000,000 payoff. Poker and 21 machines.
Baccarat: $5-$5,000, bank does not pass.
Pai Gow: $5-$5,000, bank passes.
Race & Sports Book: 54 seats, 26 TVs.
Poker: $20 buy-in, 7-Card Stud, Texas Hold 'Em.

Harolds Club, 250 North Virginia St., Reno, NV 89501 (702-329-0881).

Harolds is the oldest club in Reno, known world-wide for its "Harolds Club, Reno or Bust" signs. The casino, spread over three floors, offers blackjack, craps, roulette, keno, pai gow, and many slots. Unfortunately, employees can be curt and indifferent.

The seventh floor contains the Presidential car restaurant, serving outstanding meals from 5:00pm-11:00pm. There's an extensive wine list, and a dessert cart with choices from Harolds' own bakery (reservations suggested). The Boardwalk Diner has breakfast for $2.49, plus good pastrami and roast beef sandwiches. Also, Nevada Annie's Snack Bar is open Fri-Mon.

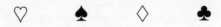

Harrah's, 219 North Center St., Reno, NV 89501 (702-786-3232 or 800-648-3773). Rates: $69-$105 weekdays, $79-$115 weekends. Two floors of non-smoking rooms.

This world-class resort offers free gaming instruction daily and extra-friendly dealers to make its casino great for beginners.

Located in the center of downtown Reno, Harrah's has recently undergone a $15 million renovation. The hotel takes pride in special touches, such as a fresh rose in your room every morning, Godiva chocolates at night, and a complimentary airport shuttle that runs continuously. The health club is complete with sauna, whirlpool, and an in-house masseur and masseuse. There's also an outdoor heated pool, a 24-hour video arcade, and a gift shop. The 15,000 square foot convention center on the third floor features championship boxing matches. And don't miss the off-premises Automobile Collection (see *Area Attractions* above).

Restaurants & Lounges
The Skyway Buffet: Breakfast (7:00am-11:00am) for $4.49, lunch (11:00am-3:00pm) for $4.99, and dinner (4:00pm-10:00pm) for $6.99. Children under 12 can eat dinner for $3.50, and there's a 15% senior's discount. On Friday nights, seafood is featured for $12.95. Sunday brunch is served 7:00am-5:00pm and costs $6.50. A lavish assortment of desserts is sure to tempt.
The Garden Room: Open 24 hours with breakfast, lunch, dinner, and a variety of snacks. Made-to-order pastries are a specialty.
Steak House: Steak, seafood, and a wide selection of wines. Open 11:00am-2:30pm, and for dinner from 5:00pm.
Headliner Room: Features a Revue and top entertainers. Dinner and cocktail show. There's also lounge entertainment in the Skyway Vintage Court and in the Rendezvous Bar.

Games
Blackjack: 70 tables, $2 minimum bet, $1,000 maximum bet at $25 tables, single-deck, double-deck, and six-deck shoes. Dealer hits soft 17, Insurance offered, double on 10 or 11.
Craps: eight tables, $1-$500, some tables $100-$1,000, double odds available.
Roulette: five tables, 25 cents-$1,000.
Keno: $2 minimum ticket, any way ticket $1 a way, $250,000 maximum payout for 7 and 8 spots, $500,000 maximum payout for 9-15 spots. With Keno-to-Go, you can collect winnings up to a year after the game, up to 1,000 tickets.
Slots: Over 2,000 machines. 5 cents-$100, $5 progressive ma-

chines, MegaBucks linked to all Harrah's properties in Nevada, video poker throughout the hotel.

Mini-Baccarat: $5-$1,000.

Pai Gow: $5-$1,000. Asian games section (Sic Bo, Pai Gow Poker, Super Pan 9).

Sports Book: 120 seats with 14 TVs.

Race Book: 60 seats in Champions Lounge, parimutuel betting, 5 ft. screen. Total of 28 screens. Each table has individualized lighting and computer betting. Snack Bar open 8:00am-9:00pm.

Poker: Separate room with eight tables, 7-Card Stud, Texas Hold 'Em, Razz.

Holiday Hotel, Mill & Center Streets, Reno, NV 89502 (702-329-0411 or 800-648-5431). Rates: $46 weekdays, $60 weekends.

A small hotel and casino, the Holiday is one of Reno's older hotels, built directly on the Truckee. There are 200 rooms, a gift shop, and a large coffee shop, with windows overlooking the river. The casino is not especially good for beginners.

Games

Blackjack: six tables, $2-$1,000, all single-deck games, dealer hits soft 17, Insurance offered, double on 10 or 11.

Craps: one table, $1-$1,000, double odds available.

Keno: $1 ticket, way tickets, $50,000 maximum payout.

Slots: 300 machines, 5 cents-$1, progressive machines, poker and 21 machines.

Holiday Inn—Monte Carlo Casino, 1000 E. 6th St., Reno, NV 89512 (702-786-5151 or 800-648-4877). Rates: $59-$79 for rooms, $125 for suites.

The Holiday Inn, away from the action downtown, has a small casino and friendly dealers. The hotel offers an airport shuttle, outdoor swimming pool, a shuttle to Virginia Street downtown, a gift shop, and a lounge in both the hotel and the casino, with occasional entertainment. Two restaurants are open 24 hours: one's a snack bar, the other offers fine dining.

Games

Blackjack: eight tables, $2-$200, single-deck games, dealer hits soft 17, Insurance offered, double on 10 or 11 only.

Craps: one table, $2-$300, double odds available.

Keno: 70-cent ticket, way tickets, $25,000 maximum payout.

Slots: 302 machines, 5 cents-$1, MegaBucks, progressives, poker machines from 5 cents-$1, 21 machines.

♡   ♠   ◇   ♣

Horseshoe Club, 229 North Virginia, Reno, NV 89501 (702-323-7900).

This small downtown casino, an okay place for beginners, has a Sizzler Steak House open 24 hours.

Games

Blackjack: nine tables, $2-$200, all single-deck games, dealer does **not** hit soft 17, Insurance offered, double on 10 or 11.

Craps: one table, $1-$500, double odds available.

Roulette: one table, 25 cents.

Keno: $1 ticket, $50,000 maximum payout.

Slots: 500 machines, 5 cents-$1, MegaBucks, progressive machines.

♡   ♠   ◇   ♣

Nevada Club, 224 N. Virginia, Reno, NV 89501 (702-329-1721).

One of three casinos owned by Fitzgerald's, the Nevada Club is a working-man's club, but it's not bad for beginning players. The coffee shop has great hamburgers and milkshakes.

Games

Blackjack: ten tables, $1-$500, single-deck games only, dealer does **not** hit soft 17, Insurance offered, double on 10 or 11.

Craps: one table, 25 cents-$5 minimum bet, double odds available.

Roulette: one table, 25 cents.

Keno: $1 ticket, $50,000 maximum payout.

Slots: 795 machines, 5 cents-$1, no progressives, poker and 21 machines.

♡   ♠   ◇   ♣

Peppermill Hotel Casino, 2707 South Virginia St., Reno, NV 89502 (702-826-2121 or 800-648-6992). Rates: $35-$125 for rooms, $225-$400 for suites.

This resort hotel has a small, crowded casino that caters to the big money. Dealers are not especially friendly.

Hotel amenities include a heated outdoor swimming pool and a complete fitness center with spa and sauna. The complex is close to walking and jogging paths and a major mall. A free shuttle will take you downtown and to and from the airport. There's also a hair salon, gift shop, a video arcade, snack bar, baby sitters on call, a staff fluent in seven languages, and 24-hour room service. Ask for the complimentary fun book.

Six theme bars and lounges are open 24 hours. The Peppermill Cabaret features live entertainment nightly, and the Fireside Lounge serves free *hors d'oeuvres* with your cocktail from 4:00pm-8:00pm weekdays.

The original 24-hour restaurant, opened in 1971, serves everything from bacon and eggs to fettucini alfredo. There are also low-cholesterol selections. Breakfasts $4.95 from midnight-6:00am. Entrees $5-$15. Other restaurants include Le Moulin, the Peppermill's gourmet restaurant, where many dishes are prepared at your table; and the Island Buffet, with delicious appetizers, salads, fresh fruits, entrees, and bakery-fresh desserts. Breakfast, lunch, and dinner, with Friday night seafood buffet and Sunday brunch. Buffet $5.50-$14.95.

The casino has standard rules for blackjack, craps, roulette, baccarat, poker, pai gow poker, and keno, plus over 800 slot and video poker machines. The poker machines have a 98.3% payback. Non-smoking tables are available in the casino.

Pioneer Inn, 221 South Virginia St., Reno, NV 89501 (702-324-7777 or 800-879-8879). Rates: $24 weekdays, $38-$75 weekends.

This motel-like inn and small casino two blocks south of the river could be friendlier, but it does have three good restaurants. The Iron Sword Room is a dinner house with fine steaks, open 5:00pm-11:00pm. The coffee shop is open 24 hours for pancakes and other breakfast treats, and the Prime Rib Company serves gourmet meals 5:00pm-11:00pm daily. There are also three bars, one with live entertainment.

Games
Blackjack: seven tables, $2-$500, single-deck games, dealer hits soft 17, Insurance offered, double on 10 or 11.
Craps: one table, $1 minimum, double odds available.
Keno: $1 ticket, $50,000 maximum payout.
Slots: 250 machines, 5 cents-$1, MegaBucks, poker and 21 machines.

Reno Turf Club, 280 North Center, Reno, NV 89501 (702-323-1046).

This race and sports book (85 seats, 24 TVs) has a few slot machines but no table games. All slots are 25-cents with a $1,000 maximum payoff. The snack bar serves the best pastrami sandwich in town. Players get complimentary drinks.

Riverboat Hotel & Casino, 34 West 2nd St., Reno, NV 89501 (702-323-8877 or 800-888-5525 in the U.S., 800-321-4711 in Canada). Rates: $22-$40 and up.

The Riverboat, patterned after an old Mississippi River paddle-wheeler, is a lovely new hotel with a very friendly casino. Everyone here smiles—including the dealers.

One block off busy Virginia Street, the hotel has 120 rooms and suites decorated with satin wallpaper, Tiffany-style lamps, carved molding, and bougainvillea. The front courtyard has brick walkways, an outdoor bandstand, and park benches. The casino even has willow trees dropping from the ceiling, and small alcoves hold slot machines next to tree trunks!

The Oyster Bar features a variety of special drinks, and the Riverboat Restaurant is open 24 hours for chicken and ribs with Cajun sauce, plus steak and eggs at a bargain price after 10:30pm.

Games
Blackjack: 13 tables, $2-$500, all single-deck games, dealer hits soft 17, Insurance offered, double on 9, 10, or 11.
Craps: one table, $1-$500, double odds available.
Roulette: one table, $1-$1,000.
Keno: $1 ticket, way tickets, $150,000 maximum payout.
Slots: 381 machines, 5 cents-$1, progressives, unlimited maxi-

mum payoffs. Poker, 21, and keno machines. The free Slots Ahoy Club gives members 10% off food and rooms, plus free gifts and bonus points that can be redeemed at the gift shop.
Pai Gow Poker: $5-$500, bank passes.

Sands Regency Hotel Casino, 345 North Arlington, Reno, NV 89501 (702-348-2200 or 800-648-3553). Rates: $49-$69.

This beautiful new hotel, three blocks west of Virginia Street, unfortunately has a newly enlarged casino with indifferent dealers. The Sands has 1,000 rooms and suites, two pools, a state-of-the-art health club, and many shops. Owned by a local Greek family, the hotel features a steak house called Antonio's, which also offers special Greek dishes. The casino has standard rules for blackjack, craps, keno, and roulette, plus lots of slots, but the employees could be friendlier, and there are better places to stay.

Sundowner Hotel & Casino, 450 North Arlington, Reno, NV 89503 (702-786-7050 or 800-648-5490). Rates: $20 weekdays, $25 weekends.

This nice, inexpensive hotel has a very friendly casino that's great for beginning players. Three blocks west of Virginia Street, the Sundowner has three restaurants: G.K.'s Steak House, open 5:00pm-11:00pm for fine dining (frog legs, escargot, and stuffed quail), a buffet nightly, with all-you-can-eat seafood on Friday and a Sunday champagne brunch, and a 24-hour coffee shop.

Games
Blackjack: 15 tables, $2-$200 and $25-$1,000, single- and double-deck games, dealer hits soft 17, Insurance offered, double on 10 or 11.
Craps: two tables, $2-$500, triple odds available.
Roulette: one table, 25-cents weekdays, 50-cents weekends, $1,000 maximum payout.
Keno: $1 ticket, 50-cent way tickets, $50,000 maximum payout.
Slots: 636 machines, 5 cents-$5, progressives, unlimited maximum payoff, poker and 21 machines.

The Virginian, 140 North Virginia St., Reno, NV 89503 (702-329-4664 or 800-874-5558). Rates: $25 weekdays, $38 weekends.

In the middle of the downtown action, the Virginian has a friendly casino on two floors, 118 rooms, and a 24-hour restaurant with a $1.49 breakfast. It's a good spot for beginners.

Games
Blackjack: 18 tables, $2-$500, single-deck games, dealer hits soft 17, Insurance offered, double on 10 or 11.
Craps: one table, $2-$500, double odds available.
Roulette: one table, 25 cents-$5.
Keno: $1 ticket, 50-cent way tickets, $50,000 maximum payout.
Slots: 458 machines, 5 cents-$1, video poker and 21 machines, progressive machines.

Gaming Instruction

The following clubs offer free lessons in some or all of the games: **Bally's, The El Dorado, Harrah's**, and the **Sands**. The **Flamingo Hilton** and the **Horseshoe** have learner's tables where dealers explain the game and minimum bets are reduced.

Sparks

Reno's sister city, Sparks was originally little more than a railroad yard outside Reno. Today it's growing at twice the rate of its sibling, and millions of dollars are being spent developing the casino district and an eight-block festival marketplace called Victorian Square. Located on B Street, the Square has a turn-of-the-century theme with a bandstand, gazebo, fountain, Victorian store fronts, and an amphitheater seating 300 people. Plans call for a museum and shopping mall soon.

The whole town is getting into the Victorian spirit. The Nugget, Sparks' largest casino, sports a new facade consistent with the plaza's theme. Several smaller casinos have also remodeled in the same look.

The Square also hosts a variety of special events throughout the year: the Rodeo Chili Cook-off, a jazz festival, bicycle races, and the beautiful Victorian Christmas Parade and Celebration. In the summer, the amphitheater offers frequent concerts.

The city limits of Sparks touch the city limits of Reno, and you won't know when you leave one and enter the other.

Area Attractions
Of course, the attractions listed for Reno apply to Sparks, but Sparks has a few of its own:

Wild Waters Fun Resort: A fun spot for the family, with wild currents, deep drop-offs, tides, slides, and a children's recreation area. Open May-Sept at Interstate 80 and Sparks Boulevard, 10:00am-8:00pm daily. Admission is $12.95 for adults, $9.95 for children and seniors. Phone: 702-785-5961. Wild Island, part of Wild Waters, has a mini-golf course called Adventure Golf. Greens fees are $3.95 for 18 holes or $5.95 for 36 holes.

Sierra Nevada Ice Arena: Next door to Wild Island, this complete skating facility offers lessons, hockey, broom ball, and performances. Admission for two hours is $4.50 for children under 12 and $5 for adults. Phone: 702-355-1033.

Golf:
Wildcreek Golf Course—18 holes, par 72. Open all year. Carts mandatory. $32 greens fee. A stream, seven lakes, clubhouse, lounge, snack bar, and pro shop. 3500 Sullivan Lane (702-673-3100).

Brookside Municipal Golf Course—9 holes, par 70. Open all year. Greens fees $3.50 for 9 holes, $6 for 18 holes. Snack bar, putting green. 700 South Rock Boulevard (702-322-6009).

Swimming pools:
Alf Sorenson Pool, 1400 Baring Blvd. (702-356-2385).
Deer Park Pool, 1700 Prater Way (702-356-2385).

Tennis:
Aimone Park—two courts, lights, Puccinelli Drive & Queen's Way.
Burgess Park—three courts, lights. Pyramid & Holman Way.
Oppio Park—three courts, lights. 18th Street & York Way.
Shelly Park—two courts, lights. 2901 Baring Blvd.
For more information, call the Sparks Recreation Department at 702-359-7930.

Paradise Park: 49-acre lake with fishing, small boat sailing, soccer, picnic areas, restrooms, and a playground. Oddie Blvd. & El Rancho Drive.

Rock Park: On the banks of the Truckee River. Picnic area, BBQs, a pavilion, horseshoe courts. 1515 Rock Blvd.

The Lazy 5 Trap Shooting Club is located on Pyramid Lake Highway. Phone 702-673-1370.

Casinos, Resorts, Hotels, & Games
Baldini's Sports Casino, 865 South Rock Blvd., Sparks, NV 89431 (702-358-0116).

This is a small, friendly casino, with a snack bar open 11:00am-11:00pm and a 24-hour restaurant. The Cabaret Lounge has live music.

Games
Blackjack: six tables, $2-$100, all single-deck games, dealer hits

soft 17, Insurance offered, double on 10 and 11.

Keno: 5-cent ticket, must play $1 minimum, way tickets, $25,000 maximum payout.

Slots: Over 300 machines, 5 cents-$1, progressive machines, poker machines.

Bingo: Free Bingo games, two cards per board, $1,000 blackout game.

Race & Sports Book: 50 seats, over 70 TVs.

Giudici's B Street Gambling Hall, 1324 B St., Sparks, NV 89431 (702-359-8868).

Located on Victorian Square, this is a tiny casino with an Italian-style coffee shop open 24 hours. Giudici's has just three black-jack tables, with $1-$50 bets, single-decks, Insurance, and the dealer hits on a soft 17. There's also a keno counter with 70-cent tickets and a $50,000 maximum payout, plus 206 slot machines from 5 cents-$1.

Gold Club, 1201 B St., Sparks, NV 89431 (702-355-8600).

This small, very friendly casino next door to the Nugget is a great place for beginning players to learn blackjack. They're planning to add poker soon, too.

The Gold Club has an extensive coupon program, with free plays on the tables, free sandwiches, free drinks, etc. There's also a deli specializing in pizza, ribs, and chicken wings, open 24 hours.

Games

Blackjack: four tables, all single-deck games, $1-$50, dealer hits soft 17, Insurance offered, double on 10 or 11.

Slots: 84 machines, 5 cent-$1, 5-cent video progressive poker machines.

Pai Gow Poker: $1-$5. Bank does not pass.

John Ascuaga's Nugget, 1125 B St., Sparks, NV 89431 (702-356-3300 or 800-648-1177). Rates: $28-$85.

One of the largest complexes in the Reno-Sparks area, the Nugget has a huge, crowded casino, where the dealers are sometimes too busy to be friendly.

Locally owned, the Nugget has over 1,000 rooms, a rooftop indoor swimming pool, a health spa, beauty parlor, and gift shop. The Celebrity Cabaret, a spectacular showroom, features top stars, and a casino lounge features live entertainment nightly. Parents will appreciate "Dial-A-Sitter," where you can phone for a babysitter from your room. There's also an arcade for children on the main floor.

Restaurants & Lounges
Pub and Pantry: Snacks, sandwiches, pizza, and over 50 beers. Open 24 hours.
Farm House Coffee Shop: Breakfast, lunch, and dinner. Open 24 hours.
Rotisserie Restaurant and Buffet: Breakfast, lunch, and dinner. Sunday brunch special 11:00am-2:00pm.
Nevada General Store: Country-style breakfast, lunch, and dinner. Open 24 hours.
The Steak House: Prime rib and steaks. Open for lunch and dinner 11:00am-11:00pm.
John's Oyster Bar: Fresh seafood served in a restaurant resembling the deck of a sailing ship. Open 10:00am-10:00pm daily.
Trader Dick's: Beautiful Polynesian restaurant serving exotic cocktails and Asian and American cuisine amid tropical flowers and waterfalls. Dancing in the lounge. Open 10:00am-10:00pm.

Games
Blackjack: 40 tables, $1-$500, single- and six-deck shoe games, dealer hits soft 17, Insurance offered, double on 10 and 11.
Craps: eight tables, $1-$500, double odds available.
Roulette: six tables, 25 cents-$5.
Keno: $1 ticket, 50-cent way tickets, $50,000 maximum payout.
Slots: 1,363 machines, 5 cents-$1, progressive machines, $25,000 maximum payoff, poker and 21 machines.
Bingo: 120-seat room, four cards per board, $5,000 coverall.
Race & Sports Book: 75 seats, 8 TVs.
Poker: Buy-in $10, 7-Card Stud.
Also: **Red Dog**.

Mint Casino, 1130 B St., Sparks, NV 89431 (702-359-4944).

This tiny casino at Victorian Square is okay for learning black-jack. The Mint has just three blackjack tables, with $1-$50 bets, all single-deck games, Insurance, and the dealer hits soft 17. There's also a keno counter with a 70-cent ticket and a maximum payout of $50,000, plus 265 slots and Quartermania. The coffee shop is open 24 hours.

Plantation Club, 2121 B St., Sparks, NV 89431 (702-359-9440).

This small casino has friendly dealers and a 24-hour restaurant. On weekends, the lounge offers live entertainment.

Games
Blackjack: five tables, $2-$50, all single-deck games, dealer hits soft 17, Insurance offered, double on 10 and 11.
Craps: one table, $1-$50, double odds available.
Roulette: one table, 25 cents-$500.
Keno: 70-cent ticket, way tickets, $25,000 maximum payout.
Slots: 250 machines, 10 cents-$1, Quartermania and Dollar-mania, progressive machines, poker and 21 machines.
Race & Sports Book: 20 seats, 10 TVs.
Poker: $10 buy-in, 7-Card Stud.

Silver Club, 1040 B St., Sparks, NV 89431 (702-358-4771 or 800-648-1137). Rates: $28 rooms, $45 suites.

This Victorian-style hotel has a hospitable, crowded casino that's good for beginners, plus 234 rooms and parking for RVs. "Dial-A-Sitter" brings a babysitter to your room.

The Gazebo Lounge has nightly live entertainment, and the Rails Bar and Grill features traditional tavern fare. The Town Square Restaurant, open 24 hours, has a buffet for all three meals, and Victoria's Steak House offers fine dining with chef specials (open 5:00pm-9:00pm daily).

Games
Blackjack: 13 tables, $1-$200, all single-deck games, dealer hits soft 17, Insurance offered, double on 10 and 11.

Craps: one table, 25 cents-$500, double odds available.
Roulette: one table, 25 cents-$5.
Keno: $1 ticket, 50-cent way tickets, $50,000 maximum payout.
Slots: 631 machines, 5 cents-$1, progressive machines, Quartermania, $20,000 maximum payoff. Poker and 21 machines.
Pai Gow Poker: $5, bank does not pass.
Race & Sports Book: 150 seats, 10 TVs.

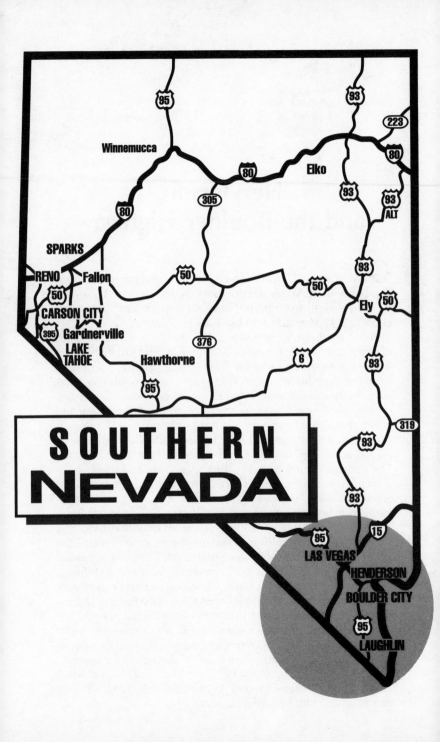

Henderson
and the Boulder Highway

On your way to Laughlin, you'll pass through Henderson, midway between Las Vegas and Boulder City. Henderson's big attraction is its small town friendliness, so stop for lunch, visit the chocolate factory, and try your luck in a casino.

In the southern tip of Nevada, Henderson is 13 miles south of Las Vegas, 11 miles north of Boulder City, and just eight miles from Lake Mead and Hoover Dam. It was originally a mining town and then home to the construction workers who built the dam. At the start of World War II, the government built a magnesium plant nearby, and the town flourished. After the war, the government sold the plant to private industry, and Henderson became a company town. The population gradually grew to nearly 70,000, and today Henderson is the fourth largest city in the state. The climate is mild and dry; the elevation is 1,940 feet.

Henderson's interesting **Clark County Heritage Museum** (1830 S. Boulder Hwy., 702- 455-7955) gives you a chance to see a pueblo, historic homes with period furnishings, a ghost town, and a 1905 steam engine and caboose. Its desert frontier exhibit tells the story of southern Nevada from prehistoric times through the 20th century. The museum, open daily from 9:00am-4:30pm (except major holidays), costs just $1 for adults, 50 cents for children.

If the thought of a candy bar or a hot fudge sundae makes your mouth water, don't miss the **Ethel M Chocolate Factory** (2 Cactus Dr., 702-458-8864; just 15 minutes from the Las Vegas Strip), where some of America's most delicious chocolates are made. It's open daily 8:30am-6:00pm, and admission is free. Imagine how Grandma's kitchen smelled when she baked a chocolate cake, and then multiply that by a hundred. Ethel M also has a large **Cactus Garden** with over 350 species of cactus and desert plants, many with beautiful flowers.

Casinos and Hotels

The Gold Strike Inn & Casino, Highway 93, Boulder City, NV 89005 (702-293- 5000 or 800-245-6380). Rates: $31.95-$57.95.

Boulder City is the only city in Nevada that prohibits gambling. So, the Gold Strike, a small, friendly hotel-casino with 155 rooms, is not in the city but on the highway that connects Henderson and Boulder City. An arcade, gift shop, and three restaurants including a steakhouse and a buffet are on the property, as well as a lounge with entertainment. The Gold Strike is a quiet alternative to the big-city glitz palaces.

Games

Blackjack: 12 tables, $1-$200, single decks and four-deck shoe games. Insurance available, dealer hits soft 17, double on 10 or 11 only.

Craps: one table, $1-$200, double odds available.

Roulette: one table, 25 cents-$200.

Keno: 50-cent ticket, way tickets, maximum payout $50,000.

Slots: 640 machines, 5 cents-$1, progressive machines, Mega-Bucks, poker, and 21 machines.

Bingo: 250 seats, free cards, maximum progressive payout.

Poker: Minimum buy-in $20, 7-Card Stud, Texas Hold 'Em.

Nevada Palace Hotel & Casino, 5255 Boulder Highway, Las Vegas, NV 89122 (702-458-8810 or 800-634-6283). Rates: $29 weekdays, $45 weekends.

Casual, elegant hotel with small, very friendly casino. A nice change from the Strip, and good for beginning play. 220 rooms and suites, pool and spa, gift shop, three beautiful restaurants, and a video arcade.

Restaurants & Lounges

Gold Mine Restaurant: Open 24 hours. Simple snacks and full-course meals.

Klondike Louie's: Chinese cuisine. Open 5:00pm-1:00am daily.

La Bella Pasta: A delicious selection of pasta, traditional Italian food, and antipasto salad and soup bar, all served from 4:00pm-10:00pm nightly. Champagne Brunch 9:00am-2:00pm Sunday.

Games

Blackjack: 10 tables, $1-$200, single-deck and six-deck shoe games, dealter hits soft 17, Insurance offered.

Craps: one table, 50 cents-$200, double odds offered.

Roulette: two tables, 10 cents-$200.

Keno: 50-cent ticket, 35-cent 3-way ticket, $50,000 maximum payout.

Slots: 650 machines, 5 cents-$5, progressive machines, poker and 21 machines.

Bingo: 280 seats, free Bingo sessions, Super Coverall $250,000.

Poker: Buy-in $20, 7-card Stud, Texas Hold 'Em.

Race & Sports Book: 4 huge screens.

Railroad Pass Hotel & Casino, 2800 S. Boulder Hwy., Henderson, NV 89015 (702-294-5000 or 800-654-0877). Rates: $31.95-$57.95.

Friendly casino good for beginning play. On the road leading to Boulder City from Henderson. 120 rooms, pool, children's arcade, gift shop with Indian pottery, three restaurants (one open 24 hours), buffet open for breakfast, lunch, and dinner. The International Dinner Buffet has over 45 hot and cold dishes, with a different nation's cusine featured each night. Bar with glass wall overlooking the desert, well-lit RV parking.

Games

Blackjack: 10 tables, $1-$100, single-deck games, four-deck shoes, dealer hits soft 17, Insurance offered, double on 10 or 11 only.

Craps: one table, $1-$100, double odds available.

Roulette: one table, 10 cents-$100.

Keno: 50-cent minimum ticket, way tickets, maximum payout $50,000.

Slots: 640 machines, 5 cents-$1, progressive machines, Mega-Bucks, poker and 21 machines.

Bingo: 250 seats, free boards, progressive payout.

Rainbow Club, 122 S. Water St., Henderson, NV 89015 (702-565-9776).

A casino in downtown Henderson, the Rainbow serves good food at reasonable prices 24 hours a day.

Games
Blackjack: six tables, $1-$100, double-deck hand-held games, dealer hits soft 17, Insurance offered, double on any first two cards.
Keno: 70-cent ticket, three-ways or more 35 and 50 cents a way, six ways or more ticket is 25 cents a way, maximum payout $50,000.
Slots: 426 machines, video poker, Keno, progressive, 5 cents-$1, rapid bonus progressives. Maximum payoff for 5-cent machines is $40,000.

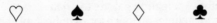

Skyline Restaurant & Casino, 1741 N. Boulder Hwy., Henderson, NV 89015 (702-565-9116).

Friendly casino, lots of goodies available, plus three restaurants open 24 hours a day. Silhouette Lounge features live music and dancing. Children's arcade open 24 hours. Ask at cashier's cage for Fun Book containing a souvenir, free drink with popcorn and pretzels, free nickles, coupons for drawings, discounts on food, etc. Free lighted parking for RVs and trucks.

Games
Blackjack: four tables, $1-$100, only four-deck shoes, dealer hits soft 17, Insurance available, double on any two cards.
Slots: Over 300 machines, 5 cents-$1, progressive machines, unlimited maximum payoff, poker and 21 machines.
Poker: Buy-in $10, 7-card Stud.

Las Vegas

Set among the vivid colors of the desert southwest, Las Vegas is Nevada's largest, most exciting city, where you'll discover a huge variety of attractions and endless possibilities for entertainment. Terrific weather, recreation galore, top-name stars, and wonderful hotel/resort facilities all make for an unbeatable combination.

Named by explorers in 1829, Las Vegas is Spanish for "The Meadows." In 1843, John C. Fremont explored the Great Basin to conduct the first mapping expedition of what would become the state of Nevada. By 1902, Senator William Clark had decided to build a railroad between Los Angeles and Salt Lake City, but he needed the artesian springs near Las Vegas to do it, so he auctioned his land. The buyers made a wise investment—today that land is the site of Hoover Dam, an engineering marvel built by 5,000 men over five years.

In 1931, the state legislature made gambling legal in Nevada, but it wasn't until 1946 that Bugsy Siegal and Meyer Lansky built the Pink Flamingo hotel/casino in the middle of the desert. It was the first of the lavish hotels and resorts on what is now "The Strip," the stretch of enormous buildings and gaudy neon signs for which the city is famous.

Today, over 18 million people—many of them attending a trade show or convention—come to see Las Vegas' spectacular nightlife and surrounding attractions every year. Breathtaking scenery, 24-hour gambling, entertainment, and fun are abundant. Las Vegas really is a different world, an exciting, vibrant city alive with extravagance in every form.

Even non-gamblers can have a full vacation in Las Vegas. There are numerous recreation areas and resorts where you can swim, fish, or water ski. A flight to the Grand Canyon makes a terrific daytrip, or visit one of the area ghost towns. Annual events such as rodeos and hot air balloon races abound, and tours of the area are available by bus, car, plane, and helicopter.

The hotels in Las Vegas offer everything except the ordinary. Some are mini-cities, where you can find anything from a toothbrush to an 18-hole golf course. You can relax in a private whirlpool, drink champagne on your terrace, or indulge in an extravagant meal. Best of all, prices are quite reasonable, and the hotels provide many services such as a multi-lingual staff, gaming lessons, and child care.

Throughout Las Vegas, you'll feel a unique magic that helps you leave the rest of the world behind.

Area Attractions

Hoover Dam: Constructed during the Depression, Hoover Dam has long been recognized as one of the world's greatest engineering feats. The dam retains the Colorado River and provides electricity to three states and Mexico. Seventeen generators provide enough power annually for a million homes, and over 14 million people rely on the dam for water.

Hoover Dam is 30 miles southeast of Las Vegas on the Boulder Highway. Tours run Memorial Day to Labor Day every 35 minutes from 8:00am-6:45pm. (Other times, tours run 9:00am-4:15pm.) The fee is $1 for adults, 50 cents for seniors, and children under 16 are admitted free.

Boulder City has a **Hoover Dam Visitors Bureau** at 1228 Arizona St., which shows a free movie daily from 8:30am-4:00pm, describing the history and construction of the dam.

Valley of Fire: About 55 miles east of Las Vegas, Valley of Fire State Park got its name from the red sandstone formations shaped by erosion into seemingly man-made objects, like beehives. You'll also find many Indian petroglyphs, petrified wood, and white domes that provide a startling contrast to the sandstone. The park has a visitors' center, self-guided trails, two campgrounds, and picnic areas with water and restrooms. Pets are welcome but must be kept on a leash. All the artifacts and signs of the Indian civilization are protected by state and federal law.

Near Red Rock Canyon, **Bonnie Springs Ranch** was built in 1843 as a stopover for wagon trains. There's a fine dinner house, cocktail lounge, petting zoo, and a large stable where horses are available for hire. Call 702-875-4292 for prices and hours. The drive through **Red Rock Canyon** is one of the most scenic drives in the West, past cacti, desert plants, and unique trees. **Old Nevada,** near Bonnie Springs, is a western town with a wax museum, shops, an opera house, a saloon, a restaurant and ice cream parlor, a miniature train, a silent movie house, and gunslingers who stage shootouts daily on Main Street. The **Bonnie Springs Motel** has family units, a pool, hiking trails, cocktails, and fine dining. For reservations and rates, call 702-875-4400.

Lake Mead National Recreation Area: Just 25 miles southeast of Las Vegas, Lake Mead extends 115 miles, with a 500-mile shoreline, making it the largest man-made lake in the northern hemisphere. The National Park Service governs the area, and they operate a visitors' center (open daily 8:00am-4:30pm) four miles northeast of Boulder City. Recreational activities include swimming, boating, waterskiing, camping, and fishing (largemouth bass, rainbow trout, catfish, and bluegill are abundant). Six marinas provide boat docking and restaurants. You can rent power boats and houseboats that sleep ten people at **Calville Bay** (800-255-5561). If you have your own boat, there are 600 slips available with an easy grade launch ramp. A marina store provides last minute supplies, along with gifts, beach wear, and ice.

The **Las Vegas Boat Harbor** (4635 Boulder Hwy, Las Vegas, 702-565-9111) is a full-service marina on the lake with patio boat rentals, restaurant and lounge, tackle shop, 24 hour fuel, and fishing boat rentals. The **Lake Mead Resort** (322 Lakeshore Blvd., Boulder City, 800-752-9669) has a floating restaurant and lounge, boat rentals, marina storage, and a lakeview hotel with a pool.

You can also cruise Lake Mead to Hoover Dam in about an hour. Boats depart daily from the Lake Mead Marina at 10:30am, noon, 1:30pm, and 3:00pm. Cost: $7.50/adults, $4/children 12 and under.

Ghost towns of the area include **Potosi**, site of Nevada's oldest lode mine (on the Old Spanish Trail, 25 miles southwest of Las Vegas); **Goodsprings**, a mining camp in the early 1900's, 35 miles southwest of the city; **Sandy Valley**, 13 miles west, with an old gold mine; and **Eldorado Canyon**, 40 miles southwest, the site of the Techatticup Mine, which produced over $2 million in gold before 1942.

Liberace Museum: Extravagant fashions, stage jewelry, furs, pianos, and other memorabilia from "Mr. Showmanship" fill this museum. A Baldwin grand piano inlaid with thousands of etched mirrors rests on a revolving stage, and you can view Liberace's customized cars up close. Many people consider this the best attraction in Las Vegas. Address: 1775 Tropicana Ave., 702-798-5595. Hours: Mon-Sat 10:00am-5:00pm, Sunday 1:00pm-5:00pm. Admission: $6.50/adults, $4.50/over 60, $2.00/children, $3.50/students.

The Lost City Museum: This ghost town at Overton, 60 miles northeast of Las Vegas, features a collection of early Pueblo Indian artifacts and exhibits relating to the early Mormon settlers. Open daily except major holidays from 8:30am-4:30pm. Admission for adults 18 and over is $1.

Old Las Vegas Fort: Tour the remnants of the oldest original buildings in the Las Vegas Valley and the first Anglo settlement, dating to 1855. Address: Las Vegas Blvd. North & Washington St. Hours: Saturday & Monday 10:00am-4:00pm, Sunday 1:00pm-4:00pm. Donation of $1 for adults, 50 cents for children requested.

Southern Nevada Zoological Park: This family attraction with lions and tigers and bears—and lots of monkeys—also offers a great children's petting zoo. Address: 1775 North Rancho Dr., 702-648-5955. Hours: Open daily 9:00am-5:00pm. Admission: $3.50 for adults, $2 for children under 16 and Seniors.

Mt. Charleston: Part of the Toiyabe National Forest, Mt. Charleston (elevation 12,000 feet) is a year-round recreation area. There's skiing in the winter, camping and hiking in the summer, and picnic areas throughout. Bristlecone pines, the oldest living trees on earth, exist at the highest peaks. The **Mt. Charleston Inn** offers dining and accommodations. Call 702-872-5500 for rates. In the winter, **Lee Canyon** is a fine ski facility, with three chairlifts, a beginners' hill, and cross-country trails. Snow-making is provided on all lifts, and you can ski at night. Call 702-658-1931 for more information.

Wet 'N Wild: On the Las Vegas Strip, this 26-acre water park boasts the world's highest and fastest water slide, flumes, lagoons, waves, rivers, and an indoor arcade. Bring your own picnic and lunch by the pool. Address: 2600 Las Vegas Blvd. South, 702-737-3819. Hours: April-September, 10:00am-6:00pm. Admission $15.95 for adults, $12.95 for kids.

Guinness World of Records Museum: This museum of the exceptional has 5,200 square feet of space devoted to exhibits, rare film footage, and computerized data banks from space, the arts and entertainment, sports, and the theater. You'll also see replicas of the world's tallest man (8 ft., 11 inches), the most-tattooed lady, and the heaviest man. The data banks provide information from many fields: Did you know that 38 different buildings and monuments tell you the world's largest palace is the Imperial Palace in Peking? You'll also discover the world's strongest beer and how much the world's biggest lemon weighed. Address: 2789 Las Vegas Blvd. South, 702-792-0640. Hours: Sun-Thurs 9:00am-10:00pm (until 11:00pm on Fri and Sat). Admission: $2.95/children, $3.95/students and seniors, $4.95/adults.

Black Canyon Raft Tours: Take a one-day raft trip down the Colorado River from Hoover Dam to Willow Beach Resort. The trip, which is free of rapids, covers 11 miles and takes you past Indian shelters, waterfalls, and magnificent geological formations. You can arrange for a pickup at your hotel in Las Vegas or drive to the Gold Strike Casino near the dam. The cost is $59.95 for adults, $35 per child under 12. A hot lunch is furnished, and reservations are required. Call 702-293-3776 for more information.

Golf:

Desert Inn Golf Club, 3145 Las Vegas Blvd. South, 702-733-4444. Par 72, 7,111 yds., clubhouse, pro shop, driving range, deli. Fee includes carts. Hotel guests $60 weekdays, $75 weekends; general public $100.

Desert Rose Golf Course, 5483 Club House Dr., 702-438-4653. Municipal course. Par 71, 6,507 yds., pro shop, rental clubs, driving range, restaurant. Fee includes carts. $29 for 18 holes, $11.50 for 9 holes.

Dunes Country Club, 3650 Las Vegas Blvd. South, 702-737-4747. Considered the toughest course in Las Vegas. Par 72, 7,240 yds., clubhouse, pro shop, restaurant, rental clubs. Fee includes carts. Hotel guests $65, public $90.

Sahara Country Club, 1911 E. Desert Inn Rd., 702-796-0016. Par 71, 6,815 yds., clubhouse, pro shop, driving range, rental clubs. Rates are seasonal; call for current fees.

Tennis:

Aladdin Hotel, 3366 Las Vegas Blvd. South, 702-736-0111. 3 courts, lighted.

Bally's Casino-Resort, 3645 Las Vegas Blvd. South, 702-739-4111. 10 outdoor courts, 7 lighted.

Caesars Palace, 3570 Las Vegas Blvd. South, 702-731-7110. 4 outdoor courts.

Desert Inn Hotel, 3145 Las Vegas Blvd. South, 702-733-4444. 10 outdoor courts, 5 lighted, equipment rental, pro shop, daily clinics.

Flamingo Hilton, 3555 Las Vegas Blvd. South, 702-733-3344. 4 lighted courts.

Riviera Hotel, 2901 Las Vegas Blvd. South, 702-734-5110. 2 outdoor lighted courts.

Sports Club, 3025 Industrial Blvd., 702-733-8999. Total fitness and sports facility, located behind the Stardust.

Union Plaza, 1 Main St. (downtown), 702-386-2110. 4 outdoor lighted courts.

Sightseeing & Tour Services

Gray Line Tours offers a choice of trips to Las Vegas nightclubs, Hoover Dam, Lake Mead, Red Rock Canyon, and Mount Charleston. One especially good bargain is an eight-hour tour to Laughlin for $14.50 per person, including hotel pick-up and a buffet dinner. Call 702-384-1234 for information and reservations.

Ray & Ross Transport has many fun tours, including a "party bus" that visits the city's dancing spots. Snacks, drinks, and tips are included for $38 per person, including hotel pick-up. They also have a nightclub tour, a trip to Laughlin through Searchlight, NV, a rafting trip down the Colorado, and an air excursion to the Grand Canyon. Call 702-636-4661 for details.

The Grand Canyon is a short flight from Las Vegas, and several companies offer daily sightseeing flights. **Scenic Air** (702-739-1900) provides planes with huge windows and high wings so nothing impedes your view. **America West** (800-247-5692) has low fares, including cocktails, and flies to the Canyon twice daily. **Air Nevada** (702-736-8900 or 800-634-6377) has personalized air/ground tours and flies daily. **Lake Mead Air** (702-293-1848) uses high-wing aircraft and has flights from $15. For the ultimate thrill, take a helicopter ride over the Canyon, to Hoover Dam, or to Death Valley with **Helicop-Tours** (135 Reno Ave. 702-736-0606). **Grand Canyon West** (702-736-7511 or 800-543-3077) offers tours by bus, helicopter, or plane to the Grand Canyon. Their trips include an Indian picnic on the edge of the Canyon, Indian war canoe rides on the Colorado, or a one-day rafting trip. Free hotel pick-up, camera rentals, and multi-lingual guides make this a complete service.

Allstate Tours, 999 E. Tropicana (702-798-5606 or 800-634-6787), can get show tickets for you, arrange for a car rental, or take you on a tour to Laughlin, Hoover Dam, or Lake Mead.

RV Parks & Campgrounds

California Hotel RV Park Downtown, Stewart and Ogden Sts., 702-388-1222 (or -2602). 222 full hook-ups, pool, Jacuzzi, laundry, showers, groceries, convenience store.

Circus Circus Hotel Casino, 2880 Las Vegas Blvd. South, 702-734-0410 or 800-634-3450. 421 spaces, total resort complex.

Desert Sands RV Park, 1940 N. Boulder Hwy., 702-565-1945. 300 spaces, full-service, free cable TV, mini-mart. Near Lake Mead.

Preferred RV Resort, Hwy. 160 & 372 at Pahrump (60 miles west of Las Vegas), 702-727-6429. 156 full hook-ups, golf course, Jacuzzi, pool, bowling, tennis, showers, laundry.

Riviera Travel Trailer Park, 2200 Palm, 702-457-8700. Pool, Jacuzzi, laundry, tree-shaded spaces. Daily, weekly, and monthly rates.

Sam's Town RV Park, 4040 Nellis Blvd. and 5225 Boulder Hwy., 702-454-8056. 500 spaces total, with full hook-ups, Jacuzzi, pool, showers, laundry.

Stardust Hotel RV Park, 3000 Las Vegas Blvd. South, 702-732-6466 or 800-824-6033. 375 full hook-ups, pool, laundry, showers. Reservations suggested.

Weddings

The most popular wedding days are New Year's Eve and, of course, Valentine's Day. To obtain a marriage license, both parties must appear at the **County Clerk's Office** at 200 South Third. The license costs $27, blood tests are not required, and there is no waiting period. Office hours are 8:00am-midnight Mon-Thurs, 8:00am Friday to midnight Saturday, and 24 hours on holidays. Ceremonies may be performed by the Commissioner of Civil Marriages at 309 South Third or at any of the chapels in the city. Chapels usually offer flowers, music, pictures, and even witnesses. A few of the best:

Candlelight Wedding Chapel, 2855 Las Vegas Blvd. South, 702-735-4179 or 800-882-3379. Free limo service from your hotel, all the amenities.

Cupid Wedding Chapel, 1515 Las Vegas Blvd. South, 702-388-0242 or 800-543-2933. If you call ahead, they will make hotel reservations and all arrangements to make your wedding special.

Las Vegas Wedding Gardens, 200 W. Sahara, 702-387-0123 or 800-843-2362. Weddings performed next to a waterfall surrounded by indoor gardens. They also provide a marriage planning service to take care of everything.

The Little Church of the West, 3960 Las Vegas Blvd. South, 702-739-7971. Famous for the celebrities who've married there, the Little Church looks exactly like a postcard chapel and has an altar with flowers and a steeple whose bells chime after the ceremony. Complimentary champagne.

Mission of the Bells Wedding Chapel, 1213 Las Vegas Blvd. South, 702-386-1889. A southwest-style mission accommodating up to 200 guests. Religious, civil, or nondenominational services performed. Complimentary champagne, cake, and limo service.

Climate and Dress

The sun shines over 300 days a year in Las Vegas, and the air is desert dry. Daytime temperatures often reach over 100° during the summer, but the dry air makes the heat tolerable. Spring and fall temperatures run in the 70's in the daytime, and the winter months have temperatures in the 50's and 60's. The average rainfall is very low, so forget the umbrella.

Casual clothes are the norm, except for dinner shows, when women will want a cocktail dress and men wear jackets and often a tie. Shorts and sundresses are essential during the summer. You'll want a light sweater in the evening from November through March, and you may want some sort of wrap for the dinner shows year-round, since the rooms are often chilly with air-conditioning.

Driving Mileage from Las Vegas

Albuquerque, NM—588   Portland, OR—1,026
Denver, CO—944   Reno, NV—447
Grand Canyon (S. Rim)—253   Salt Lake City, UT—450
Los Angeles, CA—272   San Francisco, CA—587
Phoenix, AZ—293

Air Services

Flying into Las Vegas is easy. **McCarran International Airport**, just a mile from The Strip and five miles from downtown, handles over 500 flights a day. People-movers help with the long walk from your plane, and the airport is full of good shops—and slot machines! Airlines currently serving Las Vegas:

Air Nevada (702-736-8900)
America West (702-736-1737 or 800-247-5692)
American Airlines (702-385-3781 or 800-433-7300)
Continental Airlines (702-383-8291 or 800-525-0280)
Delta Airlines (702-731-3111 or 800-221-1212)
Golden Pacific (602-754-2545 or 800-352-3281)
Hawaiian Airlines (702-796-9696 or 800-227-7110)
Northwest Airlines (702-732-0722 or 800-225-2525)
Scenic Airlines (702-739-1900)
Southwest Airlines (702-739-5929 or 800-531-5601)
StatesWest Airlines (800-247-3866)
Trans World Airlines (702-385-1000 or 800-221-2000)
United Airlines (702-385-3222 or 800-241-6522)
USAir (702-382-1905 or 800-772-4368)

Casinos, Resorts, Hotels, & Games

We've listed the casinos in Las Vegas by location, either on The Strip or downtown. The distance between casinos on The Strip can be considerable, so if you don't have a car and want to avoid taxis, consider staying downtown, where you can easily walk from place to place.

Downtown

The California Hotel and Casino, 12 Ogden St., Las Vegas, NV 89101 (702-385-1222 or 800-634-6255 toll free). Rates: $40 Sun-Thurs, $50 weekends.

This 650-room hotel provides some of the friendliest service in town—a great spot for beginning gamblers. There's a banquet room seating 300, a children's game room, gift shop, Hawaiian specialty shop, Ethel M candy store, pool, Jacuzzi, and a 222-space RV park with full hook-ups and its own swimming pool.

Restaurants & Lounges
Market Street Cafe: 24-hour coffee shop, with Oriental specialties, continental food, and graveyard specials.
Pasta Pirate: A pasta and seafood restaurant with pasta made fresh on the premises. Mesquite broiled seafood: prawns, lobster, and the catch of the day. Open 5:30pm-11:30pm nightly. Reservations suggested.
Redwood Bar and Grill: Fine dining, steaks, chicken, and seafood. Cozy atmosphere with a stone fireplace. Open 5:30pm-11:30pm daily. Reservations suggested.

The Cal Club Snack Bar: A quick service snack bar with a side-walk cafe feeling. Pizza, sushi, shrimp tempura, desserts, and drinks. Open 9:00am-11:00pm Sun-Wed, 24 hours Thurs-Sat.

The Lounge has live entertainment and dancing nightly from 9:00pm-3:00am. The **Main Street Bar** is open 24 hours in the west end of the casino. Progressive poker machines in the bar. The **San Francisco Pub**, located in the east end of the casino, is open 24 hours and has progressive poker machines.

Games

Blackjack: 24 tables, $2-$1,000.

Craps: six tables, $2-$1,000, double odds.

Roulette: two tables, 25 cents-$1,000.

Keno: Separate lounge. 50-cent ticket, $50,000 maximum payout.

Slots: 1,000 machines, 5 cents-$5, MegaBucks, video keno, poker machines.

Sports Book: Open every morning at 9:00am until the last event of the day is over. All major sports, prop bets on the Super Bowl, future betting odds.

Mini-Baccarat and **Pai Gow Poker** are also available.

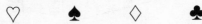

El Cortez Hotel and Casino, 600 Fremont St., Las Vegas, NV 89101 (702-385-5200 or 800-634-6703). Rates: $23-$32.

Small hotel, friendly casino, 316 rooms, 24-hour gift shops and convenience stores, fine dining in Roberta's Cafe (lobster, prime rib, and steaks), gourmet meals in the Emerald Room, and a 24-hour snack bar. Children's arcade open 24 hours. The Celebrity Lounge has TV, and there's a Carnival Bar as well. The El Cortez offers a Fun Book, available at motels around Las Vegas or by request through the mail.

The casino offers blackjack, craps, roulette, keno, a poker room, race and sports book, baccarat, hundreds of slots, video poker, and video keno.

Fitzgerald's, 301 East Fremont St., Las Vegas, NV 89101 (702-388-2400 or 800-274-5825). Rates: $28-$78.

An especially fun place with a casino that caters to beginners, Fitzgerald's has an Irish theme, including a Lucky Forest where

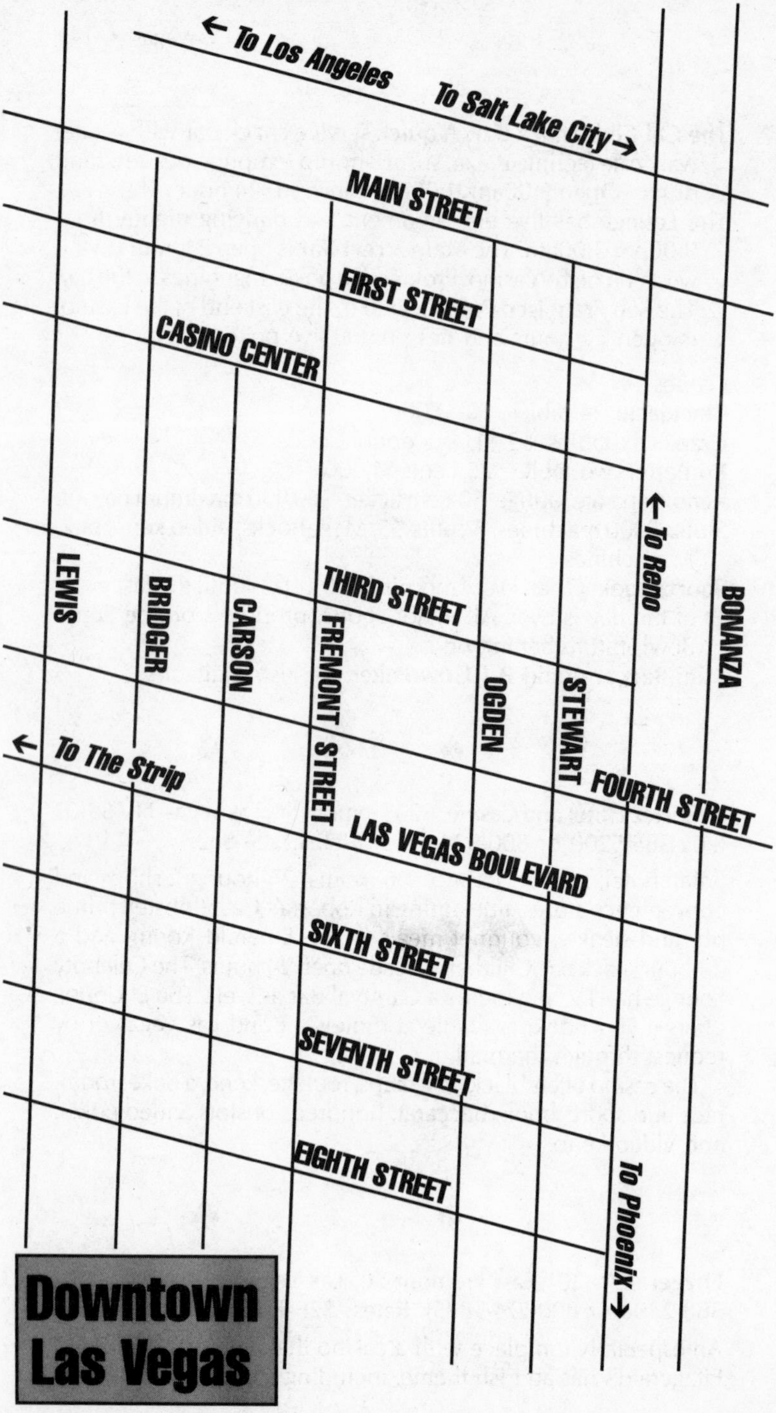

← To Los Angeles   To Salt Lake City →

MAIN STREET

FIRST STREET

CASINO CENTER

← To Reno

BONANZA

LEWIS

BRIDGER

CARSON

THIRD STREET

FREMONT STREET

OGDEN

STEWART

FOURTH STREET

← To The Strip

LAS VEGAS BOULEVARD

SIXTH STREET

SEVENTH STREET

EIGHTH STREET

To Phoenix →

Downtown Las Vegas

you can win gifts, toss a coin into the Lucky Wishing Well, touch a horseshoe from a Triple Crown Winner, and walk the Lucky Wishing Steps. Fitzgerald's, the tallest building in the state, has 652 rooms, a 10-story parking garage, health club, gift shop, and live entertainment.

Restaurants & Lounges

Chicago Joe's: Italian food. Open 11:00am-10:30pm Tues-Fri. Open at 5:00pm Mon and Sat. Closed Sunday.

Cassidy's Steak House: Fine dining with steaks, seafood, and Mexican dinners. Open 9:00am-11:00pm daily.

Molly's Coffee Shop: Open at 6:00am for breakfast and stays open through lunch and dinner until 2:00am.

Games

Blackjack: $2 minimum, single-deck games, four-deck shoes, double on any two cards, Insurance offered.

Craps: $1, double odds.

Roulette: 25 cents, 0 and 00 wheels.

Keno: Special ticket games, $50,000 maximum payout.

Slots: 850 machines, non-smoking slot area on 2nd floor, $1 slots in Blarney Castle certified the "loosest slots in Las Vegas" with 101% payback. MegaBucks, Quartermania, Nicklemania, and video poker quarter machines.

Also: new 90-seat **Bingo Parlor**, **Red Dog**, and **Nine's Up**.

Classes in all games daily from 10:00am.
Fun coupons available at the 2nd floor redemption center.

Four Queens Hotel and Casino, 202 East Fremont St., Las Vegas, NV 89101 (702-385-4011 or 800-634-6045). Rates: $47 mid-week, $57 Friday and Saturday.

In addition to the Ripley's Believe It or Not Museum, the Four Queens offers a casino with $1-minimum blackjack and a friendly, relaxed atmosphere. The hotel has 720 rooms, a gift shop, a 24-hour children's arcade, and the French Quarter Lounge, which features well-known jazz musicians. The Ripley's museum boasts treasures discovered by Robert Ripley in his world travels. It's open Sun-Thurs 9:00am-midnight, and 9:00am-1:00am Friday and Saturday ($1.50 for adults, $1 for children).

Restaurants & Lounges
Hugo's: Gourmet cuisine, open 6:00pm-11:00pm.
Magnolia's: Open 24 hours for you to indulge in the Ice Cream Shoppe.

Games
Blackjack: 27 tables, $1-$1,000, single-deck and six-deck shoe games, dealer hits soft 17, Insurance offered.
Craps: six tables, $2-$1,000, double odds available.
Roulette: two tables, 50 cents-$1,000.
Keno: $1 minimum ticket, 50 cents 3-ways, 25 cents 6-ways, unlimited progressive payout.
Slots: 955 machines, 5 cents-$25, maximum payoff $1,000,000, poker machines.
Baccarat: $5-$1,000, bank does not pass.
Poker: $10 buy-in, Hold 'Em, 7-Card Stud, Omaha.
Also: **Big Six Wheel.**

Fremont Hotel and Casino, 200 East Fremont St., Las Vegas, NV 89101 (702-385-3232 or 800-634-6182). Rates: Sun-Thurs $26-$75, Fri-Sat $42-$100. Non-smoking rooms available.

Smaller, inexpensive hotel, casual atmosphere in casino. The hotel has 452 rooms, a 24-hour gift shop, and live entertainment.

Restaurants & Lounges
The Hulapai: Fine dining, open 5:30pm-midnight daily.
Overland Stage Cafe: Open 24 hours, featuring gourmet Chinese cuisine.
The Paradise Buffet: Open 7:00am-11:00pm, with all-you-can-eat buffets—breakfast $3.79, lunch $4.50, and dinner $5.95. Sunday brunch, too.
Tony Roma's: National chain featuring ribs. Open 5:00pm-11:00pm Sun-Thurs, 5:00pm-midnight Fri-Sat.
Roxy's: Top lounge acts 8:00pm-2:00am Mon-Tues, 2:00pm-2:00am Wed-Sun.

Games
Blackjack: 26 tables, $2-$1,000, single-, double-, and six-deck shoe games, dealer hits soft 17, Insurance offered, double on any first two cards.
Craps: four tables, $2-$1,000, double odds available.

Roulette: three tables, 25 cents-$100 straight up, $1-$100,000 on outside.

Keno: 50-cent ticket, way tickets, 20 game multi-ticket, $100,000 maximum payout.

Slots: 1,000 machines, 5 cents-$5, MegaBucks, Quartermania, progressive poker, 21 machines.

Mini-Baccarat: $2-$500, bank passes.

Pai Gow: $5-$500, cards, bank passes.

Race & Sports Book: 140 seats, 20 TVs.

Poker: Buy-in varies with each game. 7-Card Stud, Hi-Lo Split, Texas Hold 'Em, 5-Card Draw, Lo-Ball.

Gold Spike Hotel & Casino, 400 East Ogden, Las Vegas, NV 89101 (702-384-8444 or 800-634-6703). Rates: $18 (includes breakfast).

Here's the place for truly inexpensive fun. The Gold Spike has 109 rooms, a famous 50-cent shrimp cocktail, penny slots with $10,000 payoffs, 40-cent keno, and free bingo.

Golden Gate Hotel & Casino, 1 East Fremont St., Las Vegas, NV 89101 (702-382-3510 or 800-426-0521). Rates: $25 weekdays, $32 weekends.

Small, budget hotel (106 rooms) with some non-smoking rooms. The Golden Gate's restaurant is the home of the original, giant 50-cent shrimp cocktail—the same price for over 20 years. The small, intimate casino offers blackjack, keno, craps, slots, and video poker.

Golden Nugget of Las Vegas, 129 East Fremont St., Las Vegas, NV 89101 (702-385-7111 or 800-634-3454). Rates: standard rooms $58-$110, Peach Suites $210-$300, Spa Tower Suites $500-$750.

An upscale resort hotel with a friendly, often crowded casino, the Golden Nugget is one of the most luxurious hotels in downtown Las Vegas. The lobby features Oriental rugs, Grecian marble, and crystal; the guest rooms are richly decorated; and the staff overwhelms you with personal service. Two gift boutiques offer clothing, jewelry, and souvenirs. Relax in the spa and salon or sunbathe by the tropical pool. The Golden Nugget, a AAA Four-Diamond Hotel, has also received four stars from the Mobile Travel Guide.

Restaurants & Lounges

Elaine's: Gourmet continental cuisine. Open 6:00pm-11:00pm Thurs-Mon.

Stefano's: Superb Italian food. Open 6:00pm-11:00pm daily.

Lillie Langtry's: Exquisite Cantonese cuisine. Open 5:00pm-11:00pm daily.

Carson Street Cafe: Open 24 hours.

The Buffet: Breakfast (7:00am-10:30am) for $4.75, lunch (10:30am-3:00pm) for $7.50, and dinner (4:00pm-11:00pm) for $8.75. There's also a Sunday Champagne buffet from 8:00am-10:00pm for $9.50.

The **Cabaret Showroom** features such stars as Don Rickles and Kenny Rogers. Cocktail shows only, hours vary. Call for current information.

Games

Blackjack: 46 tables, $1-$1,000 and $100-$5,000, single-deck and six-deck shoes, dealer hits soft 17 on single-deck games but **not** on shoe games, double on first two cards.

Craps: six tables, $1-$5,000, double odds available.

Roulette: three tables, $2-$5,000 outside.

Keno: 70-cent ticket, way tickets, $100,000 maximum payout.

Slots: 1,128 machines, 5 cents-$100, 183 progressive machines, $5,000,000 on $5 machine, 21 and video poker machines. High limit slot area.

Baccarat: Separate room, open 24 hours, $25-$15,000. Also Mini-Baccarat game, $5-$1,000.

Pai Gow & Pai Gow Poker: $5-$1,000, tiles and cards.

Race & Sports Book: 60 seats, 27 TVs.

Also: **Big Six Wheel** and **Red Dog** with $1,500 maximum payoff.

Binion's Horseshoe Hotel and Casino, 128 Fremont St., Las Vegas, NV 89101 (702-382-1600 or 800-622-6468). Rates: $24-$55.

A small, extra-friendly hotel and casino geared to all kinds of action from $1 to whatever, Binion's is a good place to play and a fun place to watch the high-rollers. The original Horseshoe consisted of 83 rooms. Now there's a 256-room highrise addition, but you can still stay in the old hotel with its quaint rooms. There's a rooftop pool open April-Nov, two gift shops, a boutique, and a liquor store. Be sure to see the display of 100 $10,000 bills. Six restaurants and two snack bars assure you of something to eat at any hour.

Restaurants & Lounges

The Skye Room: Atop the tower. Piano lounge, gourmet cuisine, huge wine selection, and an unbeatable view. Open 5:00pm-11:00pm.

Spaghetti Red's: Fantastic Italian food. Open 5:00pm-11:00pm.

The Steak House: Prime cuts. Open 5:00pm-11:00pm.

Mexican Bar: Adjoining The Steak House. Open 5:00pm-11:00pm.

Coffee Shop: Open 24 hours.

The Buffet: On the 2nd floor. Breakfast 7:00am-11:00am, lunch 11:30am-4:00pm, dinner 4:30pm-10:00pm. Night Owl buffet served 10:00pm-3:00am.

Games

Binion's has long been known by high-rollers as the house of "no-limit action" —the place where they can bet any amount of money, regardless of the house limit. The only restriction: your first bet establishes your personal limit. Stories circulate of gamblers placing a $300,000 bet on one roll of the dice—and winning. Myths? Maybe, maybe not. . .

Blackjack: 53 tables, $1-$25,000, single-deck games, four-deck shoe games, dealer hits soft 17, Insurance offered, double on any first two cards.

Craps: 14 tables, $1-$20,000, ten times odds.

Roulette: four tables, $1-$100,000.

Keno: 70-cent ticket, 50-cent way tickets, $200,000 maximum payout.

Slots: 865 machines, 5 cents-$100, progressive machines, poker and 21 machines, unlimited payoff.

Bingo: 500-seat room, $4-$12, $50,000 maximum payout.

Baccarat: Separate room open 24 hours, $5-$25,000, bank passes.

Race & Sports Book: 162 seats, 21 TVs.

Poker: Home of the World Series of Poker. $20-$200 buy-in, 7-Card Stud, Texas Hold 'Em, Omaha.

Red Dog: $1 minimum.

Lady Luck Casino Hotel, 206 North Third St., Las Vegas, NV 89101 (702-477-3000 or 800-523-9582). Rates: $39 Sun-Thurs, $52 weekends & holidays. Suites are $500.

The Lady Luck is elegant but quite affordable, with a casual casino offering $1 blackjack and craps. The hotel's twin towers, encircled in bands of gold, hold over 800 rooms and suites—all with refrigerators and Jacuzzis. Also: free airport shuttle, outdoor pool, gift shop, and a block-long casino, plus five restaurants and the Lucky Dome Showroom, with 1,000-square-foot dance floor, dance bands, and entertainers.

Restaurants & Lounges

Burgundy Room: Open 5:00pm-11:00pm daily. American and French gourmet, steaks, and seafood.

Marco Polo's: Italian specialties. Open 6:00pm-11:00pm daily.

Emperor's Room: Chinese cuisine. Open 5:00pm-11:00pm daily.

Brasserie Coffee Shop: Open 24 hours. Breakfast and dinner served any hour.

The Lady Luck Buffet: Open 6:00am-2:00pm daily. Prime Rib dinner and all-you-can-eat salad bar for $3.95 from 4:00pm-11:00pm.

Snack Bar: Open 8:00am-11:00pm daily.

Games

The Lady Luck has a free gaming school, a Casino Fun Book, and blackjack tournaments for hotel guests (prizes can run to $2,500). Special events happen year-round. Slots players can get a Mad Money VIP card for special room rates, entry in slots tournaments, a suite with a fully stocked refrigerator, complimentary meals, champagne, and the use of a stretch limo. Check with the management to see how to qualify.

Blackjack: 24 tables, $1-$1,000, single-deck and six-deck shoe games, dealer hits soft 17, Insurance offered, double on any two cards and after splitting.

Craps: four tables, $1-$1,000, double odds available.

Roulette: two tables, $1-$1,000.

Keno: 50-cent ticket, way tickets, $50,000 maximum payout.

Slots: 1,000 machines, 5 cents-$5, Quartermania, MegaBucks, progressives, poker and 21 machines, $260,000 maximum payoff.

Baccarat: $10-$4,000, bank passes, noon-4:00pm.

Pai Gow: $10-$1,000, played with cards, bank passes.

♡   ♠   ♢   ♣

Las Vegas Club Hotel & Casino, 18 East Fremont St., Las Vegas, NV 89101 (702-385-1664 or 800-634-6532). Rates: $32-$125, depending on the season.

Despite the small, crowded casino, baseball fans will enjoy staying here. The Las Vegas Club's Sports Hall features the most complete collection of baseball memorabilia outside Cooperstown, with a World Series Bat Collection, autographed baseballs, and photos. The Great Moments dining room features gourmet dining and is open 5:00pm-11:00pm daily. There's also the 24-hour Dugout Coffee Shop. Child care is available through the bell desk.

Games
Blackjack: "The most liberal 21 rules in the world." 14 tables, $1-$500, six-deck shoe games only, dealer hits soft 17, Insurance offered.
Roulette: one table, $1-$500 outside, $25 straight up.
Keno: 70-cent ticket, $1 way tickets, $50,000 maximum payout.
Slots: 642 machines, 5 cents-$1, progressive machines, $175,000 maximum payoff, poker and 21 machines.
Sports Book: 30 seats, six 25-inch screens.

Leroy's Horse and Sports Place, 114 South First Avenue, Las Vegas, NV 89101 (702-382-1561).

Strictly a race and sports book, with 80 seats and 10 viewing screens.

Pioneer Club, First & Fremont, Las Vegas, NV 89101 (702-382-4576).

A casino only, the Pioneer offers a good buffet from 11:00am-11:00pm daily. You can get their Fun Book by showing an out-of-state I.D. The casino is casual and good for beginners.

Games
Blackjack: 14 tables, $1-$500, single-deck and four-deck shoe games, dealer hits soft 17, Insurance offered, double on any two cards.
Craps: one table, $1-500, double odds available.
Roulette: one table, 10 cents-$500.

Slots: 510 machines, 5 cents-$1, progressive machines, Mega-Bucks, poker and 21 machines.

Union Plaza Hotel & Casino, 1 Main St., Las Vegas, NV 89101 (702-386-2110 or 800-634-6575). Rates: $40 mid-week, $50 weekends. Holidays slightly higher.

This is a large (over 1,000 rooms), moderately priced hotel with low-minimum tables and very crowded games in the casino. Fitness enthusiasts will enjoy the Sports Deck, with a heated pool, exercise equipment, a 1/4-mile jogging track, and four lighted tennis courts. It's also the most convenient hotel for Amtrak riders—the depot is in the hotel. Lovebirds will find a wedding chapel in the complex, too. And within the five acres of buildings, you'll find most everything else: a shopping arcade, barber and beauty shops, a video arcade, a liquor store, an ice cream parlor, etc.

Restaurants & Lounges
Center Stage: Fine dining from 5:00pm-11:00pm.
The Coffee Shop: Open 24 hours.
Kung Fu: Oriental cuisine from 11:00am-11:00pm.
Snack Bar: Open 24 hours.
Plaza Theater Showroom: Dinner and cocktail shows featuring top-name entertainment. Meals from $16, cocktail shows from $9. Closed Monday.
Center Stage Lounge: Live entertainment 3:00pm-3:00am daily.

Games
Blackjack: 26 tables, $1-$2,000, six-deck shoe games only, dealer hits soft 17, Insurance offered, double any two cards.
Craps: five tables, 25 cents-$1,000, ten times odds.
Roulette: four tables, 25 cents-$2,000.
Keno: 70-cent ticket, 35-cent 3-way ticket, $50,000 maximum payout.
Slots: 1,464 machines. One cent-$1, progressive machines, 21 machines.
Baccarat: $5-$1,000, bank passes, mini-game.
Pai Gow: $10-$1,000, cards, bank passes.
Race & Sports Book: 170 seats, 34 TVs.
Poker: Pan, 7-Card Stud, Omaha Hi-Lo, Texas Hold 'Em, Pineapple Hi-Lo.

Western Hotel & Casino, 899 East Fremont St., Las Vegas, NV 89101 (702-384-4620 or 800-634-6703). Rates: $16-$20.

The Western is a very small, budget hotel—just 115 rooms—with a casino that has a can't-be-bothered attitude. Guests can get free breakfast and a Fun Book. There's also a snack bar, 50-cent well drinks at the bar, progressive penny slots, a 400-seat bingo room with free cash bingo, 40-cent keno, 10-cent roulette, blackjack, and daily lunch and dinner specials.

Casinos On or Near "The Strip"

Aladdin Hotel & Casino, 3667 Las Vegas Blvd. South, Las Vegas, NV 89109 (702-736-0111 or 800-634-3424). Rates: $25-$2,500.

This luxury resort with a large casino catering to the serious player is located in the heart of The Strip. The Aladdin has three fantastic pools, three lighted tennis courts, many shops, and a beauty and barber salon. Its 7,000-seat Theatre of the Performing Arts showcases top stars, and the Bagdad Showroom features extravagant production shows.

Restaurants & Lounges
Oasis Coffee Shop: Features prime rib dinners, open 24 hours.
40 Banditos Mexican Cantina: Open 6:00pm-11:00pm.
Fisherman's Port: Fresh seafood flown in daily. Open 5:00pm-11:00pm.
The Florentine Buffet: Open 6:00pm-11:00pm daily.
Wellington Steak House: The finest beef, served 5:00pm-11:00pm daily.
International Buffet: Japanese, Chinese, and American food. Open 7:30am-9:00pm daily.
Snack Bar: Open 24 hours.
The Sinbad Lounge: Nightly entertainment.

Games
Blackjack: 33 tables, $2-$2,000, single-deck and six-deck shoe games, dealer hits soft 17 only on single-deck games, Insurance offered. Double on any two cards on shoe games, on 9, 10, & 11 only with single-deck games.
Craps: four tables, $2-$2,000, double odds available.
Roulette: four tables, $2-$50 any way.
Keno: $1 tickets, 50-cent way tickets, $50,000 maximum payout.
Slots: 900 machines, 5 cents-$25, Quartermania, MegaBucks, 21 and poker machines.

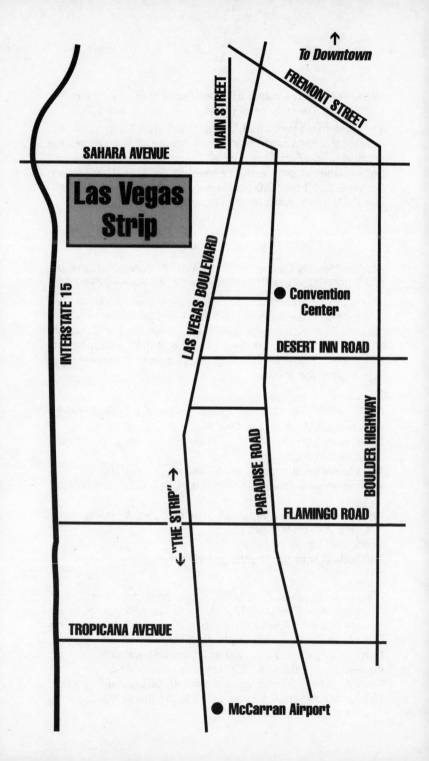

Baccarat: Separate room, $5-$2,000, open noon-4:00am.
Pai Gow Poker: $5-$2,000.
Race & Sports Book: 215 seats, 19 TVs.
Poker: Buy in $20-$40, Stud, Hi-Lo Split, Hold 'Em.
Also: **Red Dog, Head and Tails**.

Anthony's Club and Casino—Quality Inn, 377 East Flamingo, Las Vegas, NV 89109 (702-733-7777 or 800-634-6617). Rates: $55 weekdays, $75 weekends.

Anthony's, a Quality Inn franchise, has nice rooms and a small casino that is not especially good for beginners. The hotel offers 320 mini-suites with wet bars and refrigerators, a pool, a whirl-pool spa, laundry facilities, and free shuttle service to The Strip. Its Speakeasy Cafe serves inexpensive meals and is open 24 hours.

Games
Blackjack: six tables, $2-$50, single deck, four- and six-deck shoe games, dealer hits soft 17, Insurance offered, double on any-thing.
Craps: one table, 50 cents-$50, double odds available.
Roulette: one table, $2-$50.
Slots: 287 machines, 5 cents-$1, progressive machines, Mega-Bucks, poker and 21 machines.

Arizona Charlie's, 740 South Decatur Blvd. (west of The Strip), Las Vegas, NV 89107 (702-258-5200 or 800-342-2695). Rates: $35 weekdays, $40 weekends.

With 50 bowling lanes and a country music lounge, this Western-style hotel is fun, but its casino is aloof. There's indoor and out-door dining facilities, entertainment nightly, a pool, a video ar-cade, and the Wild West's 32-foot, all-you-can-eat buffet with recipes from around the world ($2.49/breakfast, $2.99/lunch, $3.99/dinner; Sunday crêpes-and-champagne brunch). The casino is smoke-free, with Megabucks, Quartermania, a Slot Club, video poker and keno machines, a race and sports book, craps, black-jack, and a 400-seat bingo parlor with cash prizes up to $20,000.

Bally's Casino Resort, 3645 Las Vegas Blvd. South, Las Vegas, NV 89109 (702-739-4111 or 800-634-3434). Rates: $79-$105, suites $115, penthouse suites $1,000.

A world-class resort with a huge casino geared to high-limit play, Bally's is virtually a city in itself—and one of the world's largest luxury resorts, with 2,900 guest rooms and suites. The recreation area has an outdoor pool and cabanas, ten tennis courts (seven lighted), and health club facilities for men and women with steam rooms, saunas, gyms, whirlpools, tanning lamps, massages, and soap rubs. Bally's Mall is the largest hotel shopping mall in Las Vegas, with 40 shops offering fine art, salons, secretarial services, souvenirs, and clothing. Travel agents, laundry and dry cleaning, bus tours, and many other services are available through the hotel. And there's a children's video arcade, too.

Restaurants & Lounges
Gigi's: Classic French cuisine in a setting reminiscent of Versailles.
Caruso's: Northern Italian specialties.
Barrymore's: Steaks, chops, and fish in an atmosphere of a New York private club.
Tracy's: Gourmet Chinese cuisine and traditional American food, with a panoramic view.
Orleans Room: Open 24 hours. Simple snacks to full-course meals.
The Deli: Overstuffed sandwiches and traditional deli food.
Celebrity Room: Top-name stars entertain at dinner and cocktail shows.
Ziegfeld Theatre: Spectacular production shows twice each evening (closed Wednesday).
Celebrity Bar: Live music from 2:00pm-late.
Catch a Rising Star: Comedy club.

Games
Bally's casino is enormous, with 84 blackjack tables, 11 craps tables, nine roulette wheels, and two baccarat games, almost 1,000 slot and poker machines, a poker room, and a race and sports book.

Barbary Coast Hotel & Casino, 3595 Las Vegas Blvd. South, Las Vegas, NV 89109 (702-737-7111 or 800-634-6755). Rates: $50 weekdays, $75 weekends.

In the center of the Strip, the Barbary Coast is a small, attractive hotel with a tiny, can't-be-bothered casino. The hotel employs a Victorian theme throughout, including the world's largest Tiffany-style stained glass mural. The 198 rooms are decorated to evoke old San Francisco. Fine dining is a specialty at Michael's, a gourmet restaurant, or enjoy Chinese cuisine in the 24-hour Victorian Room. There's live lounge entertainment nightly and 24-hour room service. The casino features a race and sports book open 24 hours, craps, blackjack, roulette, poker, "Million Dollar Jackpot Slots," and keno.

Bourbon Street Hotel & Casino, 120 East Flamingo, Las Vegas, NV 89109 (702-737-7200 or 800-634-6956). Rates: $45 weekdays, $65 weekends. Suites $65 and up.

Just off The Strip on Flamingo Road, the Bourbon Street is a small hotel (150 rooms) patterned after a New Orleans hotel with "hot jazz and Southern hospitality." There's a friendly atmosphere in its small casino, and the hotel features live Dixieland music, great food (buffets $2.25-$4.25), a champagne brunch, and an airport courtesy shuttle. The lounge offers entertainment from late afternoon to early morning, with no cover charge and no minimum. The casino has Quartermania and video slots, blackjack, craps, roulette, keno, and poker.

Caesars Palace, 3570 Las Vegas Blvd. South, Las Vegas, NV 89109 (702-731-7110 or 800-634-6661). Rates: $95-$160. (Call for specials and changing rates.)

"Why settle for a hotel when you can have an empire?" Caesars Palace asks with a sly grin. And it *is* an empire: world-class sporting events, spectacular fountains, majestic cypress trees, gleaming marble statuary, beautiful landscaping—and you may even see Caesar and Cleopatra (protected by their centurions, of course) inspecting their domain. However, gambling novices are advised to look but don't touch, as Caesars' casino is geared for high-limit, serious players.

Caesars' Olympic-size pool, inspired by the Pompeii Baths of Rome, is set in the Garden of the Gods, a luxurious area of trees, tanning pools, and gardens. A spa overlooks the pool and forms a continuous waterfall into the pool below. A second pool, on the upper level of the Garden, has three "islands" for sunbathing, just beneath the water's surface. Adjacent to the pool is Neptune's Bar and the Primavera Restaurant, with outdoor seating for brunch and dinner.

The hotel has 1,500 rooms, nine restaurants, three casinos, the Appian Way shopping center, tennis courts, and a showroom. The rooms—rated among the best in the world—have marble baths and whirlpools, while suites have in-room saunas, steam rooms, Jacuzzis, and mirrored ceilings (!).

In addition to its renowned theater with top performers, Caesars offers an Omnimax Theatre for thrilling movies. The Forum Shops (a mall, Caesars-style) resemble an ancient Roman landscape, with tall columns and arches, central piazzas, fountains, and statuary. Lighting effects create morning sunrises, blue skies, sunsets, and twinkling stars, all synchronized with the actual time of day. Computers also control the fountains and make the statues appear lifelike.

Restaurants & Lounges

The Palace Court Restaurant: Award-winning gourmet restaurant serving classic French and American contemporary cuisine. Superb selection of wines. Gallery of art treasures.

Empress Court: Exotic Chinese gourmet food. Giant aquarium in the kitchen holds daily shipments of fresh fish. Lobster, crab, prawns with walnuts, and Buddhist vegetarian foods are featured. Multi-lingual staff. Dinner only.

Ah'So: Japanese food, sushi and sashimi. Fixed-price menu has six courses. Everything is prepared at your table. Asian waitresses in authentic kimonos pour "a most humble offering" of sake for you.

The Spanish Steps Steak and Seafood House: Featuring a la carte selections of seafood, traditional Spanish and Mediterranean dishes, and steaks. Fine sangria and margaritas. Gazpacho Andaluz, red snapper, and Paella Valenciana are specialties. Strolling musicians make for a romantic atmosphere. Dinner only, reservations suggested.

Primavera: Set in the gardens near the pool, the Primavera is open for breakfast, lunch, and dinner. Italian kitchen with selections from both northern and southern Italy. Each table has a view of the pool and surrounding gardens.

Cafe Roma: 24-hour restaurant for informal dining, quick snacks, breakfast, lunch, and dinner. Moderately priced. Breakfast served 24 hours.

Palatium Buffet: Open daily. Features a separate breakfast, lunch, and dinner menu Mon-Fri. Special brunch on weekends. $5.95-$10.50.

La Piazza Food Court and Lounge: Multi-cuisine restaurant and late-night lounge. Morning specialties, internationally themed food stations, make-your-own pizzas. Deli, grill, and daily "Blue Plate Special." Salad bar, yogurts, and beverage buffet. Moderately priced. Live entertainment at night, 24-hour cocktail service.

Games

Caesars has three casinos: The **Palace Court** is small, with blackjack, roulette, baccarat, and Pai Gow. The **Roman Forum Casino** is huge, with nine craps tables, 37 blackjack tables, six roulette wheels, four baccarat tables, 589 slots, a Wheel of Fortune, two Pai Gow tables, and two Pai Gow Poker tables. The **Olympic Casino** is even larger, containing the Olympiad Race & Sports Book, which seats 547 people and has 38 video screens (one measures 32-feet by 26-feet). Caesars can show any broadcast sporting event. The Olympic Casino also has three craps tables, 30 blackjack tables, two roulette wheels, 1,374 slot machines, a Wheel of Fortune, two Pai Gow tables, keno, one Super Pan 9, and a mini-baccarat table.

Caesars tables have no low-minimum bets; you can't play there for $2.

Circus Circus, 2880 Las Vegas Blvd. South, Las Vegas, NV 89109 (702-734-0410 or 800-634-3450). Rates: $19-$33 weekdays, $24-$44 weekends.

A great place for a family vacation, Circus Circus emphasizes fun, family activities, with a friendly casino good for beginning players. There are 2,793 rooms, two swimming pools, an RV park with 421 spaces, a wedding chapel, and various shops (including a toy store). But the main gimmick is, of course, circus acts, which run free of charge 11:00am-midnight every day. Trapeze artists perform directly above slot players, and clowns, jugglers, etc. roam throughout the complex. The kids (and more than a few adults) will enjoy the inexpensive "carnival midway" with all the standard carnival games—the softball throw, skeeball, etc.—and prizes of stuffed animals. Circus Circus' promotion of clean, silly fun is a refreshing change from the relentless pursuit of money elsewhere in town.

The Pink Pony Coffee Shop and the Skyrise Dining Room are both open 24 hours. The Circus Buffet serves breakfast 6:00am-11:30am ($2.29), brunch noon-4:00pm ($2.69) and dinner 4:40pm-11:00pm ($3.89). The Pizzeria is open 11:00am-midnight, and the Steak House is open 5:00pm-midnight.

Games

Blackjack: 88 tables, $1-$1,000, single-deck, four- and six-deck shoe games, dealer does **not** hit soft 17, Insurance offered, double on any two cards.

Craps: six tables, $1-$500, double odds available.

Roulette: six tables, 25 cents-$1,000.

Keno: $1 minimum ticket, 3-ways or more 50 cents, 10-ways or more 25 cents, 100-ways or more 10 cents a way, $100,000 maximum payout.

Slots: 2,664 machines, 5 cents-$5, progressive machines, $100,000 maximum payoff, 21 and poker machines.

Race & Sports Book: 274 seats, 30 screens from 13"-52".

Poker: Buy-in $20, Texas Hold 'Em, 7-Card Stud.

Continental Hotel Casino and Resort, 4100 Paradise Rd. (Flamingo & Paradise), Las Vegas, NV 89109 (702-737-5555 or 800-634-6641). Rates: $35-$55.

A moderately priced, pleasant hotel with a crowded, friendly casino, the Continental offers 400 rooms, handicapped facilities, an Olympic-size pool, 24-hour room service, a gift shop, and baby sitters. Its Renaissance Room has 24-hour dining, and the Continental Buffet serves a daily lunch and dinner buffet. The lounge has an afternoon comedy show and live music at night.

Games

Blackjack: 11 tables, $2-$200, single-deck and six-deck shoe games, dealer hits soft 17, double on any two original cards.

Craps: two tables, 25 cents-$100, double odds available.

Roulette: one table, 25 cents minimum, $1 minimum on the outside, $800 maximum payoff.

Keno: 70-cent ticket, way tickets 35 cents a way, $50,000 maximum payout.

Slots: 650 machines, 5 cents-$1, progressive machines, $9,999.99

maximum payoff, 100 poker machines.

Bingo: 400 seats, two cards per board, $1-$4, $8,000 maximum payout.

Poker: Buy-in $20, 7-Card Stud, Hold 'Em.

Race & Sports Book: Six seats and two TVs.

Desert Inn Hotel & Casino, 3145 Las Vegas Blvd. South, Las Vegas, NV 89109 (702-733-4444 or 800-634-6906). Rates: $90-$135, suites $150-$1,500.

The Desert Inn, commonly called "The D.I.," is a luxury resort that will appeal especially to the fitness-minded. The casino caters to the big money, and there are no low-limit games, so it's not a place for beginning play.

The D.I.'s recently renovated rooms reflect a desert-Southwest motif. Some rooms have whirlpools, wet bars, refrigerators, and private patios. Guests can enjoy the 18-hole golf course, lighted tennis courts, complete health and fitness spa (open 7:00am-7:00pm), aerobics classes, 10 outdoor whirlpools, swimming pool, Turkish steambath or Finnish sauna, exercise equipment, and a jogging track. The hotel provides robes, warm-up suits, leotards, shorts, sandals, towels, and toiletries.

Restaurant & Lounges

Ho Wan: Chinese specialties—Mandarin, Cantonese, and Szechuan. Open 6:00pm-11:00pm.

La Vie En Rose: Exquisite French cuisine. Open 6:00pm-11:00pm.

Portofino: Northern Italian cooking. Open 6:00pm-11:00pm.

La Promenade: Open 24 hours, serving favorites of American Continental food. More than just a coffee shop.

The Grill Room: Deli beside the golf course. Open 7:00am-5:00pm for breakfast and lunch. Bar service.

The Winner's Choice Lounge: Live entertainment nightly.

The Crystal Room: Headliner showroom with dinner and cocktail shows. An intimate nightclub with top entertainment.

Games

Blackjack: 26 tables, $3-$5,000, six-deck shoe games only, dealer does **not** hit soft 17, Insurance offered, double on anything and after splits. Re-split aces.

Craps: eight tables, $5-$5,000, double odds available.

Roulette: two tables, $3-$5,000, outside maximum, $100 any way.

on inside numbers.

Keno: $1 ticket, way tickets, $50,000 maximum payout.

Slots: 450 machines. 5 cents-$25, progressive machines, Mega-Bucks. Poker and 21 machines.

Baccarat: Separate room open 24 hours, $25-$15,000, bank does not pass.

Pai Gow: $10-$5,000, tiles, bank passes.

Race & Sports Book: 40 seats, 12 TVs.

Poker: 7-Card Stud and Hold 'Em.

Also: **Pai Gow Poker**.

The Dunes Hotel Casino and Country Club, 3650 Las Vegas Blvd. South, Las Vegas, NV 89109 (702-737-4110 or 800-777-7777). Rates: $39-$109.

Like the D.I., the Dunes is a world-famous luxury resort catering to high-rollers, so it's also not a great place for beginning play. A complex of 24-hour excitement with 1,118 rooms and two swimming pools, the Dunes also owns the Emerald Green 18-hole golf course, a health club, a video arcade for children, a beauty salon, and a shopping mall. The four restaurants include an International Buffet in the Terrace Room, serving champagne brunch ($7.50) 9:00am-2:00pm and dinner 5:00pm-10:00pm ($6.95). Continental gourmet food is served 6:00pm-11:00pm; a seafood restaurant is open 6:00pm-11:00pm; and there's a 24-hour coffee shop. The snack bar is open 11:00am-11:00pm. Two casino lounges are open 8:00pm-2:00am, and the main showroom has a revue Tues-Sun at 8:00pm and 11:00pm.

The two casinos have slots, blackjack, craps, and roulette.

El Rancho Tower and Casino, 2755 Las Vegas Blvd. South, Las Vegas, NV 89109 (702-796-2222 or 800-634-3410). Rates: $29-$38 weekdays, $40-$48 weekends.

The El Rancho, a budget-priced hotel with a blue-collar casino that's decent for beginners, has over 1,000 rooms, an Olympic pool, a 52-lane bowling center, and five restaurants, including Joe's Oyster Bar, the Chuck Wagon (all-you-can-eat-buffet with weekend brunch for $2.99), and the Depot Steak House. For international food, try the Pizzeria or the El Taco. The Alamo Coffee Shop is open 24 hours. The casino lounge has live entertainment, and casino action includes a 450-seat bingo parlor, a race and sports book, blackjack, poker, keno, craps, roulette, and 1,000 slot machines.

Excalibur, 3850 Las Vegas Blvd. South, Las Vegas, NV 89193 (702-597-7700 or 800-939-7777). Rates: $45-$110.

This exciting "Castle on The Strip" is wonderful for the entire family. The casino has very good rules and is a great place for beginning play. The Excalibur, which opened in mid-1990, looks like every child's King Arthur dream come to life, with drawbridges, colorful turrets and spires, and 4,400 costumed employees. The restaurant and show prices are moderate, and nearly 90% of the 4,032 rooms cost just $45 a night. Though the medieval fantasy sometimes gets overdone (when someone is paged, the operator calls for "My Lord or Milady"), the Excalibur is a lot of fun, with jousting matches and strolling troubadors in the Medieval Village and a Renaissance Faire. In addition, there are two movie theaters, two swimming pools, and 23 shops, plus gypsy carts spread throughout.

Restaurants & Lounges
Above, below, and around the casino are the theme restaurants, shops, arcades, rides, and shows. Both **Lance-A-Lotta Pasta** and the **Oktoberfest** restaurants are open 11:00am-midnight. Lance-A-Lotta serves a complete dinner for $4.95; the minstrels are free. Other restaurants:

The Roundtable: Open 7:00am-10:00pm.

The Sherwood Forest Cafe: Open 24 hours.

Sir Galahad's: Fine dining, open 5:00pm-midnight.

Robin Hood's & Little John's: Open 24 hours.

Camelot: Gourmet dining, open 6:00pm-midnight.

Hansel & Gretel's: Open 10:00am-1:00pm.

King Arthur's Arena: Two dinner shows nightly (6:00pm and 9:00pm), with *King Arthur's Tournament*, an amazing show about the King Arthur legend, with knights and horses in jousting and sword-fighting action. The Arena seats 1,000.

Contemporary bands perform in the 150-seat lounge at 2:30pm, 8:30pm, and 3:00am.

Games

100,000 sq. ft. of casino space.

Blackjack: 78 tables, $2-$1,000, single-deck and six-deck shoe games, dealer does **not** hit soft 17, no Insurance is offered, double on any two cards.

Craps: six tables, $1-$1,000, double odds available.

Roulette: four tables, 25 cents-$1,000.

Keno: $1 tickets, 3-ways for ½ price, $100,000 maximum payout.

Slots: 2,646 machines, 5 cents-$25, 97.4% payback on $1 carousels, win a boat on 25-cent machines. Poker machines.

Race & Sports Book: 250 seats, 16 screens.

Poker: $20 buy-in, Stud and Hold 'Em.

Also: two **Big Six Wheels**.

Flamingo Hilton, 3555 Las Vegas Blvd. South, Las Vegas, NV 89109 (702-733-3100 or 800-732-2111). Rates: $65-$115 rooms, $200-$480 suites.

One of the first world-class resorts on The Strip, the Flamingo Hilton has a colorful history and a friendly, crowded casino with good blackjack rules—good for beginning play. Opened in 1947, the hotel was the plaything of "Bugsy" Siegel, the millionaire mobster who controlled the Los Angeles underworld. Decorated like a set from a big-budget Hollywood movie, the Flamingo set the standard for lavish elegance on The Strip, complete with Oriental date palms and tuxedo-clad employees.

Today the Flamingo is one of the largest resort hotels in the world, with 3,530 rooms and luxury suites. The hotel's facilities include a tennis club with four lighted courts, a practice alley and pro shop, an Olympic-size pool with Jacuzzi, a sports deck, sundeck, and video arcade. The health spa offers a sauna, steam room, hot therapy pools, exercise equipment, tanning beds, and massages. Translators can assist with 29 languages, the tour desk can arrange trips to popular nearby attractions, and a variety of shops are open daily in the shopping arcade.

Restaurants & Lounges

Alta Villa: The feel of an old Italian village with stone walkways, fountains, and vine-covered trellises. Italian specialties, seven-course dinners for families. Open daily, moderate.

Flamingo Room: Continental and American cuisine. Overlooking the pool. Seafood salad bar available for lunch and dinner.

Beef Barron: Western style dining room, open nightly for dinner. Known for gourmet beef selections.

The Peking Market: Each area is an authentic recreation of a small Chinese market. Features a nine-course family dinner. Open each evening for dinner.

Food Fantasy: Open for breakfast, lunch, and dinner. Cafeteria-style or made-to-order items.

Crown Room Buffet: Open for breakfast and dinner. Great variety of food at reasonable prices. Outdoor terrace.

Lindy's Deli: Coffee shop open 24 hours. Specializes in deli platters and sandwiches.

Terrace Cafe: Snack and beverage bar.

Sushi Bar Hamada: Features fresh fish, sake, and Japanese beer, take-out orders. Open daily for dinner.

Flamingo Showroom: Dinner show at 7:45pm ($24.95). Cocktail show at 11:00pm ($17.95). Closed Sunday. Ice skating production show, plus other acts. Reservations: 702-733-3333.

Games

Blackjack: 39 tables, $2-$2,000, double deck and six-deck shoe-games, dealer does **not** hit soft 17, Insurance offered, double on first two cards, split aces only once.

Craps: eight tables, $2-$2,000, double odds available.

Roulette: six tables, $2 minimum bet.

Keno: $1 ticket, $280,000 progressive to $1,000,000 payout.

Slots: 1,601 machines, 5 cents-$5, progressives from $250,000 to over $1,000,000. Pot-O-Gold dollar machines pay huge jackpots. Poker and 21 machines.

Mini-Baccarat: $5-$2,000, bank passes.

Pai Gow: $5-$1,000, bank does not pass.

Race & Sports Book: 25 seats, two 25" TVs.

Poker: 7-Card Stud and Hold 'Em.

Also: **Sic Bo**.

Frontier Hotel & Gambling Hall, 3120 Las Vegas Blvd. South, Las Vegas, NV 89109 (702-734-7110, 702-794-8200, or 800-634-6966). Rates: $35 Sun-Thurs, $55 Fri-Sat. Suites $65-$85.

Though the Frontier's 930 rooms have been recently remodeled, they still need to renovate their attitude. The casino is not very friendly and is uninterested in beginning players.

Restaurants & Lounges

Michelle's: 24-hour coffee shop.

St. Thomas: Features seafood. Breakfast 8:00am-11:00am, dinner 5:00pm-10:00pm.

Justin: Gourmet dining room open 5:00pm-11:00pm. Closed Monday & Tuesday.

Margarita's: Open 11:00pm-2:00am. Features Mexican food.

Games

Casino has blackjack, craps, baccarat room, poker room, race and sports book, and slots.

Gold Coast Hotel & Casino, 4000 W. Flamingo Road, Las Vegas, NV 89103 (702-367-7111 or 800-331-5334). Rates: $35-$45.

With Nevada's largest country-western dance hall, including live entertainment and free dance instruction, you might expect the Gold Coast to be a very friendly hotel with a relaxed casino and low-limit games. You'd be right.

Just five minutes west of The Strip, the Gold Coast has a Western motif throughout its 750 rooms. It also offers hourly shuttles to and from The Strip, a 72-lane bowling alley, free daycare for children, a travel agency, two lounges, an ice cream parlor, and two movie theaters.

Restaurants & Lounges

Monterey Room: 24-hour coffee shop. Chinese menu 11:00am-5:00am prepared by Chinese chefs. Lunches are $3.75, dinners $3.95-$11.95.

Gold Coast Buffet: Hot and cold specialties for breakfast, lunch, and dinner. Complimentary Bloody Mary for breakfast and frozen cocktail for lunch and dinner. Casual dining. Breakfast 7:00am-10:30am, $2.95. Lunch 11:00am-3:00pm, $3.95. Dinner 4:00pm-10:00pm, $5.95. Sunday brunch 8:00am-3:00pm, $4.95.

The Cortez Room: Complete dinners. Generous servings of prime rib. Casual dress. Open for lunch Mon-Fri 11:00am-3:00pm. Dinner 5:00pm-11:00pm ($5.95-$15.95). Reservations suggested.

The Mediterranean Room: Italian specialties, fresh seafood. Open 5:00pm-11:00pm. Entrees from $3.95.

Terrible Mike's: A build-your-own hamburger place open 10:00am-midnight.

Games

Blackjack: 32 tables, $1-$1,000, two-deck shoe games, dealer hits soft 17, Insurance offered, double any two cards and after splits.

Craps: six tables, 25 cents-$1,000, double odds available.

Roulette: three tables, 25 cents-$100.

Keno: 75-cent ticket, three ways for 50 cents, $250,000 maximum payout.

Slots: 2,018 machines, 5 cents-$5. Slot Club with bonus points redeemable for gifts. Keno and poker machines.

Bingo: 750-seat room, $3 minimum board, $7,500 coverall, $10,000 on Bonanza board. 10 sessions daily, 7:30am-midnight.

Mini-Baccarat: $2-$2,000. Bank does not pass.

Pai Gow: $5-$1,000. Bank does not pass.

Race & Sports Book: 190 seats, 43 TVs.

Poker: Separate room, 11 tables, 7-Card Stud, Texas Hold 'Em, Omaha.

Hacienda Resort Hotel & Casino, 3950 Las Vegas Blvd. South, Las Vegas, NV 89119 (702-739-8911 or 800-634-6713). Rates: $36-$46 weekdays, $56-$66 weekends. Suites $125.

Neither accommodating, friendly, nor close to the action on The Strip, the Hacienda is a place we would avoid. The casino is not for beginners, and the dealers have an attitude problem.

The hotel offers 840 rooms, an RV park, two pools, six lighted tennis courts, a shopping arcade, and an ice-and-dance spectacular in the showroom. The Garden Room has a buffet breakfast, lunch, and dinner from $3.99 to $4.99. There's also a deli, the Bolero Lounge, and Minsky's Theater. The casino has blackjack, craps, roulette, and slots.

Las Vegas Hilton, 3000 Paradise Rd. (east of The Strip), Las Vegas, NV 89109 (702-732-5111 or 800-732-7117). Rates: $89 weekdays, $102 weekends.

Though the Las Vegas Hilton is every bit as luxurious as the Flamingo Hilton, its casino caters to big money players and is not as friendly as the Flamingo's.

In addition to the spectacular Benihana Village, the Japanese restaurant where every meal is a show at your table, the hotel features over 3,000 luxury rooms, a state-of-the-art health spa, sauna, pool, tennis courts, and 14 restaurants, including Andiamo, serving Italian food, and the Hilton Steak House. The showroom features top-name stars, and there's live music in the lounge.

The huge casino (over 85,000 square feet) includes all the standard games, plus a Race & Sports Book with 46 video screens— one of the largest video displays in the world.

Harrah's Las Vegas, 3475 Las Vegas Blvd. South, Las Vegas, NV 89109 (702-369-5123 or 800-634-6765). Rates: $59-$89.

As you may expect, Harrah's Las Vegas, formerly a Holiday Inn, is a friendly hotel, and its casino has good limits for beginning players.

The world's largest Harrah's (1,725 rooms), it's often called "The Ship on The Strip." There's a health club, pool, shops, an arcade for children, and a babysitting service. The theater features "Keep Smilin' America," a cocktail show about a musical journey across the USA. This extravaganza costs only $12.50, including two drinks. The hotel also offers a Casino Funbook and free gaming instruction.

Restaurants & Lounges
Claudine's Steak House: Fine dining from 5:30pm-11:00pm.
Veranda: Italian specialties from 5:00pm-10:30pm.
Joe's Bayou: Southern cuisine and seafood, open 5:30pm-11:00pm.
Galley Restaurant: All-you-can-eat buffets, breakfast, lunch, and dinner from $2.99-$3.99. Open 7:00am-11:00pm.
Deli: Open 8:00am-11:00pm.

Games
Blackjack: 54 tables, $2-$1,000, two- and six-deck shoe games, dealer does **not** hit soft 17, Insurance offered, double on any first two cards.
Craps: six tables, $2-$1,000, double odds available.
Roulette: six tables, 25 cents-$1,000.
Keno: $1 ticket, 3-ways or more 50 cents a way, $100,000 maximum payout.
Slots: 1,788 machines, 5 cents-$25, progressive machines, Mega-

Bucks, poker and 21 machines.

Bingo: 250-seat parlor, 3 cards per board, 2 or 3 minimum, 12 maximum. Computerized bingo. $12,500 maximum payout.

Baccarat: $3-$1,000, bank does not pass.

Pai Gow Poker: $5-$1,000, bank passes.

Race & Sports Book: 155 seats, 25 screens of varying sizes.

Poker: 7-Card Stud with $20 buy-in, Hold 'Em 1-4-8, $30 buy-in, 1-4-8-8 with $40 buy-in. Omaha has a $30 buy-in.

Also: **9's Up** and **Red Dog**.

Imperial Palace Hotel & Casino, 3535 Las Vegas Blvd. South, Las Vegas, NV 89109 (702-731-3311 or 800-634-6441). Rates: $45 weekdays, $65 weekends. Suites $65-$125.

This large, luxurious hotel has a crowded and not very friendly casino. The 2,700 rooms have an Oriental theme, and there are men's and women's health clubs and a pool with waterfall and heated spa. The Imperial is also renowned as the home of an antique auto collection (over 200 classic cars) and the award-winning "Legends in Concert" show, with live re-creations of yesterday's stars, in the Imperial Theatre.

The Emperor's Buffet serves breakfast, lunch, and dinner from 7:00am-11:00pm for $2.99-$3.99 and features a champagne brunch Saturday and Sunday from 8:00am-3:00pm for $6.50.

As well as the standard games, the Imperial has the best-equipped Race & Sports Book in town. Each of the 106 seats has its own 8" color TV, and you can watch any sporting event in progress. Plus, two 10-foot front projection TVs and nine 5-foot rear projection screens provide great views. There's also a special area for VIP bettors and a 24-hour payout window.

King 8 Hotel and Casino, 3330 West Tropicana Ave., Las Vegas, NV 89103 (702-736-8988 or 800-634-3488). Rates: $35 weekdays, $55 weekends. Suites $90.

This small hotel ¼-mile west of The Strip has a casino that's okay for beginners, but it could be friendlier. It's mostly a popular spot for truckers, who receive special promotions.

The King 8 has over 300 rooms, a heated pool and spa, and

a general store. Its lounge features country-western entertainment with no cover or minimum. There's also an elaborate buffet, 24-hour restaurant, and free airport transportation. The casino has craps, blackjack, roulette, poker, keno, and video slots.

Little Caesars Gambling Casino, 3665 Las Vegas Blvd. South, Las Vegas, NV 89109.

"Little" is appropriate. This casino is for the truly budget-minded, but it's friendly and fun. There's a small gift shop for souvenirs, and a cart selling hot dogs and drinks. Complimentary coffee, soft drinks, and draft beer for players.

Games

Blackjack: four tables, $1-$200, six-deck shoe games, dealer hits soft 17, Insurance offered, double on 9, 10, or 11.

Craps: one "Crapless Craps" game, 25 cents weekdays, $1 on weekends. Double odds available.

Slots: 90 machines, one penny-$1, poker and 21 machines.

Race & Sports Book: three 19" screens.

Also: **Video keno**.

Mahoney's Silver Nugget, 2140 Las Vegas Blvd. North, North Las Vegas, NV 89030 (702-399-1111).

This small, very friendly casino is good for beginning craps players. There's no lodging, but an RV park is nearby (phone 702-649-7439), with a pool and Jacuzzi. Mahoney's 24-hour restaurant features prime rib for $3.99.

Games

Blackjack: six tables, $2-$200, four-deck shoe games, dealer hits soft 17, Insurance offered, double on any first two cards.

Craps: one table, 25 cents-$500, five times odds available.

Keno: 50-cent ticket, 35 cents a way, $50,000 maximum payout.

Slots: 410 machines, 5 cents-$1, progressive machines, Mega-Bucks, over $1,000,000 payoff, poker machines.

Bingo: 400-seat room, three cards per board, $10,000 coverall.

Race & Sports Book: 50 seats, 7 screens.

Poker: $20 buy-in, 7-Card Stud, Texas Hold 'Em. Poker tourna-

ments every Tuesday at 7:00pm.
Also: **Video keno**.

Maxim Hotel & Casino, 160 E. Flamingo (east of The Strip), Las Vegas, NV 89109 (702-731-4300 or 800-634-6987). Rates: Sun-Thurs $29.50, Fri-Sat $49-$68. Suites $140 and up.

This moderately priced, elegant hotel has a small, friendly casino good for casual play. Close to the airport, the Maxim is also a minute's walk from The Strip. The hotel has 795 rooms, a pool, arcade, gift shop, and men's store. Suites feature in-room Jacuzzis. The Cloud Nine Lounge offers nightly entertainment from 11:00pm-4:00am, and there's a Comedy Club in the Cabaret Showroom. The Cabaret shows at 7:00pm and 9:00pm include a prime rib buffet.

Restaurants & Lounges
Tree House Restaurant: Open 24 hours with a prime rib buffet Mon-Sat 5:00pm-10:00pm. Sunday champagne brunch (9:00am-3:00pm) costs $6.95.
J.B.'s Sidewalk Cafe: Open 7:00am-11:00pm.
The China Stop: Open 6:00pm-2:00am.
DaVinci's: Gourmet dining daily 6:00pm-11:00pm.

Games
Blackjack: 26 tables, $2-$1,000, four-deck shoe games, dealer does **not** hit soft 17, Insurance offered, double on any first two cards, no double after split.
Craps: three tables, $2-$500, double odds available.
Roulette: two tables, $1 minimum, even-money payoffs to $1,000, 2-to-1 payoffs to $500, others $50.
Keno: 65-cent ticket, 50 cents for 3-ways, 10 cents for 120-ways, $50,000 maximum payout.
Slots: 681 machines, 5 cents-$5, MegaBucks, Quartermania, $25,000 maximum payoff, poker and 21 machines.
Mini-Baccarat: $5-$500, bank does not pass.
Pai Gow Poker: $2-$500, bank passes.
Race & Sports Book: Features nine 19" screens and two 25" screens.
Poker: Buy-in $40-$500, 7-Card Stud, Hold 'Em, any game requested.
Also: **Big Six Wheel**.

The Mirage, 3400 Las Vegas Blvd. South, Las Vegas, NV 89109 (702-791-7111 or 800-627-6667). Rates: $89-$115. Suites $225-$450. Children under 12 free.

You might expect this world-class luxury resort to be snobbish and cater only to high-rollers, but The Mirage is very friendly, with a huge, fun casino and happy dealers. Though there are no single-deck blackjack games, it's a good place for beginners to learn craps.

There's no other destination resort like it in the world. A live, so-help-me-it's-real volcano erupts every 10 minutes near the front entrance, and that's just the beginning. A realistic habitat provides a beautiful setting for the exotic white tigers employed by magicians Siegfried and Roy. Behind the front desk, a 20,000-gallon aquarium contains sharks, rays, and angelfish, and the entire lobby is a tropical rainforest with waterfalls, orchids, and towering palms.

The 3,000 rooms are decorated with colors from the South Seas, and each has views of the pool, mountains, or The Strip. The Esplanade is a collection of shops including high-fashion swimwear, formal wear, a shop featuring new designers, etc. The Spa has men's and women's facilities, an exercise room, aerobic studio, sauna, steam bath, whirlpool, and massage. The beauty salon offer total personal care for both men and women. The swimming pool is a series of connected lagoons that link two palm tree-covered islands where you can enjoy the sun.

Siegfried and Roy perform nightly, three weeks a month, in the 1,500-seat Theatre Mirage. If you love magic, you'll love their show. One week a month the Theatre features top-name entertainment.

Restaurants & Lounges

Kokomo's: Specializing in steaks and seafood, set in a tropical rainforest surrounded by waterfalls and a lagoon. Reservations suggested. Open for lunch 11:00am-2:30pm, for dinner 5:30pm-11:30pm.

Mikado: Japanese gourmet cuisine, lobster, steak, chicken, and shrimp served *teppan yaki* style. Dinner 6:00pm-11:30pm. Reservations suggested.

Moongate: Chinese courtyard serving Szechuan and Cantonese cuisines. Open 5:30pm-11:30pm. Reservations suggested.

Ristorante Riva: A northern Italian restaurant featuring home-made pastas, seafood, and veal dishes. Open 6:00pm-11:30pm. Reservations suggested.

The Bistro: French food served in a Left Bank setting. Open

6:00pm-11:30pm. Reservations suggested.

Caribe Cafe: 24-hour coffee shop patterned after a Caribbean village. Serves breakfast, lunch, sandwiches, exotic desserts, and dinner entrees.

Bermuda Buffet: Breakfast 7:00am-11:00am, lunch 11:00am-3:00pm, and dinner 3:00pm-11:00pm.

The California Pizza Kitchen: Wood-fired gourmet pizza, located in the Race & Sports Book. Sun-Thurs 11:00am-11:00pm, Fri & Sat 11:00am-2:00am.

Coconuts Ice Cream Shop: Fresh ice cream, sorbets, and frozen yogurts.

Lagoon Saloon: Tropical drinks and nightly entertainment.

Baccarat Bar: In the center of the casino.

Sports Bar: Overlooking the Race & Sports Book, next to the Pizza Kitchen.

Games

Blackjack: 100 tables, $2-$5,000, two- and six-deck shoes, dealer hits soft 17 **only** on double decks, Insurance offered, double on anything.

Craps: 12 tables, $2-$5,000, double odds available.

Roulette: eight tables, $5-$5,000 outside, $100 inside any way.

Keno: $1 ticket, $250,000 maximum payout, Keno-To-Go (play 21 to 1,000 consecutive games with a year to collect winnings.)

Slots: 2,200 machines, 5 cents-$500, MegaBucks, poker, and 21 machines.

Baccarat: $25-$15,000, separate room, open 24 hours.

Pai Gow: $5-$5,000, tiles and cards, bank passes.

Race & Sports Book: Large room, huge screens.

Poker: Stud, Hold 'Em, and Omaha. Separate room.

Also: **Red Dog** and **Big Six Wheel**.

Paddlewheel Hotel & Casino, 305 Convention Center Dr., Las Vegas, NV 89109 (702-734-0711 or 800-782-2600). Rates: $32 Sun-Thurs, $49 weekends.

This small hotel has a small casino with friendly dealers, good for beginners. Each room has a private balcony; suites have Jacuzzis. There's a also a spa and sauna, pool, gift shop, restaurant (open 24 hours) featuring country cooking with all-you-can-eat baby back ribs, snow crab, and fried shrimp, a lounge with live entertainment and dancing, and a video poker bar.

Games

Blackjack: eight tables, $2-$100, single- and two-deck shoe games, dealer hits soft 17, Insurance offered, double on any two cards.

Craps: one table, $1-$100, double odds available.

Roulette: one table, $1-$100.

Keno: 80-cent ticket, $50,000 maximum payout.

Slots: 444 slots, 5 cents-$5, progressive machines, MegaBucks, poker and 21 machines.

Bingo: 250-seat room, two cards per board, $1-$3, $5,000 maximum payout.

Poker: Buy-in $20, 7-Card Stud.

Palace Station Hotel & Casino, 2411 West Sahara Ave., Las Vegas, NV 89102 (702-367-2411 or 800-634-3101). Rates: mid-week $35-$45, weekends $55-$90.

This moderately priced hotel has a large, crowded, friendly casino, plus a complimentary shuttle service to and from The Strip, 457 rooms, two pools and Jacuzzis, in-room gaming instructions, a gift shop, and beauty and barber shops. The Loading Dock Lounge has live entertainment.

Restaurants & Lounges

The Pasta Palace: Italian specialties.

Fisherman's Broiler: Seafood restaurant.

The Iron Horse: Open 24 hours.

The Feast: An all-you-can-eat buffet serving breakfast for $3.95, lunch (until 2:30pm) for $4.95, and dinner (4:30pm-10:00pm) for $6.95. Sunday brunch (7:00am-3:00pm) costs $5.49.

Burger King: In the Palace Station.

Games

Blackjack: 30 tables, $2-$1,000, four-deck shoe games, dealer hits soft 17, Insurance offered.

Craps: four tables, $1-$1,000, double odds available.

Roulette: three tables (25 cents, 50 cents, and $1 minimum, $1,000 maximum).

Keno: 70-cent ticket, 35 cents on way tickets, $250,000 maximum payout.

Slots: 1,700 machines, 5 cents-$5, progressive machines, Mega-Bucks, $1,000,000 maximum payoff, poker and 21 machines.

Bingo: 550-seat room, two cards per board, $10,000 Super Coverall payout.

Mini-Baccarat: $2-$2,000, bank does not pass.
Pai Gow Poker: $5-$1,000, bank does not pass.
Race & Sports Book: 200 seats, 42 TVs.
Poker: Buy-in $20-$40, 7-Card Stud, Texas Hold 'Em.

Ramada Hotel San Remo Çasino & Resort, 115 East Tropicana Ave., Las Vegas, NV 89109 (702-739-9000 or 800-522-7366). Rates: $50 Sun-Thurs, $65 weekends. Suites $150-$777.

The San Remo is a small, elegant, European-inspired hotel with 322 rooms (soon to be over 700 with the tower under construction). It's very friendly, with a casino that's small and fun and dealers who are helpful to beginners.

The hotel offers free indoor parking, 24-hour room and valet services, a swimming pool and spa, gift shop, and car rental agency.

Restaurants & Lounges
Bonne Chance Bar: Live entertainment nightly 6:00pm-3:00am, except Monday.
Parisian Cabaret: Name entertainment nightly 8:00pm-2:00am.
Ristorante dei Fiori: Open 24 hours for casual dining. Buffet in a garden setting.
Le Panache: Gourmet dining, continental and American cuisine, 6:00pm-3:00am Wed-Sun.

Games
Blackjack: 16 tables, $1-$500, six-deck shoe games, dealer does **not** hit soft 17, Insurance offered, double on any first two cards.
Craps: one table, $1-$500, double odds available.
Roulette: one table, $1 minimum.
Keno: 90-cent ticket, 25-cent way tickets 10 or more ways, 10 cents a way 100 or more ways, $100,000 maximum payout.
Slots: 600 machines, 5 cents-$5, progressive machines, Mega-Bucks & Quartermania, 21 and poker machines.
Baccarat: $2-$500, bank passes. Open 16 hours a day.
Pai Gow: $5-$500, bank does not pass.
Poker: $20 buy-in, 7-Card Stud and Texas Hold 'Em.
Also: **Big Six Wheel**.

Rio Suites Hotel & Casino, Flamingo at Valley View, Las Vegas, NV 89109 (702-252-7777 or 800-888-1808). Rates: $78 Sun-Thurs, $98 weekends.

This beautiful new hotel—with the only sand beach in Las Vegas—unfortunately has a small, crowded, can't-be-bothered casino. The 430 rooms all have a Brazilian theme, and there's a full health club, a swimming pool with fountains, volleyball on the beach, and gift shops.

Restaurants & Lounges
Sonny's Deli: Open 9:00am-11:00pm weekdays, 9:00am-1:00am weekends.
Carnival Buffet: All-you-can-eat buffet serving breakfast 7:00am-10:30am, lunch 11:00am-2:30pm, and dinner 5:00pm-10:00pm.
Antonio's: Gourmet dining 6:00pm-midnight. Closed Monday.
The Beach Cafe: Open 24 hours.
All-American Bar & Grill: Open Sun-Thurs 5:00pm-10:00pm (to midnight on weekends).

Games
The casino has blackjack, craps, slots, Pai Gow, and poker.

Riviera Hotel & Casino, 2901 Las Vegas Blvd. South, Las Vegas, NV 89109 (702-734-5110 or 800-634-6753). Rates: $89-$140.

This world-class resort hotel unfortunately has a casino with dealers who are indifferent and interested only in big-money players.

Otherwise, the 2,000-room Riviera has everything you could want under one roof: beauty and barber salons, a gift shop, a children's clothing and toy shop, women's wear, fine jewelry, and an imaginative gadget store. The hotel offers 35 rooms equipped to accommodate people in wheelchairs, and there are two swimming pools, a Jacuzzi, lighted tennis courts, a wedding chapel, and a florist. Free parking and 24-hour room service are also available. A business center provides fax machines and copying services.

Restaurants & Lounges
Delmonico's: Complete continental dinner for $26.95. Open Thurs-Mon 6:00pm-11:00pm.
Ristorante Italiano: A four-star Italian restaurant.

Kristofer's: Mediterranean in style, featuring steaks and seafood with fixed-price dinners from $16.95, served 5:30pm-11:00pm daily. Saturday and Sunday champagne brunch 9:00am-2:00pm.

Kady's Brasserie: Overlooking the pool, this 24-hour deli has daily specials for breakfast, lunch, and dinner.

Riviera Buffet: On the 2nd floor near the shopping arcade. Open daily for breakfast, lunch, and dinner, $2.95-$7.95.

Mardi Gras Food Court: Nine quick-service restaurants, including Burger King and Baskin-Robbins.

Versailles Theatre: This 1,000-seat showroom features an aquatic extravaganza with mermaids, showgirls, diving, and swimming.

Mardi Gras Showroom: Adult entertainment with showgirls, impersonators, and comedians, three times a night.

Games
The casino bills itself as the world's largest, with 90 table games and 2,000 slot machines. There's a Race & Sports Book, craps, blackjack, slots, and video poker.

The Royal Hotel & Casino, 99 Convention Center Dr., Las Vegas, NV 89109 (702-735-6117 or 800-634-6118). Rates: $37 weekdays, $47 weekends.

The Royal is a new Best Western AAA-rated hotel. It's small (238 rooms), with a very friendly staff and a modest casino with relaxed, happy dealers—a good spot for beginning players. There's a swimming pool, gift shop, and a restaurant open 24-hours, with specials for breakfast, lunch, and dinner. The lounge has live entertainment and a dance floor.

If you can do without the renowned Las Vegas glitz, the Royal is a gem—friendly people, good food, and very reasonable prices.

Games
Blackjack: six tables, $1-$200, two- and five-deck shoe games, dealer hits soft 17, Insurance offered, double on any first two cards.

Craps: one table, $1-$200, double odds available.

Roulette: one table, $1-$200.

Keno: 75-cent ticket, 50 cents per way on way tickets, $50,000 maximum payout.

Slots: 292 machines, 5 cents-$3, progressive machines, Mega-Bucks and Quartermania, 21 and poker machines.

Sahara Hotel & Casino, 2535 Las Vegas Blvd. South, Las Vegas, NV 89109 (702-737-2111 or 800-634-6666). Rates: $60-$140.

This luxurious resort hotel has a large, crowded, friendly casino and over 2,000 rooms, including 80 suites. There are two pools, a video arcade, child care center, a beauty salon, and a wide variety of shops.

Restaurants & Lounges
La Terrazza: Italian fare from 5:00pm-10:00pm.
House of Lords: Gourmet steak house with a great wine list. Open 5:00pm-10:00pm.
Caravan Coffee Shop: Open 24 hours.
Don the Beachcomber: Polynesian food from 5:00pm-10:00pm.
Oasis Buffet: Breakfast 7:30am-10:30am ($3.33), lunch 11:30am-2:30pm ($4.44), dinner 4:00pm-10:30pm ($5.55). Weekend champagne brunches (7:30am-2:30pm) cost $5.55.
The Turf Club Deli: Open 8:00am-6:00pm.
The Congo Theatre Showroom: Home to some of the top acts in the world, the room is open for two shows nightly except Wednesday.
The Casbah Lounge: Features up-and-coming performers daily from 2:00pm-5:00am.

Games
Blackjack: 31 tables, $2-$2,000, two-and six-deck shoe games, dealer does **not** hit soft 17, Insurance offered, double on any two cards.
Craps: five tables, $2-$2,000, double odds available.
Roulette: three tables, $2-$100 straight up.
Keno: 50-cent ticket, way tickets, $100,000 maximum payout.
Slots: 987 machines, 5 cents-$5, progressive machines, $250,000 maximum payoff, poker and 21 machines.
Baccarat: $10-$2,000, bank passes. Separate room. Open Wed-Sun from noon, Mon-Tues from 7:00pm.
Pai Gow Poker: $2-$200, bank passes.
Race & Sports Book: 200-seat room, 30 TVs.
Poker: Buy-in $10, 7-Card Stud, Pan, Hi-Lo Split, Texas Hold 'Em. Also: **Red Dog**.

Sands Hotel & Casino, 3355 Las Vegas Blvd. South, Las Vegas, NV 89109 (702-733-5000 or 800-634-6901). Rates: $65-$85. Tower rooms $105.

The Sands is a complete luxury resort, smaller and friendlier than many of the huge spots on The Strip. Its casino is crowded but friendly, with good blackjack rules.

The hotel offers 720 rooms, two pools, men's and women's health spas, lighted tennis courts, a nine-hole putting green, and various shops. The Copa Room, the main showroom, features top talent, and the Winner's Circle Cabaret has nightly entertainment.

Restaurants & Lounges
The Regency Room: Gourmet dining every night 6:00pm-midnight.
House of Szechuan: Chinese food 5:00pm-11:00pm.
Garden Terrace Restaurant: Open 24 hours.
Sands Deli: Open daily 7:00am-10:30pm.

Games
Blackjack: 28 tables, $2-$2,000, six-deck shoe games, dealer does **not** hit soft 17, Insurance pays 2-to-1, double after splits.
Craps: four tables, $2-$2,000, double odds available.
Roulette: three tables, $2-$2,000 outside, $100 any way.
Keno: $1 ticket, 50 cents per way on 3-ways or more, 10 cents a way on 100-ways, $50,000 maximum payout.
Slots: 794 machines, 5 cents to $25, MegaBucks and Quartermania, over $1,000,000 maximum payoff, poker and 21 machines.
Baccarat: Separate room, $5-$4,000, bank passes. Open noon-4:00am.
Pai Gow: $10-$2,000, bank passes.
Race & Sports Book: 112 seats, 20 TVs.
Also: **Big Six Wheel**.

Showboat Hotel, Casino, and Bowling Center, 2800 East Fremont, Las Vegas, NV 89104 (702-385-9123 or 800-634-3484). Rates: $55.

This recently refurbished destination resort has over 500 rooms and a crowded casino that caters to big-money players.

The hook here is bowling, and the Showboat is home to PBA bowling stars, who often use the deluxe bowling alley (106 lanes, pro shop). There's also a sports pavilion, an 18-hole golf course with shuttle service to and from the Showboat, a restaurant, lighted tennis courts, and a pool. Child care is located in the bowling center.

Restaurants & Lounges
Coffee Shop: Open 24 hours.
Captain's Buffet: Lunch 10:00am-3:30pm ($3.79), dinner 4:30pm-10:00pm ($5.95), weekend brunch ($4.75) served 8:30am-3:30pm.
The Captain's Table: Gourmet dining, featuring prime rib. Open nightly 5:00pm-11:00pm.
The Mardi Gras Lounge: Nightly entertainment and dancing, with no cover or minimum.

Games
Blackjack: 21 tables, $2-$1,000, single- and six-deck shoe games, dealer hits soft 17, Insurance offered.
Craps: two tables, $1-$1,000, double odds available.
Roulette: two tables, $1-$100.
Keno: 70-cent ticket, $50,000 maximum payout.
Slots: 1,900 machines, 5 cents-$1, progressive machines, Mega-Bucks, over $1,000,000 payoff, poker machines.
Bingo: New 1,500-seat Bingo Gardens, three cards per board, $1-$7, $25,000 maximum payout.
Pai Gow: $5-$5,000, bank does not pass.
Poker: $20 buy-in, Stud and Texas Hold 'Em.

Silver City Casino, 3001 Las Vegas Blvd. South, Las Vegas, NV 89109 (702-732-4152).

This small, friendly casino owned by Circus Circus has some outstanding drink and food deals. The bar serves all drinks for 75 cents, and the 24-hour restaurant features prime rib for $3.99, a nine-ounce lobster tail for $9.99, and a roast chicken dinner for $2.99. Breakfast, served 11:00pm-11:00am, costs just 99 cents.

Games
Blackjack: 15 tables, $1-$200, single-and four-deck shoe games, dealer hits soft 17, Insurance offered, double only on first two cards.
Craps: one table, $1-$200 double odds available.

Roulette: two tables, $1-$200.
Keno: 75-cent ticket, 50 cents 3-ways or more, 25 cents 10-ways, $50,000 maximum payout.
Slots: 516 machines, 5 cents-$1, progressive machines, $150,000 maximum payoff, poker and 21 machines.
Red Dog: $1-$100.

The Stardust Hotel & Casino, 3000 Las Vegas Blvd. South, Las Vegas, NV 89109 (702-732-6111 or 800-634-6757). Rates: $28-$125.

A good place for gamblers of all levels to play, this resort complex has a huge casino (83,000 square feet), friendly dealers, and over 1,600 rooms and suites. The Stardust also features two pools with a tropical setting, one of the most complete athletic clubs in the country, access to three championship golf courses, numerous shops, a video arcade, and limo services.

Restaurants & Lounges
Toucan Harry's: Coffee shop open 24 hours serving snacks and full course meals. Chinese cuisine featured 5:00pm-2:00am.
Warehouse All-You-Can-Eat Buffet: 7:00am-10:00pm daily. Breakfast $4.95, lunch $5.95, and dinner $7.95. The weekend champagne brunch from 7:00am-3:30pm costs $6.95.
Ralph's Diner: Daily blue-plate specials starting at $3.95, served in a 1950's atmosphere. Old-fashioned soda fountain with milkshakes and sundaes. Tunes from the 50's and 60's on the jukebox, and dancing waitresses do the Bop (honest!). Open daily 7:00am-2:00am.
William B's Steakhouse: American cuisine from 5:00pm daily.
Tony Roma's: Open 5:00pm for dinner daily, and 11:00am for lunch Thurs-Mon. Great BBQ ribs and onion rings. There's a washtub for your hands on your way out the door.
Willie and Jose's: Mexican cuisine.
Short Stop Snack Bar: Near the Race & Sports Book. Specializing in sandwiches, open 8:00am-10:00pm.
Galaxy Piano Bar: In the casino area. Open 24 hours.
Final Score: Cocktail lounge with video poker and sporting events on TV. Open 24 hours.
Starlite: Open 24 hours with live entertainment daily and sporting events on big-screen TVs. No cover or minimum.
Landing Pad: Bar open 24 hours. In the casino area.

Dio's: Lounge near Tony Roma's. Opens at 5:00pm.

The Lido Showroom: The former home of the extravagant production show starring the Lido Girls, the Showroom now features an even more extravagant spectacle called "Into the Night." It has everything you'd expect of a multi-million dollar Las Vegas spectacular—including hard-to-get seats, so you must book at least a day in advance.

Games

Blackjack: 50 tables, $2-$1,000, all tables use six-deck shoes, dealer does **not** hit soft 17, Insurance offered, double on any first two cards only.

Craps: six tables, $2-$2,000, double odds available.

Roulette: five tables, 25 cents, $100 straight up, $25 any way.

Keno: $1, way tickets, $10,000 maximum payout.

Slots: 1,065 machines, 5 cents-$100, progressive machines, poker and 21 machines. Slot Club gives *cash* bonuses.

Bingo: 900-seat room, six cards per board, $2-$8, $5,000 maximum payout.

Baccarat: $5-$2,000, bank does not pass.

Pai Gow Poker: $5-$2,000, bank passes.

Race & Sports Book: 250 seats, 46 screens, reader boards. The Stardust's Sports Handicappers Library provides statistics on current sporting events.

Poker: Buy-in $20-$30, 7-Card Stud, 7-Card Lo, Hold 'Em.

Also: **Red Dog**.

Town Hall Casino, 4155 Koval Lane, Las Vegas, NV 89109.

This very small casino has a restaurant and casino bar, plus live entertainment and a friendly atmosphere. Complimentary food and beverages for players.

Games

Blackjack: three tables, $1-$200, five-deck shoe games, dealer hits soft 17, Insurance offered.

Slots: 177 machines, poker, 21, and keno machines.

Tropicana Resort & Casino, 3801 Las Vegas Blvd. South, Las Vegas, NV 89109 (702-739-2222 or 800-634-4000). Rates: $49-$125.

This large resort caters to big-money play, so it's not for beginners. The hotel features a health club, pool, Jacuzzis, and over 1,900 rooms. There's lounge entertainment, numerous shops, ten restaurants, and an island casino under a stained-glass dome. Also, the Tiffany Theatre features the Folies Bergere production show.

Games
Blackjack: 40 tables, $2-$3,000, single deck and six- and eight-deck shoe games, dealer does **not** hit soft 17, Insurance offered, double on any two cards and splits.
Craps: eight tables, $3-$3,000, triple odds available.
Roulette: five tables, $2-$100 inside, $3,000 outside.
Keno: $1 ticket, 50 cents for 3-ways, 25 cents for 10-ways, 10 cents for 100-ways. $100,000 maximum payout.
Slots: 1,106 machines, 5 cents-$100, progressive machines, $290,000 maximum payoff, poker and 21 machines.
Baccarat: Separate room always open, $25-$10,000.
Pai Gow Poker: $5-$500, bank does not pass.
Race & Sports Book: 30 seats, 11 TVs.
Poker: Buy-in $20, Stud and Hold 'Em.
Mini-Baccarat: $5-$500.

Vegas World, 2000 Las Vegas Blvd. South, Las Vegas, NV 89104 (702-382-2000 or 800-634-6277). Rates: $35 weekdays, $45 weekends.

This hotel and casino caters to out-of-town package deals (you may have seen their ads in *Playboy* and other national magazines). The deals are pretty good, but the hotel has an indifferent attitude toward individual reservations and casino play.

There's an Olympic-size swimming pool, 529 rooms and mini-suites, two restaurants, a showroom with super-star entertainment, and various lounges. They'll send a Fun Book to out-of-state guests on written request. The casino offers standard rules for blackjack, craps, roulette, and slots.

Westward Ho Hotel & Casino, 2900 Las Vegas Blvd. South, Las Vegas, NV 89109 (702-731-2900 or 800-634-6651 [western states], 800-634-6803 [other states]). Rates: $40 weekdays, $51 weekends.

Though the Westward Ho's rooms are quite reasonable, its casino is small and not very accommodating.

The hotel features 1,000 rooms, apartment suites with two bedrooms, seven pools, Jacuzzis, and a lounge with live entertainment. The Ca-Fae restaurant features a big breakfast, a sandwich board, plus American dinner entrees and midnight specials. The buffet for lunch (11:00am-4:00pm) costs $3.99, for dinner (4:00pm-10:00pm) $4.99. The Casino Deli is handy and quick. There's also a free airport shuttle and computerized check-in.

The casino has over 1,000 slots, $50,000 keno, blackjack, craps, roulette, and a Big Six Wheel.

Laughlin

Ninety miles south of Las Vegas on the banks of the Colorado River, Laughlin is America's newest boomtown, the fastest-growing gaming town in Nevada. Set in rugged mountain terrain in the Sonora Desert, Laughlin was a sleepy little place with a few slot machines and a fishing camp just a few years ago. What a difference a few years can make! In 1984, the population was 95. Today it's over 4,000, with 30,000 predicted by the end of the century.

In the late 1960's, Don Laughlin, for whom the town is named, bought the Riverside Bait Shop and made it the Riverside Casino. Today, a dozen high-rise towers and ten resort casinos create a glittering skyline of glass and neon.

Laughlin is about the same distance from most southern California cities as Las Vegas, but it's also an easy drive from Yuma and Phoenix. You can fly from Burbank, San Diego, and eight other cities directly to the Bullhead City/Laughlin airport. The RV guide lists 20 parks, most with full hook-ups. Some have boat docks and marinas, food stores, and swimming pools, and some provide free transportation to Casino Drive.

Every member of the family will find a form of recreation in Laughlin. Take a self-guided tour of Davis Dam with its five huge turbines, sunbathe at Lake Mojave, hike in Grapevine Canyon to look at Indian petroglyphs, visit the historic ghost town Oatman (there's an exciting gunfight staged each weekend), treat yourself to a parachute ride above the town and the river, or float down the Colorado to Havasu City to see the famous London Bridge.

You can also enjoy a friendly game of chance, relax by your swimming pool or on the beach, dine in an elegant restaurant at bargain prices, catch a star in one of the hotel showrooms, or take a sunset walk along the river.

Ask anyone who visits: the best thing about Laughlin is its friend-

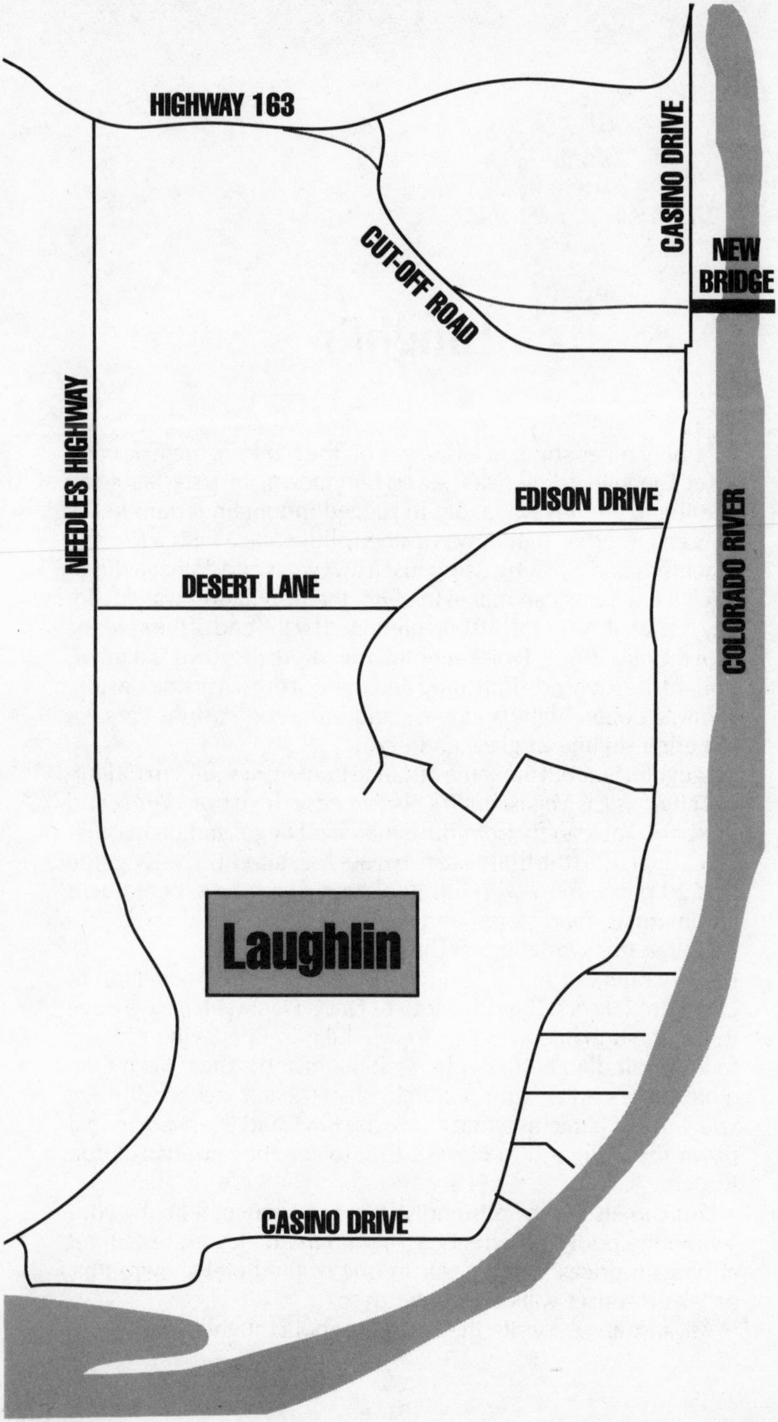
HIGHWAY 163
CASINO DRIVE
CUT-OFF ROAD
NEW BRIDGE
NEEDLES HIGHWAY
ARIZONA
EDISON DRIVE
COLORADO RIVER
DESERT LANE
Laughlin
CASINO DRIVE

liness. The small-town atmosphere contributed to the town's growth, and the powers-that-be are determined not to lose it. Though almost 15,000 people visit Laughlin every day, each receives a little extra something that makes the town special—a friendly smile, a warm hello, and courteous service.

Area Attractions

Colorado River Tours: The *Little Belle* (from the Edgewater Casino) and the *Fiesta Queen* (from Harrah's) offer daily, hour-long sightseeing cruises at 11:00, 12:30, 2:00, 3:30, and 5:00, with full service bars, air-conditioned dining rooms, and facilities for weddings. A dinner cruise runs Thursdays at 6:30pm, with live entertainment. Fare for the day-cruise is $12 adults, $6 children. Dinner cruise tickets cost $24.95. For information call Laughlin River Tours (702-298-1047 or 800-228-9825).

Blue River Safaris offers three tours daily: Tour 1 is a combination boat and bus trip to Lake Havasu's English Village and London Bridge. The bus goes from Havasu to Oatman, an old mining town. You'll also see Indian petroglyphs and Topock Gorge. This tour leaves Laughlin at 9:00am for an eight-hour journey and costs $49.95. #2 is a 130-mile round-trip on the Colorado to Lake Havasu, with two hours for lunch and sightseeing. Departure is 9:00am. The trip lasts 9½ hours and costs $49.95. Tickets for #3 cost $34.95. This tour features a round-trip by bus to the English Village and London Bridge at Havasu, a side trip to Oatman, then to Havasu City for lunch before you board a tour boat on Lake Havasu. The tour leaves Laughlin at 10:00am and lasts 7½ hours. Each of these tours includes lunch and is narrated. Call Blue River Safaris at 702-298-0910 or 800-345-8990.

Horseback Riding: Daily from Nov-April, you can take a two-hour guided tour for $25 per person. Moonlight rides are $35, and sunset rides are $15. Lessons and group packages are available. **Havasu Horse Rental**, Box 1931, Lake Havasu City, AZ (602-855-2310).

Scenic Flights: Fly to the Grand Canyon from Laughlin. High wing airplanes provide unobstructed views of the Inner Gorge and the Supai Indian Village. Tour prices range from $135-$180 per person (discounts for kids 15 and under). Call **Windrock Airlines** (602-638-9591).

Davis Dam: Built about 70 miles downstream from Hoover Dam, Davis is an earth- and rock-filled structure. Water rushes through the spillway at 214,000 cubic feet per second, and the five generating units each have a capacity of 48,000 kilowatts. The dam is part of the Colorado River storage project, designed to make the Colorado more manageable. Open for free, self-guided tours daily 9:00am-4:00pm.

Grapevine Canyon: Ten miles west of Davis Dam on Hwy. 163, you'll find sheer cliff walls with ancient Indian petroglyphs, accessible after a short, easy hike.

Emerald River Golf Course: An 18-hole championship course in Laughlin. Play from 7:00am-dusk daily. Rates: $45 weekdays, $50 weekends. Guests in a Laughlin hotel receive a $5 discount.

Oatman, Arizona: 30 miles from Laughlin on old U.S. 66, Oatman is an authentic western ghost town, where wild burros still come down from the hills early each morning, roam the streets all day, eat from tourists' hands, and then head back to the hills at dusk. For the people who migrated to California from the midwest in the 1930's, Oatman was the last stop before the Mojave Desert. Clark Gable and Carol Lombard spent their honeymoon there, and you can see their room in the Oatman Hotel. Western music is featured in three saloons, and gunfighters stage shootouts on Main Street at 2:30pm and 4:30pm each Saturday and Sunday.

Chloride, Arizona: 45 miles northeast of Laughlin, Chloride, an 1860's silver mining town, is the oldest continuously inhabited mining town in Arizona and boasts the oldest post office in the state. The town is much as it was in 1900, with several buildings registered as National Historic Sites. Melodramas are presented every first and third Saturday at 10:30am and 2:30pm. In June, there's an annual Miner's Day celebration.

Parasailing: Bright red parasails fly 200 feet above the Colorado and the resorts. A two-mile ride costs $30, and you take off and land from a boat, so your feet never touch the water. Located at the Regency Casino boat dock. Wave Runner rentals are also available at $23 for 30 minutes or $45/hour. For reservations, call **New Horizons** at 702-379-8896.

Lake Mojave: Created by Davis Dam, Lake Mojave is minutes from Laughlin and covers a 44-square-mile area. **Katherine's Landing** offers complete boating facilities, including rentals, a launch ramp, and fuel. A motel and RV sites are located on the shores of the lake. 40 spaces with full hookups are available at $15 a day. For reservations call 800-752-9669. You can also pitch a tent at the campground for $6 a day on a first-come, first-served basis. There are rest rooms and coin-operated showers.

Free **river boat rides** take you from Arizona parking lots to the Laughlin casinos. Some six million people a year shuttle across the river and from one hotel to another.

Weddings

Arizona license: **Bullhead Justice Court,** 1130 Hancock Rd., Bullhead City, AZ 86552 (602-758-0709). Fee: $24. No blood tests, bring I.D.

Nevada license: Must obtain in Las Vegas.

Wedding Chapels:
A Touch of Elegance, 626 Hancock Rd., Bullhead City, AZ 86552 (602-763-7744).
Colonial Cottage, 1051 Hancock Rd., Suite 3, Bullhead City, AZ 86552 (602-758-1615).
Diamond and Sons Silver Bell Chapel, 3300 Needles Highway, Laughlin, NV 89029 (702-646-2965).

Wedding Cruises: You can get married with all the trimmings aboard the *Fiesta Queen*, which docks at Harrah's, or on the *Little Belle* docked at the Edgewater. Advance reservations are necessary. The wedding cruises include a private room, decorations, and a glass of champagne for each guest. You can order additional services such as a minister, wedding cake, live entertainment, flowers, etc. A marriage license from either Nevada or Arizona is acceptable, since the wedding is performed on the Colorado River, a federal waterway.

Climate & Dress

Laughlin, 510 feet above sea level, is hot and dry most of the year. Temperatures range from 40°-70° in the winter and can reach 120° in the summer. Although 100° heat is not unusual in August, the low desert humidity makes outdoor activity comfortable. The average annual rainfall is only 4.2 inches, so don't worry about an umbrella.

Casual clothes are fine for daytime, and many people wear them around the clock, but women may prefer cocktail dresses for evening. Pantsuits are okay, too. Men will want a sports coat or a jacket and tie for dinner shows. Sundresses are great from spring through October, but in the winter you might like a lightweight jacket or sweater for evening, and woolens feel cozy November through March.

Air Services
The airport serves Bullhead City, AZ and Laughlin. Free transportation is provided to the casinos and hotels, and rental car services are available. For flight reservations call your travel agent or these air carriers: Mesa Airlines (800-637-2247), States West Airlines (800-247-3866), Air L.A. (800-235-4448).

Driving Distances
Flagstaff—180 miles
Grand Canyon—200 miles
Lake Havasu—79 miles
Las Vegas—90 miles
Los Angeles—300 miles
Palm Springs—220 miles
Phoenix—230 miles
Reno—460 miles
San Diego—390 miles
Tucson—350 miles
Yuma—190 miles

RV Parks
Each of the following provides full hookups, restrooms, showers, a swimming pool (unless noted), laundry facilities, and a grocery. There are several other parks in the area; not all provide full service.

Bullhead RV Park, 1610 Hwy. 95, Bullhead City, AZ (602-763-8353). 156 full hookups, TV, propane, paved streets, dump station, small pets okay.

KOA Kampground, Hwy. 95 & Merrill Ave., Bullhead City, AZ (602-763-2179). 107 full hookups, game room, propane.

Lake Mohave Resort, Katherine's Landing, Bullhead City, AZ (602-754-3245). 34 full hookups, 173 campsites, general store, dump station, no pool, gas station, propane, full service marina.

Riverside Resort Park, Casino Drive, Laughlin (702-298-2535). 600 full hookups, paved roads.

Silver Creek Camp, Silver Creek & Gold Rush Dr., Bullhead City, AZ (602-763-2444). 136 full hookups, spa.

Snowbird RV Resort, 1600 Joy Lane, Fort Mojave Mesa, AZ (602-768-2141). 110 full hookups, hot tub, tennis court, golf course, BBQs, library. Children 14 and older only. 10 miles south of Bullhead City.

Casinos, Hotels, & Resorts

The Colorado Belle Hotel and Casino, 2100 Casino Dr., Laughlin, NV 89029 (702-298-4000 [NV], 602-754-4671 [AZ], 800-458-9500). Rates: Sun-Thurs $25, weekends and holidays $59.

Very friendly casino, great blackjack rules, good for beginning players. The Belle is a replica of a turn-of-the-century paddlewheel riverboat with 1,238 rooms, a 60,000-square-foot casino, two pools and a spa, five gift shops, and a video arcade. 24-hour free ferryboat rides across the Colorado, ample free parking on both sides of the river. The Riverboat Lounge has live entertainment daily with no cover or minimum. Five restaurants and a bar.

Restaurants & Lounges
Mark Twain's Chicken & Ribs: Open 4:00pm-11:00pm. BBQ, steaks, desserts.
Mississippi Lounge & Seafood: Open 2:00pm-midnight. Fresh seafood, secret Cajun seasonings.
The Orleans Room: Open 5:00pm-11pm. Gourmet dining, full-course meals, seafood.
The Captain's Food Fare: Open 7:00am-10:00pm. Breakfast, lunch, and dinner buffets, dessert bar and create-your-own sundae buffet. Children's menu.
The Paddlewheel Coffee Shop: 24-hour service. Full menu, light lunches.
Huckleberry's Snack Bar & Bakery: Open 7:00am-10:00pm. Snacks, fast-food, ice cream, fresh pastries.

Games
Blackjack: 44 tables, $1 minimum, single-deck games, Insurance offered, dealer does **not** hit soft 17.
Craps: three tables, $1 minimum, single odds.
Roulette: three wheels, 25-cent minimum.
Keno: Lounge, 50-cent minimum, way tickets, $50,000 maximum payout.
Poker Room: 7-card Stud $1-3 & $1-4, Texas Hold 'Em $1-5 and $1-5-10-10. $10 and up buy-in.
Slots: 1,200 machines, 5 cents-$5, progressive machines, poker machines.
Also: **Red Dog**.

The Edgewater Hotel and Casino, 2020 S. Casino Dr., Laughlin, NV 89029 (702-298-2453 [NV], 602-754-3262 [AZ], 800-257-0300). Rates: Sun-Thurs $25, weekends & holidays $50.

Nice hotel and casino with very friendly dealers. Expanding to 1,492 rooms, 30 suites, handicapped facilities, pool and Jacuzzi, video arcade, 32-lane bowling alley, pro shop, gift shop, medical facilities, three restaurants and a snack bar.

Restaurants & Lounges
Edgewater Lounge: Live entertainment 9:00pm-3:00am nightly.
Fountain Room: Open 24 hours. Full breakfasts 'round the clock, salads, sandwiches, prime rib dinner for $5.95, great desserts.
Embers: Open 5:00pm-midnight. Fine dining with aged beef and gourmet seafood.
Edgewater Buffet: Giant all-you-can-eat buffet open daily. Breakfast 7:00am-11:00am $2.29. Lunch 11:30am-3:30pm $2.49. Dinner 4:00pm-10:00pm $3.69.
Snack bar in the bowling center: Open 9:00am-10:00pm.
Winner's Circle Deli: Open 9:00am-11:00pm daily. Sandwiches, hot dogs, shrimp cocktail.

Games
Blackjack: 32 tables, $1-$500, single-deck games, dealer hits soft 17, Insurance offered, double on 10 or 11.
Craps: three tables, $1-$500, single odds.
Roulette: two tables, $1-$1,000 payoff.
Keno: 75-cent tickets, minimum way tickets (10 cents per way), maximum payout $75,000.
Poker Room: 7-card Stud, buy-in $10 1-3, $20 1-4, Texas Hold 'Em $20 1-3-6-6.
Slots: Over 1,200 machines, 5 cents-$5, progressive machines, maximum payoff $75,000, poker & 21 machines.
Race & Sports Book: 200 seats, 20 TVs.
Also: **Big Six Wheel** & **Red Dog**.

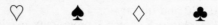

Flamingo Hilton, 1900 S. Casino Dr., Laughlin, NV 89029 (702-298-5111 or 800-445-8667). Rates: Sun-Thurs $22, Fri-Sat $45, holidays $65, suites $200.

Casino prefers big-money play. The newest hotel in Laughlin, opened in 1990 with 2,000 riverview rooms, RV parking, pool, lighted tennis courts, show lounge, gift shop, video arcade, candy store, hair salon, and five restaurants.

Restaurants & Lounges
Alta Villa: Italian food.
The Steak House: Famous steaks.
Lindy's Deli-Coffee Shop: Open 24 hours.
The Flagship Buffet: Gigantic buffet.
Flavors Snack Bar: Open 24 hours.
Burger King (!).

Two revues in the show lounge: *Broadway Varieties* 7:00pm & 9:00pm and *Zippity Do Revue* 2:00pm & 4:00pm.

Games
Blackjack: $2-$5 minimum bets, single-deck and six-deck shoe games, dealer hits soft 17, Insurance offered, double on 10 or 11.
Craps: three tables, $2-$500 minimum, double odds.
Roulette: three tables, $1 minimum, $500 maximum payoff.
Keno: $1 minimum ticket, $100,000 maximum payout.
Poker: 7 tables, Stud, Omaha, Hold 'Em, Razz, $20 buy-in.
Slots: 1,500 machines, 5 cents-$25, progressive Megabucks machines paying $5,000,000, poker and 21 machines.
Pai Gow Poker: $5-$500 bets, played with cards and a bank.
Race & Sports Book: 250 seats, 25 TVs.

The Golden Nugget, 2300 Casino Dr., Laughlin, NV 89020 (702-298-7111 [NV], 602-754-3128 [AZ], 800-237-1739 or 800-237-2512). Rates: Sun-Thurs $33, weekends & holidays $42.

Small, friendly casino. The Nevada Club Inn on the Arizona side, which serves as the Golden Nugget's hotel, has 72 rooms. River Bar open 24 hours. Gift shop, pool, spa, tennis courts, Jacuzzi. Complimentary pickup from the airport. Free 24-hour ferry service across the river.

Restaurants & Lounges
Wheelhouse Coffee Shop: Open 24 hours. $1.98 breakfast, dinner specialties include filet mignon and lobster.
Quarterdeck Buffet: Open 7:00am-10:30pm. $1.99 breakfast, $2.69 lunch. Daily dinner theme specials.
Nugget Nibbles Snack Bar: Open 8:00am-midnight. Hot dogs, pizza, deli sandwiches.

Games

Blackjack: 13 tables, $2-$2,000, single-deck games and six-deck shoes, dealer hits soft 17, Insurance offered, double on any two original cards.

Craps: two tables, $2-$2,000, triple odds available.

Roulette: one table, 25-cents, $50 straight up.

Keno: 70-cent minimum ticket, $1.05 way tickets, $50,000 maximum payout per game.

Slots: 860 slots, 5 cents-$25, progressive machines including poker, no cap on progressive machines—the sky's the limit. Over 300 poker machines, also progressive.

Pai Gow Poker: $5-$500, played with cards, bank passes.

Harrah's Laughlin, 2900 Casino Dr., Laughlin, NV 89029 (702-298-4600 or 800-447-8700). Rates: Sun-Thurs $25-$34, weekends & holidays $49-$59. Patio rooms $75, mini-suites $90.

Luxury hotel. Casino dealers have a can't-be-bothered attitude. Laughlin's next-to-newest, with the look of a sunny Mexican resort, 958 rooms, pool, gift shop, video arcade, and handicapped facilities. The only hotel with a private beach on the Colorado. Paddle-wheeler rides, jet ski and small boat rentals on the beach. Resort-wear boutique, fine jewelry, art gallery, and gift shop. Three bars, five restaurants, a lounge with cabaret shows, a banquet hall, RV plaza convenience center with gas, shopping, and parking.

Restaurants & Lounges

Rosa's Cantina, Margarita, Amigo's Bar, and **GuadalaHarrah's** all offer a variety of exotic drinks and entertainment.

The Buffet: Breakfast 7:00am-10:00am $3.49 with omelettes cooked to order. Lunch 11:00am-5:00pm $4.49 Mon-Sat. Dinner 5:00pm-10:00pm $4.79 Sun-Thurs. Champagne Brunch Sunday 10:00am-3:30pm $7.95.

The Colorado Cafe: Open 24 hours. Coffee shop and tortilla factory, burgers, salads, sandwiches, prime rib.

Gringo's Grill: Fast-food.

La Hacienda: 5:00pm-11:00pm Sun-Thurs (till midnight Fri-Sat). The oven imported from France gives unique taste to Mexican-American food.

William Fisk Steakhouse: Gourmet dining, steaks, seafood, Continental cuisine.

The **Leinani Tropic Island Dancers** perform in two shows nightly, Sun-Thurs at 7:00pm and 8:30pm. The poolside dinner show includes a luau buffet and entertainment for $14.95 per person.

Games
Non-smoking gaming area. 40,000- square-foot casino, over 1,000 slot machines including Megabucks and Quartermania, a full variety of table games, a poker room, keno, sports book, and Pai Gow poker.

The Pioneer Hotel and Gambling Hall, 2200 Casino Dr., Laughlin, NV 89029 (702-298-2442 [NV], 602-758-5557 [AZ], 800-634-3469). Rates: Sun-Thurs $28, weekends & holidays $39, riverview $50.

Nice hotel. Casino likes high-roller play. 417 rooms, pool, gift shop, tennis, banquet rooms, free airport shuttle, sandy river beach, boardwalk along the Colorado. The Pioneer is proud of its old-fashioned Western hospitality. Outside is an huge cowboy mascot, inside life-sized one-armed bandits (working antique slot machines) line the casino floor. Three restaurants and a bar are available.

Restaurants & Lounges
Fast Draw Snack Bar: Open 10:00am-10:00pm. Chili dogs, burgers, sandwiches.
Boarding House Restaurant: Open 24 hours. 7:00am-10:00am 49-cent breakfast daily, breakfast buffet $2.95. Lunch buffet 11:00am-3:00pm daily $3.25. Dinner 4:00pm-10:00pm: prime rib $3.95, steak & lobster buffet $5.95. Features real, old fashioned mashed potatoes, the kind Grandma used to make. Try them!
Granny's Gourmet Room: 5:00pm-11:00pm Tues-Sat. Gourmet dining: steaks, broiled elk, wild game, swordfish. Champagne Brunch Sunday 8:30am-2:15pm for $12.95. Adults only, dress code, reservations required.

Games
Note: The Pioneer offers the highest betting limits on the river.
Blackjack: 12 tables, $2-$2,000, single-deck, dealer hits soft 17, Insurance offered, double on any first two cards.
Craps: two tables, $2-$2,000, double and single odds available.

Roulette: one table, $1-$75.
Keno: Minimum ticket $1, way tickets 50 cents a way, 3 ways $5, payout $50,000.
Slots: 813 slots, 5 cents-$5, double jackpot time every 15 minutes, free membership in the Round-Up Slot Club with free gifts, slot tournaments, 100 high-paying progressive machines, video poker machines.

Ramada Express, 2121 Casino Dr., Laughlin, NV 89029 (702-298-4200 [NV], 602-763-2010 [AZ], 800-272-6232). Rates: Sun-Thurs $29-$34, weekends & holidays $59. Children under 12 free. No pets.

A fun place to stay and play, with a very friendly casino. The Ramada has a railroad theme, complete with free train rides on a replica steam locomotive from the parking lot to the Victorian-styled railroad station casino. The hotel offers 406 rooms, a pool, video arcade, railroad memorabilia, gift shop, handicapped facilities, RV park, non-smoking rooms, lounge, and four restaurants.

Restaurants & Lounges
The Caboose Lounge: Open 3:00pm-2:00am Tues-Sun. Entertainment.
Dining Car Coffee Shop: Open 24 hours.
The Steakhouse: Open 5:00pm-11:00pm. Fine dining, seafood, ribs, lamb, chicken, mesquite broiled meats. Unlimited Champagne Brunch on Sunday 9:00am-2:00pm for $7.95 per person. Reservations suggested.
The Roundhouse Buffet: $1.99 breakfast from 7:00am-11:00am. $2.99 lunch from 11:30am-4:30pm. $3.99 prime rib dinner from 5:00pm-10:00pm.
Whistle Stop Snack Bar: Open 6:00am-10:00pm daily. Quick meals and snacks, ice cream.
Hobo Buffet: Poolside dining 6:00pm-10:00pm Saturday only. All-you-can-eat steak, ribs, chicken buffet.

Games
Blackjack: 26 tables, $2-$2,000, single-deck games, four-deck shoes, dealer hits soft 17, Insurance offered, double on any first two cards.
Craps: three tables, $1-$2,000. Triple odds available.
Roulette: two tables, 25 cents-$50 bet per number.

Keno: 50-cent minimum ticket, way tickets, max. payout $50,000.
Slots: 964 machines, 5 cents-$25, progressive machines, maximum payoff $145,000. 400 poker machines/four 7's pay triple.
Mini-Baccarat: $2-$2,000, bank does not pass, varied hours.
Pai Gow Poker: $5-$2,000, played with cards, optional bank pass.
Sports Book: Parlay cards only, 4 TVs.

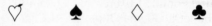

Regency Casino, 1950 Casino Dr., Laughlin, NV 89029 (702-298-2439).

The smallest but one of the friendliest casinos on the river. Lounge with piano bar and live entertainment. Snack bar serves breakfast 24 hours. Also features the Royal Room Restaurant, open 7:00am-midnight daily, with steak, seafood, prime rib, and wonderful cheese bread.

Games
Blackjack: four tables, $2-$50.
Slots: 75 machines, 5-cent, 25-cent, and $1. Six progressive machines.

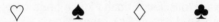

The Riverside Resort and Casino, 1650 Casino Dr., Laughlin, NV 89029 (702-298-2535 [NV], 602-763-7070 [AZ], 800-227-3849). Rates: Sun-Thurs $35, weekends & holidays $48, riverview $58.

Large, friendly hotel and casino, good for beginners. 660 rooms, handicapped facilities, two outdoor pools, courtesy airport shuttle, RV park, convention rooms, dance studio, U.S. Post Office, gift shop, hair salon, three cinemas, video arcade, lounges, four restaurants, and a showroom. The hotel raises its own cattle for the restaurants on a ranch east of town and also has an on-premise bakery.

Restaurants & Lounges
Celebrity Theatre: 1,000-seat theater with house shows 7:00pm & 9:00pm Sun-Thurs and big-name entertainment Fri-Sat 7:30pm & 10:30pm.
Loser's Lounge: Bands for dancing 1:00pm-5:45am daily.
Riverview Room: Open 24 hours. Light meals.
Gourmet Room: Open 5:00pm-11:00pm. Fine dining, elegant

desserts, wines & liqueurs. Reservations suggested.

The Prime Rib Room: Open 4:00-11:00pm. Prime rib carved at the table with potato, salad, vegetable, and dessert bar.

The East Buffet Room: $1.99 breakfast 7:00am-10:00am Mon-Fri. $2.69 lunch 11:00am-2:00pm. $3.69 dinner 3:00pm-10:00pm. Champagne Brunch 7:00am-2:30pm Sat ($2.49) and Sun ($4.49).

The West Buffet Room: $1.49 breakfast 7:00am-10:00am. Chicken & fish buffet 10:30am-8:30pm $2.49. Champagne Brunch 7:00am-10:00am $2.49.

Snack Bar: Open 24 hours.

Games
Non-smoking area available.

Blackjack: 28 tables, $2-$500, single-deck games, six-deck shoes, dealer hits soft 17, Insurance offered, double on 10 and above.

Craps: three tables, $1-$500, double odds.

Roulette: one two-sided table, $1-25 cent chip or $2-50 cent chip minimum buy-in, $500 max.

Keno: 70-cent minimum ticket, 3-10 ways for 50 cents, 10 ways 35 cents, 100-ways 10 cents, $50,000 payout.

Slots: 1,344 machines, Megabucks $3,000,000.

Poker Room: glass enclosed room, 7-card Stud, 7-card Hi-Lo Split Stud, Texas Hold 'Em, Omaha Hi-Lo Split, one-, three-, and seven-card Stud buy-in $10, other games $20.

Bingo: 400 seats, $3 minimum on all sessions, payout $100 on $2 card.

Race & Sports Book: 40 seats, 4 TVs.

Sam's Town Gold River, 2700 Casino Dr., Laughlin, NV 89029 (702-298-2242 [NV], 602-754-4628 [AZ], 800-835-7903). Rates: Sun-Thurs $19, weekends & holidays $45-$50.

Luxury resort hotel. Dealers friendly and helpful. 1,225 rooms, suites, handicapped facilities, pool, spa, dance hall, RV parking, general store, retail center, video arcade, banquet facilities, river walk, health club, beauty shop, covered parking for 1,100 cars with walkway to the casino, computer checkout, in-room service menu on TV, no pets, seven restaurants and two lounges. Lobby offers visitors a place to sit among mounted deer heads, bears, log walls, and rock fireplaces.

Restaurants & Lounges

Roxy's Lounge: Open noon-6:00am weekends, live entertainment.

Sutter's Lounge: Open 5:00pm-midnight Tues-Sun.

Opera House Buffet: Open 7:00am-11:00pm. Breakfast, lunch, and dinner. 450-seat restaurant.

The Dog House: Hot dogs in every imaginable variety.

Smokey Joe's: 24-hour coffee shop.

Sutter's Lodge: Open 5:00pm-11:00pm Wed-Sun. Prime rib, steaks, venison. Reservations suggested.

Aunt B's Ice Cream & Snack Shoppe: Open 7:00am-midnight. Snack bar and ice cream parlor.

Halftime Snack Bar: In the Race & Sports Book. Sandwiches and snacks.

Tony Roma's: Ribs.

Games

Blackjack: 38 tables, $2-$1,000, single-deck, double-deck, six-deck shoe games, dealer hits soft 17, Insurance offered, double on any first two cards.

Craps: three tables, $1-$1,000 flat with $2,000 odds or $3,000 flat, double odds available.

Roulette: three tables, 25 cents-$1,000 outside, $100 straight up.

Keno: Minimum ticket 70 cents, 10 cents a way if playing 100 ways or more, $100,000 payout, also progressive $160,000 payout.

Slots: 1,374 machines, 5 cents-$5, progressive machines, maximum payoff over $250,000, poker machines.

Bingo: Play with view of the Colorado through large windows. 307 seats, two cards per board, 3/$1, $2, $3 boards, maximum payout $5,000.

Baccarat: one mini-game Fri evening and all day Sat plus some Sun mornings, $5-$500, bank does not pass, house takes 5% commission on all winning bets.

Pai Gow Poker: two tables, $5-$1,000, bank passes, 5% commission on all winning bets.

Race & Sports Book: 200 seats, 40 TVs.

Poker: 9 tables, 1-4 7-card Stud, 4-8-8 Texas Hold 'Em, 10-20 Texas Hold 'Em, Pot Limit, 4-8-8 Omaha. Buy-in: 1-4 is $20, 4-8-8 is $40, 10-20 and Pot Limit is $100.

Also: **Big Six Wheel**.

Free Gaming Lessons

Colorado Belle Hotel and Casino: Poker, roulette, and craps lessons available on the TV in your hotel room.

Edgewater Hotel and Casino: Blackjack and roulette lessons Mon-Fri at 8:00am, craps lessons Sun-Fri 6:00pm-8:00pm.

Harrah's: Blackjack and poker lessons Mon and Tues 10:00am-6:00pm.

Ramada Express Hotel and Casino: Blackjack and craps classes Mon-Fri 9:00am-10:00am.

Riverside Resort Hotel and Casino: Instruction available to groups on request.

Sam's Town Gold River: Poker instruction Tues at 10:00am.

More Great Travel Books
from Mustang Publishing

Let's Blow thru Europe by Neenan & Hancock. The essential guide for the "15-cities-in-14-days" traveler, this is the funniest, most irreverent, and definitely the most honest travel guide ever written. With this book, you'll blow off the boring museums and stale cathedrals and instead find the great bars, restaurants, and fun stuff in all the major cities of Europe. *"Absolutely hilarious!"* —*Booklist.* **10.95**

Europe on 10 Salads a Day by Mary Jane & Greg Edwards. A must for the health-conscious traveler! From gourmet Indian cuisine in Spain to terrific take-out pizza in Italy, this book describes over 200 health food/vegetarian restaurants throughout Europe. *"Don't go to Europe without it"* —*Vegetarian Times.* **$9.95**

Europe for Free by Brian Butler. If you're on a tight budget—or if you just love a bargain—this is the book for you! With descriptions of thousands of things to do and see for free all over Europe, you'll save lots of lira, francs, and pfennigs. *"Well-organized and packed with ideas"* —*Modern Maturity.* **$8.95**

Also in this series:
London for Free by Brian Butler. **$7.95**
DC for Free by Brian Butler. **$6.95**
Hawaii for Free by Frances Carter. **$6.95**

The Nepal Trekker's Handbook by Amy R. Kaplan. This book guides trekkers through every aspect of planning and enjoying a trek through Nepal—one of the world's most magnificent adventures. From medical advice to cultural *faux-pas*, it's an essential guide. *"A must"* —*Midwest Book Review.* **$9.95**

Australia: Where the Fun Is by Goodyear & Skinner. From the best pubs in Sydney to the cheapest motels in Darwin to the greatest hikes in Tasmania, this guide by two recent Yale grads details all the fun stuff Down Under—on and off the beaten path. *"Indispensable" —Library Journal.* **$12.95**

Northern Italy: A Taste of Trattoria by Christina Baglivi. For the most delicious, most authentic, and least expensive meals in Italy, and head straight for *trattorie*, the small, unassuming cafes known only to locals. This guide, describing over 80 *trattorie* from Rome to Chatillon, is a must for the hungry traveler. *"A tasty tidbit of a tour guide" —Quick Trips Travel Letter.* **$9.95**

Mustang books should be available at your local bookstore. If not, send a check or money order for the price of the book, plus $1.50 postage per book, to Mustang Publishing, P.O. Box 3004, Memphis, TN 38173, USA.

Allow three weeks for delivery. For one-week delivery, add $3.00 to the total. *International orders:* Please pay in U.S. funds, and add $5.00 to the total for Air Mail.

For a catalog of Mustang books, send a stamped, self-addressed, business size envelope to Catalog Request, Mustang Publishing, P.O. Box 3004, Memphis, TN 38173.